Fictional Leaders

Fictional Leaders

Heroes, Villains and Absent Friends

Jonathan Gosling
Director, Centre for Leadership Studies, University of Exeter, UK

Peter Villiers

First published 2013 by
PALGRAVE MACMILLAN

Palgrave Macmillan in the UK is an imprint of Macmillan Publishers Limited,
registered in England, company number 785998, of Houndmills, Basingstoke,
Hampshire RG21 6XS.

Palgrave Macmillan in the US is a division of St Martin's Press LLC,
175 Fifth Avenue, New York, NY 10010.

Palgrave Macmillan is the global academic imprint of the above companies
and has companies and representatives throughout the world.

Palgrave® and Macmillan® are registered trademarks in the United States,
the United Kingdom, Europe and other countries.

ISBN 978–1–137–27274–4

This book is printed on paper suitable for recycling and made from fully
managed and sustained forest sources. Logging, pulping and manufacturing
processes are expected to conform to the environmental regulations of the
country of origin.

A catalogue record for this book is available from the British Library.

A catalog record for this book is available from the Library of Congress.

10   9   8   7   6   5   4   3   2   1
22   21   20   19   18   17   16   15   14   13

Printed and bound in the United States of America

Contents

PN
56
L39
-53
013

Contributors

Robert Adlam retired from the National Police Staff College at Bramshill in Hampshire, UK, as a reader in leadership studies, having previously directed the Special Course for many years. (This Home Office course identifies and develops police officers chosen for their outstanding leadership potential, from the 140,000 police officers in the UK.) He has a PhD in police ethics from the University of Surrey and is co-author of two books with Peter Villiers: *Police Leadership in the 21st Century* (2003) and *Policing a Safe, Just and Tolerant Society* (2004). He edits and publishes on art, literature, philosophy and aesthetics.

Peter Case is Professor of Management and Organization Studies at James Cook University, Australia. He is also Acting Director of the Bristol Centre for Leadership and Organizational Ethics, Bristol Business School, UK, and has taught the core executive MBA module 'Business ethics and CSR' for London Business School. He served as general editor of *Culture and Organization* (2007–10) and is currently a member of the editorial boards of *Leadership, Leadership and Organizational Development Journal, Business and Society Review* and *Journal of Management, Spirituality and Religion*. His research interests encompass corporate social and environmental responsibility, leadership ethics and organization theory. His publications include *The Speed of Organization* (with S. Lilley and T. Owens, 2006) and *John Adair: the Fundamentals of Leadership* (with J. Gosling and M. Witzel, 2007).

Jonathan Gosling is Director of the University of Exeter's Centre for Leadership Studies. He was previously Director of the Strategic Leaders Unit at Lancaster University, and he remains Chair of the International Masters in Practicing Management, a collaboration of seven business schools around the world that share in the delivery of taught modules for experienced managers in multinational companies. The group launched the Advanced Leadership Programme in 2002. His research focuses on leadership and ethics in current strategic changes, and on contemporary innovations in leadership development. His research into how leaders learn from each other led to the formation of Lead2Lead, which provides opportunities for senior directors to learn from their peers in other companies. He is a trustee of the Fintry Trust and the J H Levy Trust, a visiting professor at Lancaster University and an adviser on leadership to the Defence Academy, in effect the United Services Staff College of the armed forces of the UK.

Nathan Harter has published a range of articles on leadership, ethics and bureaucracy, and is the author of *Clearings in the Forest* (2006). In 2006–7 he chaired the section on scholarship of the International Leadership Association, and in 2011 he became Professor of Leadership Studies at Christopher Newport University, Virginia.

Beverley Hawkins is a lecturer in the Centre for Leadership Studies, University of Exeter Business School. When not watching James Bond films she is particularly interested in exploring the processes of inter-action, both formal and informal, through which people accomplish their work in organizations. She has published research on teamwork and corporate culture as well in the field of leadership studies.

Stephanie Jones is Associate Professor of Organizational Behaviour at Maastricht School of Management, teaching leadership to MBA and doctoral students. She is particularly interested in the juxtaposition of history and leadership, hence her book with Jonathan Gosling, *Nelson's Way – leadership lessons from the great commander*. She named her sailing boat after the first Hornblower novel, *The Happy Return*.

Satish Kumar has been a Jain monk and nuclear disarmament advocate, and he is the current editor of *Resurgence* magazine. He is the founder and Director of Programmes of the Schumacher College International Centre for Ecological Studies, and of the Small School in Hartland, North Devon. He organised a centenary festival in honour of Rabindranath Tagore in 2012, at which all the arts to which Tagore contributed were featured, and performances included poetry, dance, song and theatre. He continues to have a wide interest in ecology and insists that reverence for nature should be at the heart of every political and social debate.

Chris Land following a childhood in which his summers were spent tending sheep on the Cumbrian moors, Chris Land retired from the wilful companionship of his ovine wards to the cloistered groves of academe to mix his metaphors and set down in writing what he had learned out on the fells. His contribution to this collection is one in a series of works reflecting on transhumanism and conceptions of subjectivity in the organization of social collectivities. He is paid by the University of Essex to give 'senior lectures' in work and organization. They are often like 'senior moments'.

Hugo Letiche is Professor of Organization of Health and Social Care at Leicester University, UK. Previously he was Research Professor of Meaning in Organization at the Universiteit voor Humanistiek Utrecht, the Netherlands, where he was a director of the part-time PhD programme. His current interests centre on the politics and ethics of research, and the 'turn to affect'. All of these concern Blanchot, whom he (co-)writes about here.

Lynette Mitchell is Associate Professor of Greek History and Politics in the Department of Classics and Ancient History at the University of Exeter. She is interested in Greek political history and the development of Greek political thought, especially in the archaic and classical periods. She has published two monographs and three edited volumes, the last of which is on kingship in the ancient and medieval worlds. She is currently completing a third monograph on ruling ideology in the ancient Greek world: *The Heroic Rulers of Archaic and Classical Greece*.

Jean-Luc Moriceau is Professor of Accountability at Telecom Business School, France, where he is in charge of doctoral education. He was core tutor of the part-time PhD programme of the Universiteit voor Humanistiek Utrecht, the Netherlands. His research interests mainly revolve around aesthetics, literature and critical management studies.

Barbara Mossberg is President Emerita, Goddard College, Vermont; Director and Professor of Integrated Studies at California State University, Monterey Bay, California; and Host of the Poetry Showdown KRXA 540 AM. She is currently poet in residence at Poet's Perch, Monterey Bay, California.

Peter Pelzer studied economics and philosophy. He is working as an independent consultant for banks and as a visiting professor at the University for Humanistics, Utrecht, the Netherlands. He is interested in understanding the processes he experiences during his projects beyond the textbook knowledge of organisation and management theory. His book *Risk, Risk Management and Regulation in the Banking Industry: The Risk to Come* has recently been published.

Norman W. Provizer obtained his PhD from the University of Pennsylvania and is Professor of Political Science, as well as founder and Director of the Golda Meir Center for Political Leadership at Metropolitan State University of Denver. His most recent publications include chapters in *Leadership Studies: The Dialogue of Disciplines; A Companion to Franklin D. Roosevelt*; and *Lincoln's Enduring Legacy*. He is also co-editor of three books on the United States Supreme Court.

Burkard Sievers is Professor of Organization Development, Bergische Universität Wuppertal, and Co-editor of *Freie Assoziation*. He was formerly President-Elect (2005–6) of the International Society for the Psychoanalytic Study of Organizations. He has published widely on the psychotic organization and is a life-long devotee of Herman Melville.

Martyna Śliwa is a senior lecturer in international management at the University of Newcastle Business School, UK, where she obtained her MA and PhD after graduating in economics from the University of Krakow in Poland, and where she recently co-authored a book on international management.

Sverre Spoelstra is a lecturer in business administration, Lund University, Sweden. He received MAs in philosophy and in management at the University of Nijmegen, the Netherlands, and a PhD in management at Leicester School of Management. He is a member of the editorial collective of the journal *Ephemera: Theory & Politics in Organization*, an editor of the Dutch journal *Filosofie in Bedrijf* and a founding member of the Centre for Philosophy and Political Economy, Leicester. His research interests include leadership, contemporary social and political philosophy, theology and organization, literature and organization, critical management studies, customer orientation, business ethics, strategy, Spinoza, self-improvement and miracles.

Harsh Verma is a development professional working in the non-profit sector in India. He is interested in understanding the influence of dharma on leadership as enshrined in the Hindu epics, and evolving perspectives on leadership relevant to the Indian context. He is the author of *The Avatar Way of Leadership* (2006), which analyses Indian archetypes of leadership based on ancient Indian literature and contemporary leadership theory.

Peter Villiers served in the British army in Northern Ireland, Cyprus and Hong Kong, and then returned to university to take an MA. He retired from the national police staff college at Bramshill in 2006 as head of human rights and is a freelance writer who has published many books and articles on leadership, ethics and human rights, as well as a marine biography of Joseph Conrad and a study of Gavrilo Princip, the assassin who started the First World War.

David Weir is Professor of Management at CERAM Sophia Antipolis, France. He has a special interest in inter-cultural management, and he is a Companion of the Chartered Institute of Management and a Fellow of the Royal Society of Arts. He is a member of the Academy of Management, the British Academy of Management and the American Association of Anthropologists. He is an emeritus professor at the University of Northumbria, Visiting Professor in Management Development at Lancaster University and Visiting Professor in Management at Bristol Business School, University of West of England.

Introduction

This book is for people who want to understand leadership in the round, and because fiction is so well suited to giving us a rounded view, we have selected essays drawing on great works of fiction, both ancient and modern.

Why did we choose to link leadership and literature in the first place?

Writers of fiction are able to present the inner musings and unconscious drives of their characters, as if they were observed events. These are insights that we can never obtain through the surveys and personality typologies of social scientific method.

Management theory is appallingly obscure about the experience of leading. Often the more positive aspects are emphasised—excitement, potency, moral courage and the sense of achievement and affirmation. But loneliness, frustration, envy, disappointment and betrayal are probably ubiquitous and sometimes overwhelming aspects of a leader's life, yet are seldom mentioned, still less examined in any depth in standard leadership texts—and that includes the popular books supposedly written for practitioners as well as more abstract academic studies. One reason is that these experiences are difficult to study in real time, and leaders themselves are not always reliable informants about their interior lives and motives.

The aim of this book is to address these difficult-to-explore aspects of leadership, approaching them through well-known works of fiction, and to draw out the themes that emerge and render them relevant to contemporary leadership and management.

How have we chosen the contents of our book, and to review the lessons that emerge? We invited respected scholars of leadership to select a work of fiction that comes to grips with issues which are both important and hard to address through standard social science methods. Many of them selected books and characters that have been important to them since childhood, and interpreted our invitation as an opportunity to explore what has been so intriguing them all these years. Others found that substantial philosophical problems in academic leadership studies—problems of definition, generalisation, ontology and ethics, for example—could be addressed directly through novels. Overall, we were astonished at the variety and depth of our response; the book emerged as an organic growth rather than a mechanistic compilation.

One of the most exciting features of the book, we believe, is that each essay brings together a leadership scholar and a novelist or poet, mostly from different times and different continents. In each chapter we are invited to see new aspects of leadership, reaching into the predicaments of characters in ancient Persia, mythical India, pre-colonial Africa, Plato's Athens, twentieth-century Paris, wartime Europe and a whaling ship at sea. Nowhere is there an attempt to express a general theory; rather, this book is dominated by a fascination with the particular, specific personal experiences to which we as readers may relate directly. On the other hand, although there is no overarching theory of leadership in this book, there are plenty of conceptual observations and theoretical problems, and a determined focus on the humanity, rather than the techniques, of leadership.

Three parts

Part I includes seven essays on fictional characters who exemplify the predicaments of leadership in a range of circumstances. The essays in Part II do not focus on individual leaders, but question the concept of leadership itself, showing how it is used to reassure, distract or bamboozle. Part III includes chapters that speak directly to people in leadership positions, representing questions and advice posed by thoughtful critiques of poets, philosophers and novelists.

Our title, *Heroes, Villains and Absent Friends,* refers to themes that pervade the whole volume. In this book we are inviting scholars and critics to speak to us from their experience of reading powerful literature, and *then* to speculate about its implications for leaders and students of leadership.

Outline

In Part I we focus on the individual who bears the official responsibility of leadership, or aspires thereto, and whose character and virtues are on trial. All are cast within an isolated community, a world in which the legitimacy of their authority ought to be a matter of common consent. But we discover the pervasive influence of wider social and economic realities, which inform both the organisation of power and the interior struggles of individuals.

We begin with a full-blown leader: Cyrus the Great, Emperor of Persia, semi-fictionalised 150 years after his death by the Athenian author Xenophon in *Cyropaedia*, analysed here by Lynette Mitchell (Chapter 1). In Xenophon's story, Cyrus wonders how to be a ruler, and decides that the development of willing followers is the path to success. As Mitchell shows, Xenophon's account was written to appeal to the readers of his day, Athenian citizens caught up in radical changes to their mode of government, debating the rights and wrongs of democracy and strong leadership.

Then we have the first of three chapters about leadership at sea—the ambiguity is intended—and explore Joseph Conrad's *Lord Jim*. In Peter Villiers's account (Chapter 2), Jim dreams of heroism at sea, but fails to rise to the challenge when it arrives; the rest of his life is spent in trying to redeem himself from his moment of failure. Leadership is revealed here as an insecure, tenuous and doubtful burden. It is Jim's lack of heroism as a leader that makes him such a powerful hero of this novel.

We return to leadership at sea in Stephanie Jones's essay (Chapter 3) on *Captain Horatio Hornblower, RN*—one of the least confident (fictional) commanders ever to tread the quarterdeck, and a person who succeeds in command whether despite or because of his weaknesses, an issue on which Jones leaves the reader to judge. Hornblower perfectly demonstrates the isolation of command and the paucity of conventional leadership theory in accounting for his self-doubting success.

Next we meet Captain Ahab, the leader-as-villain of Melville's *Moby Dick*, often presented as a study in monomania. Here, however, Burkard Sievers (Chapter 4) foregrounds the physical and technical context in which work is done. He explores the motives, aspirations and rewards of different classes of people, and the cultural mores that determine attitudes to authority, risk, fate and death; he shows that all these are material to the specific ideas and feelings that people will have about leading and being led.

Pastoral, by Nevil Shute, explores the challenges facing an English bomber pilot in the Second World War. David Weir's essay (Chapter 5) focuses on the web of interdependency that binds the personal and work life of the protagonist. The pilot, like many of Shute's characters, is an ordinary person facing an extraordinary task, and he cannot do it alone. Weir suggests that the ability to exercise leadership depends on a readiness to be loved, and this directs us to an appreciation of dependency.

In his essay (Chapter 6) on *Things Fall Apart* by Chinua Achebe, Jonathan Gosling locates leadership in its social and political context, asking what happens when the norms of society collapse. It is the story of Okonkwo, an individual with aspirations to greatness within his Ibo village in pre-colonial West Africa; how his development, dominated by his father, is mediated by a coherent and shared culture, especially notions of masculinity, loyalty and shame; and the role of justice and luck in defining a leader's authority. The essay also points to implications for the possible collapse of social order in the industrial world, perhaps as a result of climate change.

In the final chapter of Part I, Norman Provizer (Chapter 7) examines John Hersey's *A Bell for Adano*. This reading points us to the leadership skills utilised by an American civil affairs officer in the Second World War, and his need to exercise discretion. Leadership, in Major Joppolo's hands, requires flexibility and improvisation. The leader must be clear as to what he really believes in but be flexible in how he sets out to achieve his goal. Norman Provizer draws parallels to the present day, when the American government needs more Major Joppolos to pursue its overseas interests with integrity.

Part II is a series of critiques of the concept of leadership itself—its effects on our actions and on our understanding of social life. The four essays in this section tackle an underlying implication of this volume— that all attempts to explain our actions are fictions, and subject to the same techniques of appreciation and criticism as any other fictional works.

Beverley Hawkins (Chapter 8) explores the creation of a modern myth via Ian Fleming's *James Bond* (as first introduced in *Casino Royale*). She shows how a contemporary organisation mobilises the images of Bond and Miss Moneypenny in order to enthuse their sales force with feelings of heroism and service. Bond, of course, is more of an anti-leader, yet represents the possibility of excitement in contrast to boring desk-bound bureaucracy, and at the same time speaks to the gendered roles in the workplace.

Chris Land, Martyna Śliwa and Sverre Spoelstra (Chapter 9) express mischievous delight in the possibility that the search for leadership is *A Wild Sheep Chase*—the title of a novel by Haruki Murasami. Is it a lost cause? They show, rather, that the conviction that we have lost something, and must seek it, is cause enough for us to follow.

Peter Pelzer and Peter Case (Chapter 10) pursue a similar theme through Thomas Pynchon's *Gravity's Rainbow*. The incipient disorder of the novel conjures a visceral sense of vertigo. Here the function of the CEO is purely symbolic, and the organisation functions perfectly well without a boss. However, people expect such a position to exist and to be tenanted, if only because it represents a status to which they may aspire—not that the aspiration has any substance to it either!

Maurice Blanchot, in *The Madness of the Day*, recounts a day that has no apparent cause-and-effect logic, in which events have prominence through emotional and symbolic resonance, but no a priori importance. Hugo Letiche and Jean-Luc Moriceau (Chapter 11) argue that this dissolves the notion of direction or rational intent and, along with them, leadership itself.

The essays in Part III address the 'so what?' question. If great works of literature are so relevant, what are they relevant for? Here we ask: where does literature lead us? These five essays do not focus on characters who lead, nor do they question the concept of leadership itself. Rather, they each advance advice on how to use literature to inform us about leadership, as leaders, readers, observers, teachers or students. They take us into complex territories, inviting discussion of matters such as duty, trust, inspiration and the love of beauty. These, they suggest, are proper subjects for anyone wishing to become a better leader or teacher of leaders.

Harsh Verma (Chapter 12) explores the *Mahabharata* and the *Ramayana*, concluding, among other things, that the pursuit of *dharma* (roughly translatable as 'duty') requires us to challenge the lessons of the past. We are responsible for our own destinies.

Barbara Mossberg (Chapter 13) absorbs the poetry of Alfred, Lord Tennyson, Walt Whitman and Emily Dickinson, and finds parallels between the task of the political leader and the poet in the need to bring order out of chaos. She draws on contemporary chaos theory to expose the turbulent interweaving of events and emotions confronting leaders and artists.

Satish Kumar (Chapter 14) presents a rounded picture of the Bengali polymath Rabindranath Tagore, who achieved fame as a poet, novelist, agricultural reformer and educational pioneer, and who was hugely influential in the cultural development of India, Pakistan and finally Bangladesh. Tagore, however, refused to adopt the mantle of a leader in any conventional sense, and was happiest when challenging unexamined preconceptions and stereotyped thinking.

Tagore was a challenge to those around him, but not so much as Socrates, who presented a quite exceptional challenge to authority and established views, only resolved by his death. Or was it? In the *Apology*, Socrates, via Plato and our contributor Nathan Harter, both argues and demonstrates the need for the critical questioning of those who assume the mantle of leadership; his underlying message, topically, is about the need for good citizenship.

Finally, Robert Adlam (Chapter 16) gives us a complete leadership development programme in outline, based on ten outstanding texts from world literature. In his view, the public service needs leaders who have been steeped in the lessons of literature. His chapter is in effect a short book in itself, which enables us to explore both classic and modern texts from a leadership perspective and to focus on the abiding moral challenges of leadership.

1
Xenophon and the Pursuit of Willing Obedience by Cyrus the Great

Lynette Mitchell

Introduction

The context

During the final years of the fifth century BC, the Athenians were involved in a long war with Sparta, which they eventually lost in 404. Democracy was replaced by a brutal and violent oligarchy imposed by the Spartans, although within months the democrats had ousted the regime of the so-called 'Thirty Tyrants' and democracy was restored. And yet democracy and the democratic ideal had suffered during the long years of war; particularly from among the Athenian intelligentsia there were, at the end of the fifth century BC and the beginning of the fourth, demands for new ways of conceptualising constitutional rule.

It is in this context that Xenophon, friend of Socrates, mercenary commander, prolific writer of history and philosophy, and political thinker of some standing in his own time, wrote *The Education of Cyrus*, an historical novel about the rule of Cyrus the Great, king of the Persian Empire in the mid-sixth century BC. Through his portrayal of Cyrus, Xenophon creates a model for leadership in an ideal constitution in which democratic equality is rejected in favour of a hierarchical community of the 'willing obedient' serving Cyrus, who respects the law and yet also embodies it.

The content

The purpose and content of this article is to analyse the main features of Xenophon's treatment of the ideal leader, assess its significance and offer a critique of its value as a model for leadership and rule by one man.

The adaptation

This chapter is condensed from the full text as originally published in 2008 as an occasional paper of the Centre for Leadership Studies of the University of Exeter. The original article with its full content and references may be obtained on application to the Centre for Leadership Studies. We are most grateful to Dr Mitchell for agreeing to the adaptation of her original text.

The commentary

The article is followed by a commentary in which Jonathan Gosling relates Xenophon's fictional biography of Cyrus the Great and the leadership issues arising to some contemporary issues in leadership studies.

Xenophon's portrayal of Cyrus the Great in the form of an historical novel remains of great relevance to leadership studies today, and the medium is part of the message.[1]

Cyrus the Great and the obedience of the willing

A model constitution

Xenophon begins his account with Cyrus's childhood and boyhood education first at the court of his father, the king of the Persians, and then that of his grandfather, the king of the Medes.

Under the Persian constitution children are educated by the state, and are taught justice, moderation and hunting (as preparation for war). The numbers of citizens are limited to 120,000 men, who are called 'those equal in honour' (*hoi isotimoi*), and include only those whose parents can afford formal education. Any of the *isotimoi* can hold office, but the emphasis of the constitution is on strict regulation and law, so that if any one does not fulfil any of the requisite steps in preparation for full citizenship then he is excluded from the citizen body. Likewise, in decisions regarding justice, the rule of law is strictly maintained.

When he reaches 12 years old, Cyrus leaves Persia and goes to the court of his grandfather, the king of the Medes. In contrast to Persia, life at the Medish court is excessively hedonistic. Cyrus, however, chooses to stay in Media, because there he can learn to be the best at skills in which he does not yet excel. When Cyrus's leadership comes to be tested, however, he neither accepts nor rejects either the Persian or Medish model completely, but creates a style of commanding and ruling which is a balance of the two. Calling himself a king rather than a tyrant, he rejects

Medish hedonism and assiduously practices self-control. On the other hand, he accepts that excellence can only be obtained by rivalry and pushing at limits, and that merit is not limited by class or wealth but only by opportunity.

Furthermore, while Cyrus understands that society must be regulated and that written law has its place, he also emphasises obedience to one's superiors (rather than acquiescence to the common will), and believes that a good ruler is 'seeing law', since he not only gives orders but punishes wrongdoers.

The ideal constitution?

What Cyrus produces, then, is a blend of kingship and tyranny. He rules and expects obedience; he rewards the good and punishes the wicked; he practices moderation and self-restraint; and he provides the ultimate model of virtue.

Cyrus's ideal constitution is a meritocracy where the best people are given the highest rewards, and the lazy and wicked are weeded out.[2] Cyrus rejects completely the democratic notion that all should have the same rewards and transforms his army from one based on an elite of equals, the *isotimoi*, and a 'common' mercenary contingent, into one based on 'nobility', which is defined by the pursuit of excellence irrespective of social class or nationality. Excellence is achieved through constant training and practice and never sliding into complacency despite success.

Cyrus creates a system of hierarchies rather like Isocrates's monarchic hierarchy, over which the king, as necessarily the best man, presides as ruler. The theoretical innovation here is not that either rich or poor could excel (Thucydides's Pericles had already claimed that), but the recognition that the conditions for equality of opportunity have to be created through equality of education, training and equipment so that anyone can be the best. The result, however, of allowing equality of opportunity does not produce equality of either status or reward.

A paternal analogy

The model for Cyrus's constitution is not of itself innovative, but instead reflects a radical conservatism which institutionalises domestic models of leadership and popular morality. The ruling of a state (as with Plato) is compared to the management of a household or commanding of an army. The role of a ruler, then, is like that of a father, who not only makes sure that his family has sufficient for its livelihood, but also looks to its interests and ensures the training and education of all those who manage his household.

The good ruler secures willing obedience

Willing obedience is the central pillar of Cyrus's success and security as a ruler. It is based on the good ruler, who is wiser, stronger and braver than anyone else and is generated, on the one hand, by kindness and benefaction, and, on the other, by fear and the punishment of wrong-doers. Cyrus is so successful at acquiring willing obedience that it is claimed he is a 'king by nature' and that those he leads have a 'terrible passion' (*deinos eros*) to be ruled by him no less than bees wish to obey the leader of the hive. As a result, Cyrus rules, unlike a tyrant, without slavery:

> We are different from slaves (Cyrus says to his friends) in that slaves serve their masters unwillingly, but for us, if indeed we think we are free (*eleutheroi*), it is necessary to do everything willingly which we think it is worthwhile to do.

Social and political relationships

By insisting on willing obedience, Xenophon is not only being original, but is also de-politicising political relationships. The power relation between king and subject is neutralised, since his subjects need to be ruled by him because of their desire for the relationship, rather than out of fear or compulsion. Furthermore, this social model for leadership obviates the need for written law, since society self-regulates, or at least has an internal and moral (although secular) mechanism for regulation, and does not require an external standard for measuring and imposing behaviour. In this way, Cyrus can be king rather than tyrant, provide freedom rather than slavery, rule by law and yet be law, and control his subjects through the positive pursuit of kindness and virtue rather than through fear.

The basis for successful leadership

Xenophon's political theorising was deeply embedded in contemporary trends of political thought, and yet also managed to be both conservative and innovative. The conservatism resided in the formalisation of social norms and hierarchies, whereas the turning of these values towards rule through willing obedience overturned existing anxieties about monarchy, the rule of law and rule of the best man. Nevertheless, while Xenophon's Cyrus may have been original in these respects, the question still needs to be asked whether he represented a successful or legitimate model of leadership.

Doubts and uncertainties

Xenophon's analysis of successful leadership is not convincing. In the first place, the insistence on willing obedience may theoretically neutralise power relations, but actually distorts and obscures them. Cyrus's rhetorical emphasis on kindness as the basis for benefaction masks the fact that his gift-giving often takes the form of excessive financial rewards, which necessarily impose not only personal distance in the relationship but also create a political gap. ('I do not know', Xenophon says, 'any better reason for the people's attitude towards him than that he gave large benefactions in exchange for small ones.')

Further, while Cyrus gave munificently, he was also the only one allowed to give with such generosity. Moreover, although he gave rewards according to merit, his system of rewards was intended to produce hierarchies, and so also effectively to maintain unequal power relations. Cyrus encouraged the manipulation of exchanges for securing privileges. When Hystaspas asked Cyrus why Chrysantas had been preferred to him and rewarded more highly despite the fact that Hystaspas had always offered willing obedience, Cyrus replied that Hystaspas had only done what was asked, whereas Chrysantas had looked for ways of anticipating Cyrus's wants and desires.[3]

The misuses of power

There was a darker side to Cyrus's benefactions. The boast that no one else but the Persian king could punish enemies who were a journey of many months away, or be called 'father' by those he had subdued, may have sounded little more than rhetoric: but the threat became substantial when gift-giving was used to pay informers to be Cyrus's 'eyes' and 'ears', and to report on anyone who dared to speak or act against the king, so denying freedom of action and of speech. Disobedience at court was punished not just by the withdrawal of honours, but also by the confiscation of all property, which was then given to someone else: 'In this way he would get himself a useful friend in exchange for a useless one.'

On this level, Xenophon's political theorising not only lacks transparency, but also is disingenuous in the way that it represents power relations as (more benign) social relations. It is also disturbing since, by disguising the real power inequalities in relationships behind the emotively charged rhetoric of benefaction and kindness, it distorts actual and powerfully charged relations of subordination. Viewed in this light, willing obedience appears less willing.

This politicisation of social relations is further complicated by the fact that Xenophon's Cyrus simplifies social codes and supposes an ease in relationships which they did not and could not sustain. Cyrus assumes that strong relationships would be based on a simple exchange of favours. However, as the Greeks themselves were very much aware, social relationships were by no means simple. Greek literature is littered with explorations of the problems inherent in the exchange of benefactions; and in knowing who one's friends (and enemies) are. Aristotle in the Nicomachean Ethics engages with many of these issues, and decides that balance can only be achieved by an unequal exchange, and different kinds of exchanges.

In practice, the line between friendship and enmity is not necessarily clear-cut. In Sophocles's Ajax, Ajax is all too aware of the inconstancy of friends and the ties that bind them when he cries:

> How shall we not come to be wise? I shall. For I know so much that an enemy (*echthros*) must be hated as one who will some day be a friend (*philos*), and so much in assisting a *philos*, will I wish to help him as one who will not always remain a *philos*. For to many among mortal men the harbour of companionship is faithless.

Knowing who one's friends were may have been fundamental to the maintenance of social fabric, but it was not always easy to discern. Cyrus fails to engage with these issues; for him, the natural and unwritten laws have force because of both their simplicity and their own internal momentum. While for Cyrus the social world provides a model for political life, it can only do so because he fails to offer a deep and critical examination of the real politics of social life, the intricacies of social negotiations or the drama of betrayal.

Tyranny, law and obedience

Finally, and even more unsettlingly, the emphasis on willing obedience obscures Cyrus's relationship to law. One of the chief difficulties for Xenophon's Cyrus as a paradigm for rule is the requirement that he is so far superior to the others that he can embody law. Although Cyrus continuously and assiduously pursues education in virtue, there is no objective measure for his excellence apart from the relative excellence of his subjects. Aristotle, for his part, rejected the rule of such a monarch, because, he said, that man would have to be so far unequal to the others in virtue and political ability as to be 'a god among men'.

While Xenophon suggests Cyrus has become godlike, or at least must have divine descent, Aristotle thinks it unlikely that one man could be so superior in virtue as to deserve to stand outside law, and for this reason judges that the rule of law must always be better than the rule of one man (Politics 3, 1287a8–25). Nor is there any clear sense how Cyrus's supreme virtue is to be defined except in being 'the best'.

In fact, with his emphasis on physical superiority through training, Cyrus (dubiously) seems to imagine that moral virtue and intellectual excellence (*arete*) flows from bodily strength, and there is no clear system suggested for the training and education of the mind or the soul, beyond the education he receives (and completes) as a young child in moderation and justice. However, as Plato demonstrated, being the best in strength was not necessarily the same as being the best in the pursuit of an absolute moral good.

While Cyrus claims to respect law, he is also its primary interpreter, and, as 'seeing law', is the only source for it. As a result, any sense of objective law is marginalised, and kingship itself is redefined. In traditional Greek thought kingship was rule under law and tyranny was rule outside law. Cyrus, however, replaces law with obedience (albeit willing obedience). Consequently, the legitimacy of Cyrus's rule depends wholly on obedience, which one is expected to give to one's superiors. Cyrus then becomes the single focus for the regulation of society, so that society must depend on his rule, although he himself is unregulated (and so, theoretically, can do whatever he wants: Herodotus 3.80.3).

While Cyrus underscores the importance of kindness, Xenophon is also clear that he rules with benefactions balanced by fear, and the threat of punishment. Cyrus, as the single arbiter of what constitutes obedience (and there is little room for disagreement or civil disobedience), is a king only in theory; in fact he rules by tyranny.

Aftermath

While Xenophon, at least superficially offers an unsustainable model for leadership and ruling in his Cyrus, there are also other, more ironic, ways of reading the Education of Cyrus. For, Xenophon tells us (as Plato also did), that after his death, Cyrus's ideal constitution fell into decay: there was a decline in morality; dishonesty in financial matters; a lack of physical training; and the austerity and restraint of the Persians was replaced by the luxuriousness and the effeminacy of the Medes.

While he was alive, Cyrus's empire was governed by a single mind; he honoured and cared for his subjects like children, and those he ruled honoured him like a father. As soon as he died, however, his children fought among themselves, the cities and tribes revolted, and all turned for the worse.

Text as irony

There are indications within the text that we ought to be reading it ironically. For example, Cyrus adopted Medish dress, Xenophon says, because he thought that a ruler ought not just to be superior to his subjects but even to 'bewitch' them, and the excesses of the costume would not only make him look taller, but also hide any defects. Xenophon also tells us that Cyrus encouraged prostration by initially requiring people to do it, although he tried to pass it off as a spontaneous response to his magnificence. He also suggests that Cyrus's gift-giving was destabilising, as it encouraged rivalries for his 'affection', so that the most influential men 'loved' Cyrus more than they did each other. And Cyrus did come to think (though his mother had warned against it) that it was of the utmost importance for one man to have more 'affection' than all the rest by the magnificence of his gifts. Xenophon says Cyrus made himself preferred above all others, even brothers and fathers and children. The seeds of later decline have already been planted: excess, dishonesty, lack of trust and internal rivalries.

Notes

1. By analogy, Nicolo Machiavelli's iconic portrayal of *The Prince*, as a study of the need to be ruthless in leadership in sixteenth-century Italy, is both of lasting significance *and* relates to the conflicts of Machiavelli's life and times. Although *The Prince* is not written as an historical novel, it is a very different work to any contemporary treatise on leadership.
2. The reference here is Cyropaedia 2.2.22–5. All references are to be found in the original article.
3. As we shall see in the commentary that follows this text, the corrupted relationship between Cyrus and at least some of his followers is not unknown in modern business and public service organisations, in which the modern yes-man goes further than saying yes: he has already anticipated and provided what the boss might ask for. The relationship is not so much master and slave, as emperor and acolyte. It is the subject of satire in the mass media; but that in itself can be an aspect of extended sycophancy. Modern tyrants are not necessarily tyrannical in either manner or appearance, and manipulation has many guises. We leave our readers to decide for themselves whether the minister or his senior civil servant is the smiling tyrant in *Yes, Minister*.

References

Asheri, D. et al. 2007 *A Commentary on Herodotus I-IV*, Oxford.

Avery, H.C. 1972 'Herodotus' picture of Cyrus', *American Journal of Philology* 93, 529–46.

Blundell, M.W. 1989 *Helping Friends and Harming Enemies. A Study in Sophocles and Greek ethics*, Cambridge.

Briant, P. 2002 "History and ideology: the Greeks and 'Persian decadence' " (transl. A. Nevill), in T. Harrison (ed.) *Greeks and Barbarians*, Edinburgh.

Due, B. 1989 *The Cyropaedia: Xenophon's Aims and Methods*, Aarhus.

Gomme, A.W. 1945 *Historical Commentary on Thucydides*, vol. 1, Oxford.

Gray, V.J. 2005 'Xenophon and isocrates', in C. Rowe & M. Schofield (eds) *The Cambridge History of Greek and Roman Thought*, Cambridge, 142–54.

——. 2007 *Xenophon: On government*, Cambridge.

Hansen, M.H. 1986 'The origin of the term *demokratia*', *Liverpool Classical Monthly* 11, 35–6.

——. 1991 *The Athenian Democracy in the Age of Demosthenes*, Oxford.

Harvey, F.D. 1965 'Two kinds of equality', *Classica & Mediaevalia* 26, 101–46.

——. 1966 'Corrigenda' *Classica & Mediaevalia* 27, 99–100.

Hodkinson, S. 2005 'The imaginary Spartan *politeia*', in M.H. Hansen (ed.) *The Imaginary Polis* (Acts of the Copenhagen Polis Centre no. 7), Copenhagen, 222–81.

Hornblower, S. 1991–2008 *Commentary on Thucydides* (in 3 vols), Oxford.

Huffman, C. 2005 *Archytas of Tarentum: Pythagorean, Philosopher, Mathematician King*, Cambidge.

Kerferd, G.B. 1981 *The Sophistic Movement*, Cambridge.

Mitchell, L.G. 1997 *Greeks Bearing Gifts: The Public Use of Private Relationships in the Greek World, 431–323 BC*, Cambridge.

——. 2008 'Thucydides and the monarch in democracy', *Polis* 25, 1–30.

——. 2009 'The rules of the game: three studies in friendship, equality and politics', in L.G. Mitchell & L. Rubinstein (eds) *Greek History and Epigraphy: Essays in Honour of P.J. Rhodes*, Swansea, 1–32.

Morris, I. 1996 'The Strong Principle of Equality and the archaic origins of Greek democracy', in J. Ober & C. Hedrick (eds) *Demokratia: A Conversation on Democracies, Ancient and Modern*, Princeton, 19–48, 21.

Newell, W.R. 1983 'Tyranny and the science of ruling', *Journal of Politics* 45, 889–906.

——. 1991 'Superlative virtue: The problem of monarchy in Aristotle's *Politics*', in C. Lord & D. O'Connor (eds) *Essays on the Foundation of Aristotelian Political Science*, Berkeley, Los Angeles & Oxford, 191–211.

Ober, J. 1991 'The Athenian revolution of 508/7 BC: Violence, authority and the origins of democracy', *The Athenian Revolution. Essays on Ancient Greek Democracy and Political Theory*, Princeton.

Pelling, C.B.R. 2002 'Speech and action: Herodotus' debate on the constitutions', *Proceedings of the Cambridge Philological Society* 48, 123–58.

Raaflaub, K.A. 1996 'Equalities and inequalities in Athenian democracy', in J. Ober & C. Hedrick (eds) *Demokratia: A Conversation on Democracies, Ancient and Modern*, Princeton, 139–74.

——. 2005 'Poets, lawgivers, and the beginnings of political reflection in archaic Greece', in C. Rowe & M. Schofield (eds) *The Cambridge History of Greek and Roman Thought*, Cambridge, 23–59.

Rhodes, P.J. 1972 'The Five Thousand in the Athenian revolution of 411 BC', *Journal of Hellenic Studies* 92, 115–27.

——. 1980 'Athenian democracy after 403 BC', *Classical Journal* 75, 305–23.

——. 1988 *Thucydides: History II*, Warminster.

——. 1992 'The Athenian revolution', in *Cambridge Ancient History* v2, Cambridge, 62–95.

Rusten, J.S. 1989 *Thucydides, The Peloponnesian War: Book II*, Cambridge.

Schofield, M. 2005 'Aristotle: an introduction', in C. Rowe & M. Schofield (eds) *The Cambridge History of Greek and Roman Political Thought*, Cambridge, 310–20.

Commentary

Transformational leadership, or transformational tyranny?

There are three significant themes linking this paper to contemporary leadership studies. The first is to ask, what is the basis for the leader's authority?

The ancient Greeks made a distinction between a king and a tyrant, the former subjecting himself to the law. The ideal of the good king was as attractive as many people today find the idea of the good leader. Cyrus the Great, as presented to us by Xenophon, claimed his legitimacy as a monarch on the grounds that he was the most deserving of the kingship through proven merit. There is no question that he was or should be elected into his position; rather that his personal virtues and his achievements in command would speak for themselves and be commonly appreciated by those who thus willingly became his followers.

Cyrus therefore based his claims to the right to lead on the basis that his authority to do so had become self-evident to his followers: they should recognise his qualifications to do so because they have themselves experienced his pre-eminence in creating for them a hierarchical social order.

However, in spite of these claims to the legitimacy of both bureaucratic order and proven merit, Cyrus actually strove to create enthusiasm for what might be termed transformational tyranny. His methods for doing so were primarily those of patronage and punishment informed by a carefully constructed system of spies. In this system one might assume that the primary virtue is that of partisanship and hence at least the show of friendship which brings with it inherent risks of betrayal, corruption and narcissism. If 'good behaviour' is equivalent to 'doing what the boss expects', the only way to operate is to try to get inside the mind of the leader; thus, an entire organisation can unconsciously conceive its task as being to imagine, reflect and embody the presumed will of the leader.

The dangers of corporatism

Sociologists from Max Weber onwards have remarked on the tendency of modern organisations to assert a unitary model of organisational life, bolstered by a rhetoric that the interests of each individual are, in all important respects, commensurate with those of the corporate whole.

Xenophon presents the willing obedience to a system as rational, fair and justified by the fact that people apparently choose to be part of it. In this conception, the ideal follower is one whose commitment amounts to a readiness to sacrifice his or her self-interest insofar as it differs from that of the whole, and the dangers are self-evident.

The uses and abuses of rhetoric

In contemporary organisational studies we have become accustomed to taking a somewhat critical view of the way in which people talk about matters such as 'distributed leadership', 'teamwork' and 'meritocracy'. This is not because scholars are critical of these ideas or processes; rather we are curious about the functions they perform in the realities of organisational life.

So, for example, the widespread use of the term 'distributed leadership' in public sector organisations in the UK may be seen on the one hand to authorise entrepreneurial initiative at all levels of the organisation while on the other hand obscuring the demise of formal consultative processes.

In this case, the rhetorical function of distributed leadership has what might be called a shadow side as well as its overt and intended outcome.

In this paper Mitchell shows us how the apparent reasonableness of 'obedience' allows for the establishment of a totalitarian system, masquerading as a legitimate and law-abiding bureaucratic hierarchy. Xenophon describes how Cyrus would reward those who were obedient and punish the disobedient as if this was a natural extension of the perfectly reasonable order that placed him at his pinnacle.

As Mitchell says, 'viewed in this light, willing obedience appears less willing'. The analogies to power relationships in the present day are there to be identified by any reader who chooses to do so. Rhetoric remains a useful device for leaders of many kinds, and freedom of speech will always be a contentious subject.

2
Sharing the Secret: Joseph Conrad on Leadership at Sea

Peter Villiers

I need not tell you what it is to be knocking about in an open boat. I remember nights and days of calm when we pulled, we pulled, and the boat seemed to stand still, as if bewitched within the circle of the sea horizon. I remember the heat, the deluge of rain-squalls that kept us baling for dear life (but filled our water-cask), and I remember sixteen hours on end with a mouth dry as a cinder and a steering-oar over the stern to keep my first command head on to a breaking sea. I did not know how good a man I was till then. I remember the drawn faces, the dejected figures of my two men, and I remember my youth and the feeling that will never come back any more—the feeling that I could last for ever, outlast the sea, the earth, and all men; the deceitful feeling that lures us on to joys, to perils, to love, to vain effort—to death; the triumphant conviction of strength, the heat of life in the handful of dust, the glow in the heart that with every year grows dim, grows cold, grows small, and expires—and expires, too soon—before life itself.

Joseph Conrad
Youth

Leaders or aspiring practitioners of leadership in the modern world might, at first sight, appear to have little to learn from the life, experience and writings of the writer Joseph Conrad (1857–1924), who was born in the Ukraine, served in the French and British merchant navies, and came ashore in his late thirties to become a novelist in his second adopted tongue—for French was the first foreign language in which he became fluent and in which he might have written his books.

Many of Conrad's novels and stories are set at sea on sailing ships or in the exotic location of the East as he experienced it in the late nineteenth century. Commercial sail has disappeared from the face of the earth, and the modern merchant service of tankers, container ships and colossal cruise liners would be as unfamiliar to the former Captain Korzeniowski as the colonial possessions he once visited. What can this Polish-British ex-mariner tell us about the art of leadership today?

Firstly, it would be wrong to categorise Conrad simply as an old salt who wrote entirely or mainly about the sea, and whose stories can be seen simply as maritime adventures or romances. Secondly, it would be unwise in any case to limit his contribution to our understanding of human nature and the human dilemma to a particular time and place. Conrad was a remarkably perceptive and subtle writer who showed a profound insight into human nature in any location. He did not restrict his work to the sea or exotic locations, although even had he done so, his best work would still have a universal application.

The Secret Agent is set entirely in London, which almost becomes a character in itself. There is no taste of the salt in *Under Western Eyes*, a tale set in Russia and Switzerland; nor in *Nostromo*, in which the eponymous 'hero' has served in the merchant navy but makes his mark on land; nor in many others of Conrad's works. This need not surprise us, for the subject of Conrad's curiosity is human nature itself, whether on land or sea.

What where those views, as they are revealed in his stories, and how do they relate to the study of leadership? Before we can consider Conrad the writer and his views on leadership, we need to go back to 1857, the year of his birth, and consider Conrad the man.

*   *   *

Joseph Teodor Konrad Korzeniowski was born in 1857 to a Polish family resident in the Ukraine. The once powerful kingdom of Poland had been dismembered by its neighbours three times, and in 1795, under the third partition of Poland, it had officially ceased to exist. What had been Poland was divided under Prussian, Russian and Austrian rule, and although Conrad was ethnically a Pole and spoke Polish as his first language, by birth he was a Russian subject.

Conrad described himself in later life as having been born into the *szlachta*, or land-tilling aristocracy, a class which had no precise equivalent in the England he came to adopt as his home. It was, perhaps, the equivalent of the gentry: but it was a gentry that contained about ten per cent of the Polish population and claimed to speak for the people as a whole.

Conrad's father Apollo Korzeniowski (1820–69) was an intellectual by inclination who had studied in St Petersburg but failed to take a degree.

A minor poet, unsuccessful dramatist and proficient translator, Apollo showed no aptitude for business and failed to manage the family estates to any advantage. He did, however, make a very happy marriage to a young woman named Ewa Bobrowska, and their union resulted in one child. The marriage had been opposed by the Bobrowski family, who believed that the intense, over-idealistic and impractical Apollo was an unsuitable suitor; an assessment which was unfortunately to prove correct.

Apollo was an ardent patriot, wholly committed to the active achievement of Polish independence. He conspired in Warsaw (which was under Russian rule) with his fellow-patriots, and in 1861 was sent into exile in northern Russia for his crimes, together with his frail young wife and son. The exile was a disaster from which the family never recovered. Ewa became so ill with tuberculosis that she was finally allowed to return to Poland to die. She did so in 1865, to be followed to the grave four years later by her mourning husband.

Conrad's relationship with his father, once they had returned to Poland, was an almost silent one. Although we are not always justified in linking an event in an author's life to the character and behaviour of one of his fictional creations, it is difficult to imagine that Apollo is *not* the template for the father of Axel Heyst, a lonely exile in the Malayan archipelago, who is the main character of Conrad's novel *Victory*. That is an issue to which we shall return at a later point.

Conrad described his father Apollo as:

> A man of great sensibilities; of exalted and dreamy temperament; with a terrible gift of irony and of a gloomy disposition; withal of strong religious feeling degenerating after the loss of his wife into mysticism touched with despair.

Apollo's refined sensibilities had, however, failed to impress his brother-in-law, Tadeusz Bobrowski. In his view, the Korzeniowskis were distinguished by a sort of reckless impetuosity which often resulted in disaster. The Bobrowskis, on the other hand, were more cautious, more politically skilled and more adept, reflecting their more pragmatic approach to life. Tadeusz Bobrowski himself was a successful land-owner and businessman with many interests, who had managed to reach an accommodation with the authorities, and saw nothing to be gained from a futile rebellion. The widower Bobrowski became Conrad's ward on the death of his father. Conrad was treated with extraordinary kindness by his uncle, who invested a considerable sum on his education and development, and was to exercise a careful influence on his cherished but vulnerable nephew for a long time to come.

The young Conrad was an intelligent, independent-minded boy who tended to show a keen belief in his own merits and potential, whether or not that potential had yet been justified by the facts. His education lay mainly in the hands of a tutor, and his uncle had in mind a career in business for him. When he was 15, however, he told his uncle that he wished to go to sea—an astonishing ambition for a boy from rural Poland, and one which had developed from his reading and his romantic imagination. After some consideration, Bobrowski decided that the best way to overcome this strange and probably unsuitable ambition was to give way to it: the young Conrad was despatched by train from Krakow to Marseilles to begin a career in the French merchant service.

Conrad loved Marseilles, where his uncle had business acquaintances, and he was able to serve aboard ship in a relatively privileged position as a sort of apprentice ship's officer, living aft and taking his meals with the officers. Whatever else this strange young Pole might be, he was clearly a gentleman. He sowed his wild oats with a vengeance, later claiming to have taken part in gun-running to Carlist rebels in Spain. He certainly ran up large debts, and made an attempt at suicide as a probable consequence. His uncle, who loved him dearly despite his faults, came to Marseilles, paid his debts, and resolved the crisis—for the time being. Unfailingly loyal to his ward, he described him at this time as 'not a bad boy, but one who is extremely sensitive, conceited, reserved, and in addition excitable' (Stape, 2007, Page 33).

A further crisis loomed as he neared 20 years of age, when Conrad's residential status in France would cause difficulties. He took ship for Lowestoft, where the British merchant service needed men in large numbers, of any origin.

* * *

Conrad was to spend 20 years in the merchant service, first under the French tricolour and then the British red ensign. According to his own account, he had no childhood ambition to become a writer, and his merchant service was not a means to acquire 'copy': his ambition was to master his trade and make his career as a sailor. He completed the necessary sea-time; obtained his second mate, mate and master's tickets; and, with his uncle's encouragement, obtained British nationality. However, Conrad did not entirely master his profession. He held one command, but resigned his ship, the *Otago*. His last settled position, as first officer of the *Torrens*, came to an end when the vessel was docked for repairs.

In 1895 Joseph Conrad—still known as Konrad Korzeniowski—was a 38-year-old master mariner with neither ship nor line to support him. Having been, in effect, a stateless exile, he had adopted a new language and nationality at first of necessity and then with enthusiasm; but his career had stalled. He had, however, begun to write. He had completed the manuscript for a novel called *Almayer's Folly*, which was set in the east, and on which he had been working for five years and on various voyages. He wrote that he had begun the story by chance, when he had nothing to do one morning in his lodgings. Like much of what Conrad says about himself, this may be taken with a pinch of salt. What is surprising about Conrad is not his literary inclinations, but his success in rising to the rank of master mariner in the British merchant service: an achievement that demonstrated the Bobrowski side of his character rather more than his Korzeniowski inheritance, and which was to delight his long-suffering uncle.

Within a surprisingly short time, Conrad had published his first novel to critical acclaim; married a Miss Jessie George, with whom he was to raise two sons; and settled down ashore to pursue a new career as a man of letters. Despite huge financial difficulties, he pursued his new career to the end and never returned to sea. After 18 years of hard times, he was able to achieve the monetary success that followed his literary recognition. Joseph Conrad was the acclaimed author of a number of highly respected novels, which had transformed the British approach to narration and were in the vanguard of modernism. In 1923, he had toured America as a literary lion. And he was offered a knighthood: a distinction he declined, it was said, because he was already a member of the *szlachta*. He died in 1924, his reputation secured, and the highly influential literary critic F R Leavis later went on to describe him as one of the finest novelists in English or any language.

*   *   *

The test: leadership and character

> The claims of the sea are simple and cannot be evaded.
>
> (*Chance*, 1913)

For Conrad, the sea is where man is challenged and where he finds out if he is made of 'the right stuff'. In Conrad's work, men, ships and the sea inter-penetrate each other. The sea is a perfidious environment which can never be fully trusted, for even its playfulness is deadly; sooner or later it will test everyone who ventures upon it.

The Nigger of the Narcissus (1897), *Lord Jim* (1900) and Conrad's stories 'Typhoon' and 'The Secret Sharer' (1912) show the nature of the challenges posed and the responses they evoke. As a preliminary guide to what would otherwise be an uncharted voyage into the unknown, we may say from the start that Conrad is a pessimist about life, whether at sea or ashore, and believes that many of the challenges it poses will prove insuperable to those who face them. The leader may easily become bogged down in loneliness, isolation and even despair; but he may achieve a hard-fought victory over adversity as he draws on his inner resources. Conrad is a pessimist, but not a fatalist, and resilience is the key. The challenges that leaders face in reality are nothing like the one-dimensional exercises of a management primer. They engage the leader in every part of his being, and need to be seen in their historical and social as well as their individual context.

*   *   *

The Nigger of the Narcissus is a saga of a deep sea sailing-ship voyage. We are taken aboard the *Narcissus* by an anonymous narrator, who accompanies us on her tempestuous passage from Bombay to London. The story begins with the crew being mustered to be divided into watches by the mate, Mr Baker, and ends with them being paid off in England—minus the black seaman, James Wait, who has died at the end of the voyage within sight and smell of land. The (male) crew is of mixed nationality and the story of their voyage is at least partly one of conflict: conflict within the fo'c's'l; conflict between the officers and the men, which verges on mutiny; and conflict between the ship and the sea, as it first weathers a crushing storm and then battles against prevailing head-winds. However, in the end the story is one of hope. The ship reaches its destination, and the crew lives to sail again. In the world of the sailing-ship, each completed voyage is a victory.

Formal leadership is displayed by the master and his mates, as assisted by the bo'sun. There is a parallel issue of leadership within the fo'c's'l, where there is no formal leader and various seamen exercise an influence on the rest of the crew for good or bad. Three are of special interest: Donkin, a malcontent and agitator who believes in his 'rights'; Singleton, a fine old seaman who does his duty and sets an example, but preaches no doctrine; and the black man himself, James Wait, who soon proves to be desperately ill and is removed to a deckhouse under captain's orders.

The Master: Captain Allistoun

Captain Allistoun is an effective captain who is always calm and exerts his authority only when needed. Whatever the situation, he keeps his nerve; he has seen it all before, and has an absolute conviction in his own abilities, which have been honed from a working lifetime at sea. This is how Conrad describes him, after a heavy iron belaying-pin has been thrown at him by Donkin:

> Captain Allistoun was composed and thoughtful...He was one of those commanders who speak little, seem to hear nothing, look at no-one—and know everything, hear every whisper, see every fleeting shadow of their ship's life. His two big officers towered over his lean, short figure; they talked over his head; they were dismayed, surprised and angry, while between them the little man seemed to have found his taciturn serenity in the profound depths of a larger experience...

The captain musters his crew and confronts them:

> He stood scanning them for a moment, then walking a few steps this way and that began to storm at them coldly, in gusts violent and cutting like the gales of those icy seas that had known his youth.— 'Tell you what's the matter. Too big for your boots. Think yourselves damn good men. Know half your work. Do half your duty. Think it too much. If you did ten times as much it wouldn't be enough.'— 'We did our best by her, Sir' cried someone with shaky exasperation.— 'Your best', stormed on the master; 'You hear a lot on shore, don't you? They don't tell you there your best isn't much to boast of. I tell you—your best is no better than bad.... There is another thing', said the master, calmly. He made a quick stride and with a swing took an iron belaying-pin out of his pocket. 'This!...I don't ask you any questions, but you all know it; it has got to go back where it came from.' His eyes became angry...'Donkin', he called out in a short, sharp tone.

By force of personality, the master compels Donkin to replace the pin where it belongs—much to the relief of the watching mate, who feared that Donkin would use it to strike the master down. Allistoun, however, has no such fear, although he describes the crew as a queer lot, whom he finds unpredictable. He comments to Mr Baker:

'Years ago—I was a young master then—one China voyage I had a mutiny; real mutiny, Baker. Different men, tho'. I knew what they wanted: they wanted to broach the cargo and get at the liquor. Very simple.... We knocked them about for two days, and when they had enough—gentle as lambs. Good crew. And a smart trip I made.' He glanced aloft at the yards braced sharp up. 'Head wind day after day', he exclaimed, bitterly. 'Shall we never get a decent slant this passage?'

The mate: Mr Baker

The mate is a natural second in command, who prefers someone else to make the really important decisions. He is a disciplinarian, but not a martinet. It is his task to make sure that the captain's will prevails and that the crew is licked into shape; and he does so. His credo is a very simple one: the ship must come first. When the *Narcissus* has been knocked flat by a storm and is very likely to founder, Mr Baker, while exercising an excellent duty of care by his actions in working alongside the crew and sharing the imminent danger with them, speaks to them in sardonic tones. Naturally, it is their duty to put the ship first, and they should not even think of their own safety. One of them has the temerity to claim that the master (who has refused to cut the masts and thereby save the ship) does not care for them. Mr Baker is incensed.

'Care for you!' exclaimed Mr Baker, angrily.

"Why should be care for you? Are you a lot of women passengers to be taken care of? We are here to take care of the ship—and some of you ain't up to it. Ough!... What have you done so very smart, to be taken care of? Ough! Some of you can't stand a bit of a breeze without crying over it." (Page 79)

At the end of the voyage, and after the crew has been paid off, Mr Baker has nowhere to go and lingers on board, and here Conrad shows another side to Baker's character. He has sacrificed his life ashore to his profession, and the care he might have given to a wife and family has been lavished instead on his ships and their crews. Conrad was an admirer of such men and their quiet dedication to a worthy cause; he recognised the sacrifices that being a model ship's officer imposed.

> Mr Baker, in the sudden peace of the ship, moved about solitary and grunting, trying door-handles, peering into dark places, never done— a model chief mate! No one waited for him ashore....Mr Baker sat smoking, thinking of all the successive ships to whom through many long years he had given the best of a seaman's care. And never a command in sight. Not once!—'I haven't somehow the cut of a skipper about me', he meditated, placidly ... (Page 166)

Mr Creighton, the second mate, is lightly sketched. He is a professional merchant service officer from a good background, destined for command, and he performs his duties admirably. When injured in the storm, he does not complain, but is a model of stoicism. However, unlike his senior officer, whom Conrad describes with faint irony as a model chief mate, Mr Creighton earns no such encomium—if only because his passage to the top is too assured.

The voyage of the *Narcissus* may appear as an almost idealised portrayal of leadership at sea, in which autocratic but benevolent dictatorship achieves the common good. However, although Conrad paints a gripping picture of effective captaincy, this is not just a story of leadership under crisis. It explores group dynamics in a confined environment and, in particular, the solidarity which the crew at least partially achieves on their odyssey, moulded as they are by the demands of the sea and the winds, and the incessant need to care for the ship. It is possible to analyse and interpret the story on many levels.

The black man, James Wait, has a crucial role to play, for he acts as a catalyst for the emotions of the crew and a focus for their fears, hopes and prejudices. His blackness is not only literal but symbolic, and he represents a challenge that the master cannot resolve. Wait brings out both the best and the worst in his comrades. During the great storm in which the ship is laid flat on its beam ends, he is rescued from his sick man's deckhouse by the crew at great personal risk. He is then betrayed by his treacherous admirer, Donkin, who steals his few possessions when Wait is on his deathbed and no longer able to protect himself.

The unidentified narrator describes a scene as the crew is paid off at Tower Hill, their purpose complete, their solidarity at an end—but their essential humanity still very evident:

> As I came up I saw a red-faced, blowsy woman in a grey shawl, and with dusty, fluffy, hair, fall on Charley's neck. It was his mother. She slobbered over him:—'O, my boy! My boy!'—'Leggo of me', said Charley, 'Leggo, mother!' I was passing him at the time, and over the

untidy head of the blubbering woman he gave me a humorous smile and a glance ironic, courageous and profound, that seemed to put all my knowledge of life to shame.

The crew separates, never to meet again. However, they remain in the memory of the narrator:

Good-bye, brothers! You were a good crowd. As good a crowd as ever fisted with wild cries the beating canvas of a heavy foresail; or tossing aloft, invisible in the night, gave back yell for yell to a westerly gale.

(*Narcissus*, Pages 171, 173)

Lord Jim

'Lord' Jim—the title is ironic and we never learn his surname—is a merchant service officer who goes astray. His beginnings are conventional enough. The son of a parson, he joins the merchant service as a cadet, dreaming of heroism, adventure and romance—and rises to the rank of chief officer without, it seems, encountering any of the three.

Training: a missed opportunity

Jim missed his first opportunity to perform a heroic act when training as an officer cadet on a moored ship. The sea had risen, and a nearby vessel was suddenly in difficulty.

Something's up. Come along.

He (Jim) leaped to his feet. The boys were streaming up the ladders. Above could be heard a great scurrying about and shouting, and when he got through the hatchway he stood still—as if confounded...

He was jostled. 'Man the cutter!' Boys rushed past him...Jim felt his shoulder gripped firmly. 'Too late, youngster.' The captain of the ship laid a restraining hand on that boy, who seemed on the point of leaping overboard, and Jim looked up with the pain of conscious defeat in his eyes. The captain smiled sympathetically. 'Better luck next time. This will teach you to be smart.'

A shrill cheer greeted the cutter. She came dancing back half full of water, and with two exhausted men washing about on her bottom boards.

The tumult and the menace of wind and sea now appeared very contemptible to Jim, increasing the regret of his awe at their inefficient menace. Now he knew what to think of it. It seemed to him he cared nothing for the gale. He could affront greater perils. He would do so—better than anybody. Not a particle of fear was left. Nevertheless he brooded apart that evening while the bowman of the cutter—a boy with a face like a girl's and big grey eyes—was the hero of the lower deck...

Jim thought it a pitiful display of vanity...'

In other words, Jim is able to rationalise his inability to respond to the sudden emergency that arose, but only by lying to himself—by denying the danger and denigrating his successful rival, who did not stop to dream, but acted. Jim is a romantic who is dominated by his imagination, and has failed his first test without even admitting his failure. Consequently, he has learned nothing from the experience.

The Patna

As chief officer of the *Patna*, carrying 800 Muslim pilgrims across the Red Sea to Mecca, Jim has still to find out if he is made of the right stuff, and has yet to rise above his youthful egoism. Fate again strikes when he least expects it. The *Patna*, a tramp-steamer commanded by a scoundrel and equipped only with token lifeboats, hits a submerged obstacle at sea and so damages its bow that the sea comes through to the forward bulkhead. Jim goes forward to investigate and finds that all that stands between him, the rest of the crew, the 800 pilgrims and the ocean is a thin, rusty sheet of metal that might collapse at any moment. His forestalling imagination takes hold and he enters a state of frozen panic. He goes back to the bridge, where the captain and the other officers are frantically clearing a lifeboat to save themselves, having already given up voyage, ship and passengers as a lost cause. They launch the boat and call to another crew member, whom they are unaware is already dead, to join them. It is Jim's opportunity to show heroism by remaining at his post, but he does not take it. He jumps, although it is not a conscious decision, at least as he describes it.

I had jumped... It seems, he says.

The rest of the episode is easily told. The men in the lifeboat row away from the ship. The ship's lights disappear and they assume that it has foundered. Their lifeboat is rescued by another steamer. They tell their agreed lies about the loss of their own ship, and are taken to port only to find that the *Patna* has been rescued! It was discovered, deserted by its white crew and drifting aimlessly on the seas, by a French gunboat that took it on tow—stern first. It was a magnificent feat of seamanship, and the ship made port with not a passenger lost. Would that the first officer had stayed to assist!

The inquiry: Captain Brierly

An inquiry is organised. What will Jim do? Attend and be formally disgraced, or disappear into oblivion like his fellow officers? Jim attends: and this is where he first meets the merchant service officer Marlow who will tell his story.

Jim's presence is particularly upsetting for Captain Brierly, the nautical expert at the inquiry. Why, is not at first entirely clear, for the two men could not be further apart in stature and reputation. Marlow takes up the story:

Big Brierly. Some of you must have heard of Big Brierly—the captain of the crack ship of the Blue Star line. That's the man.

He seemed consumedly bored by the honour thrust upon him. He had never in his life made a mistake, never had an accident, never a mishap, never a check in his steady rise, and he seemed to be one of those lucky fellows who know nothing of indecision, much less of self-mistrust.

He had saved lives at sea, had rescued ships in distress, had a gold chronometer presented to him.... He was acutely aware of his merits and of his rewards. I liked him well enough, though some I know—meek, friendly men at that—couldn't stand him at any price...As I looked at him, flanking on one side the unassuming pale-faced magistrate who presided at the inquiry, his self-satisfaction presented to me and to the world a surface as hard as granite. He committed suicide very soon after.

Why does he do so? Conrad, via Marlow, implies rather than states the cause. It seems that, firstly, Brierly is horrified that Jim, a white man and 'one of us' (unlike the German ship's captain, an obvious scoundrel), has let the side down. Secondly, this unexpected and catastrophic failure has caused Brierly to have doubts about himself, and he cannot live with the consequences. As he puts it to Marlow:

This is a disgrace. We've got all kinds amongst us—some anointed scoundrels in the lot; but, hang it, we must preserve professional decency or we become no better than so many tinkers going about loose. We are trusted. Do you understand?—trusted! Frankly, I don't care a snap for all the pilgrims that ever came out of Asia, but a decent man would not have behaved like this to a full cargo of old rags in bales. We aren't an organized body of men, and the only thing that holds us together is just the name for that kind of decency. Such an affair destroys one's confidence. A man may go pretty near through his whole sea-life without any call to show a stiff upper lip. But when the call comes...

(Lord Jim, Page 49)

Jim loses his certificate and profession, and with Marlow's assistance seeks other work in the East—for he cannot return home. He finds work as a harbour clerk in one port after another, desperately moving on as each time his secret is uncovered. Eventually he is taken up by a German trader called Stein, who recognises Jim to be a romantic like himself and agrees with Marlow to give him another chance. Jim becomes Stein's agent in the remote trading post of Patusan, far away from civilisation where his past should not follow him. There, he finally shows the leadership of which he has dreamed, and creates a new reputation for himself. He finds his woman, Jewel. He is admired for himself: for what he has achieved, and not for his fantasies of glory. He has made a new beginning, and put the past behind him. What could possibly go wrong?

The answer is, of course, that he cannot put the past behind him. Civilisation follows Jim to Patusan in the shape of Gentleman Brown, a piratical malcontent who is determined to raid the colony as a terrorist venture. Jim bargains with him: if Brown will leave Patusan empty-handed, then Jim will let him depart as he came. For the first time, Jim's admirers are not happy about his leadership: Brown and his colleagues are bad men and cannot be trusted. They should be killed while the opportunity is there. No, says Jim, he will not allow that; even Brown deserves a second chance. He trusts him, and will guarantee with his own life that Brown will depart with his tail between his legs and without harming anyone.

Brown is not prepared to do this: he breaks his promise and opens fire, killing the chief's beloved son, Dain Warris, who is Jim's most admiring follower. Brown and his colleagues are defeated in their turn: but the reaction is too late. Jim has given his word and he must keep it. He cannot have an ongoing series of second chances. He abandoned the *Patna*, although in fact no-one was drowned. Now he has betrayed Patusan. He is executed by the grieving father, without a second thought.

Why does Jim trust Brown, who is so patently untrustworthy? There seem to be two reasons. Firstly, Brown has touched a raw nerve in the other Englishman, for he shows a satanic skill in finding out another's weakness. On his deathbed, Brown boasts of his achievement.

He asked Jim whether he had nothing fishy in his life to remember that he was so damnedly hard upon a man trying to get out of a deadly hole by the first means that came to hand—and so on, and so on. And there ran through the rough talk a vein of subtle reference to their common blood, an assumption of common experience; a sickening suggestion of common guilt, of secret knowledge that was like a bond of their minds and of their hearts.

(Lord Jim, Chapter 42)

Secondly, Jim trusts Brown, it seems, because Stein trusted *him*; and in his arrogance he gives his word. Once he has done so, he cannot take it back, and must face the consequences.

Actions and consequences

The real-life stimulus for the creation of the fictional Lord Jim was a merchant service officer called Augustus Podmore Williams who abandoned his ship, the *Jeddah*, and its passengers in 1880 and was consequently disgraced. Podmore Williams, however, made no attempt to escape or hide his past. He stayed put and faced his critics until he was eventually rehabilitated; a display either of an extraordinary lack of imagination or an impressive reservoir of moral courage, neither of which Lord Jim was able to access.

Lord Jim fails at sea and then on land, for he can never overcome his incurable romanticism—unless we conclude that in accepting his self-imposed fate and honouring his word, he has in fact succeeded. But that is not how Conrad presents the story, which ends not on a note of tragedy but of ambiguity.

Honour, self-sacrifice and redemption

Lord Jim may be interpreted as a story of redemption, in which a young man who appears to be made of the right stuff, but proves not to be, is able to redeem his failure by self-sacrifice. Honour is not presented in this tale as an abstract quality, but as something concrete; and its loss is irrecoverable. Captain Brierly wishes that Jim had buried himself 20 feet underground, rather than expose himself and his peers to public humiliation. When he has had time to reflect on what Jim did, and to realise that the seeds of corruption are within everyone, he cannot live with the knowledge he has acquired, and kills himself: although he makes sure first that his own command will not suffer as a consequence.

The French naval officer who saved the *Patna*, and whom Marlow meets several years later in Sydney, expresses an understanding of what

Jim did, as he believes that fundamentally all men are cowards, and that it is only habit, necessity, or the scrutiny or example of others that makes them act heroically. Nevertheless, he cannot imagine acting improperly, nor how he would cope with the consequences were he somehow to do so; and at this point his conversation with Marlow comes to an abrupt end. For him, as for Brierly, honour is something tangible, and once it has been lost it cannot be regained.

Jim does what he does, because that is how he *is*, and he cannot change that. He does not resolve the question of 'how to be', as Stein puts it (Page 153). However, he does act to redeem his second disgrace, and in dying he achieves a partial if Pyhrric victory.

'Typhoon'

Conrad presents Jim's contrast in Captain MacWhirr of the *Nan-Shan* ('Typhoon', 1902), who saves his ship by sheer obstinacy from the typhoon in which it has been placed by his own stupidity. He lacks imagination, one might argue, and so he succeeds. The literally minded Captain MacWhirr is almost, but not quite, a figure of fun; and the sto- ical determination he displays in adversity may be because he simply could not imagine acting otherwise. Nevertheless, Captain MacWhirr displays what Conrad esteems as fidelity, and he is loyal to his ship, his crew and his cargo of Chinese indentured labourers ('coolies'). He sends his first mate, Jukes, forward at the height of the storm to see to their welfare; and at the end of the voyage, which the *Nan-Shan* has quite astonishingly survived, he makes sure that their silver dollars, which had been scattered throughout the hold, are fairly returned to them. MacWhirr, whose wife dreads his eventual retirement from the sea, and who is consistently described as stupid by his first officer, is a decent and honourable man; his example shows us the importance of habit in acting properly, so that the decision of 'how to be' (as Stein defines the purpose of life to Marlow) has in a sense already been made.

'The Secret Sharer'

'The Secret Sharer' explores the isolation and potential for narcissism of command and presents an ambiguous conclusion. Although the unnamed captain of his first command finally comes to grips with the responsibilities that he faces, it is at the cost of putting his ship and crew in extreme and unnecessary danger. He had formed a secret relationship with a fugitive from justice named Leggatt, whom he hides in his cabin.

Leggatt, it seems, is the only person on board ship to whom the captain can relate. He then manoeuvres his ship far too close to land, to allow the fugitive to swim ashore.

In manoeuvring his ship in this desperate venture, the master learns how to handle his first command. The story ends thus:

> I walked to the break of the poop. On the over-shadowed deck all hands stood by the forebraces waiting for my order. The stars ahead seemed to be gliding from right to left. And all was so still in the world that I heard the quiet remark, 'She's round' passed in a tone of intense relief between two seamen.
>
> 'Let go and haul.'
>
> The foreyards ran round with a great noise, amidst cheery cries. And now the frightful whiskers [the mate] made themselves heard giving various orders. Already the ship was drawing ahead. And I was alone with her. Nothing! No one in the world should stand now between us, throwing a shadow on the way of silent knowledge and mute affection, the perfect communion of a seaman with his first command.
>
> Walking to the taffrail, I was in time to make out, on the very edge of a darkness thrown by a towering black mass like the very gateway of Erebus—yes, I was in time to catch an evanescent glimpse of my white hat left behind to mark the spot where the secret sharer of my cabin and of my thoughts, as though he were my second self, had lowered himself into the water to take his punishment: a free man, a proud swimmer striking out for a new destiny.
>
> (Conrad, 1947, Page 143)

The isolation of command

In any conventional analysis, the captain's behaviour is inexplicable. Why is he unable to communicate with any other member of the crew of his new command? Why does he feel so strong an affinity to Leggatt, the first officer of the *Sephora*, who killed a member of his own crew in a storm in order, according to his own account, to save the ship? Why does he deceive the master of the *Sephora*, who comes searching for his missing first officer? Why does he believe that a jury would be incapable of understanding what Leggatt did, and why he did it? Finally, why does the captain risk the loss of his first command?

This is a strange and haunting story by a master of his art. It deals with the loneliness of command, an experience that Conrad himself had felt acutely when he was unexpectedly offered the command of the barque *Otago*. (The ship's master had walked overboard, its mate was bitterly resentful of Conrad's appointment, its crew was sick, and its accounts were in chaos—hardly an auspicious introduction to his first command!) Perhaps its most telling comment comes early in the story, when the new captain says that when he took command he was a stranger to the ship and her crew, and indeed 'if all the truth must be told, I was somewhat of a stranger to myself' (Page 95). He did not know if he was made of the right stuff; that is a puzzle he has to solve for himself.

Conclusion

Conrad was pessimistic about political idealism—his father's experience had not been an encouraging one—and at a deeper level deeply sceptical about the idea of progress as a whole. A man without illusions, he disbelieved in empire, failed to share in the contemporary enthusiasm for science and described Christianity as an oriental fable. In his popular novel *Chance* (1913) he ridiculed both the great financier de Barral as an obvious confidence trickster and the public who so easily believed in him. He was a natural conservative who believed in the enduring values of family and nation, even if he had lost his own. He was unlikely, in other words, to be seduced by the charisma, real or apparent, of any populist leader: and indeed his major novel *Nostromo* points to the futility of any such adherence.

His contemporary admirer, Bertrand Russell, remarked that Conrad 'thought of civilised and morally tolerable human life as a dangerous walk on a thin crust of barely cooled lava which at any moment might break and let the unwary sink into fiery depths' (Russell, 1969, Page 87). But that did not mean that no-one should venture onto the crust.

Conrad believed that life is a struggle in which the odds are stacked against us, and in which happiness is an unlikely outcome. As one biographer put it, he admired the virtues of honour, courage, communal spirit and professional skill (Gurko, 1963, Page 278) but believed that even if they could be acquired, they were not enough to ensure success, and were, in any case, more easily applied at sea than on land.

The underlying quality needed was resilience:

> In the end the individual had to discover in himself the resources to withstand misfortune, a process which the novels of Conrad defined with exquisite precision. Misfortune consisted not only of pressures from the outside, but of private snares and demons from

within.... His characters had to learn, like Marlow, to live with (the) Kurtz inside themselves....

> (Gurko, Page 278. The reference is to
> Conrad's novella *Heart of Darkness*.)

Post-script: *victory*

Lord Jim is the perfect antidote to what might be called the boy's own school of leadership, which so misled its main character (and had encouraged the young Konrad Korzeniowski to dream of a life of adventure at sea). Conrad's work contrasts effectively with those glib and superficial instruction manuals—how to be a leader in seven easy lessons—of which our shelves on management and leadership are so full, and which provide little more than a placebo for the credulous. Life does not lend itself to easy solutions, nor does leadership: but that does not mean that we should withdraw from the arena. To avoid commitment is to avoid involvement, and that is to fail not only as a leader but also as a human being, who can only fully exist as a member of a community.

Heyst, the main character of Conrad's novel *Victory,* has refused to engage with life, but finally he does so in rescuing the girl, Lena. Both die, and in losing his life, Heyst obtains victory. He has triumphed over the tradition and philosophy of his father, a pessimistic philosopher who advocated disengagement and withdrawal from life. Like Heyst, Conrad confronted his own demons and overcame them. His flawed protagonists offer more insights into leadership and its pressures than almost any textbook.

*   *   *

Bibliography

There are many editions of Joseph Conrad's works, published both before and after his death in 1924. The authoritative edition of the works of Joseph Conrad is by J M Dent and Sons, Limited. References here include the date of first publication as well as the edition that I have consulted.

Conrad, Joseph (1897; 1984) *The Nigger of the Narcissus*. Oxford: Oxford University Press.

Conrad, Joseph (1900; 2002) *Lord Jim*. Oxford: Oxford University Press: Oxford World's Classics.

Conrad, Joseph (1903; 1998) *Three Sea Stories: Typhoon; Falk; The Shadow-Line.* London: Wordsworth Classics.

Conrad, Joseph (1904; 1994) *Nostromo.* London: Penguin Popular Classics.

Conrad, Joseph (1906; 2008) *The Mirror of the Sea & A Personal Record.* London: Wordsworth Literary Lives.

Conrad, Joseph (1907; 2007) *The Secret Agent.* London: Penguin Classics.

Conrad, Joseph (1911; 1996) *Under Western Eyes.* London: Penguin Classics.

Conrad, Joseph (1912; 1947) The Secret Sharer, in *Twixt Land and Sea.* London: J.M. Dent and Sons Ltd.

Conrad, Joseph (1915; unknown) *Victory.* London: Penguin Modern Classics.

Conrad: The Secret Agent (1973) *A Selection of Critical Essays*, Edited by Ian Watt. London: Macmillan.

Gurko, Leo (1965) *Joseph Conrad: Giant in Exile.* London: Frederick Muller Ltd.

Sherry, Norman (1966) *Conrad's Eastern World.* Cambridge: Cambridge University Press.

Stape, John H. (2007) *The Several Lives of Joseph Conrad.* London: William Heinemann.

Villiers, Peter (2006) *Joseph Conrad: Master Mariner.* Suffolk: Seafarer Books.

3

The Isolation of the Spirit: Captain Horatio Hornblower, RN

Stephanie Jones

C S Forester's (1937) novel *The Happy Return*, which introduced Captain Horatio Hornblower, RN, effectively 'created the most renowned sailor in contemporary fiction' (Foreword, Penguin edition, 1951). Sir Winston Churchill described him as 'admirable, vastly entertaining'. But for all his swashbuckling adventures, Hornblower was a tortured, isolated, lonely man, always dissatisfied with himself and questioning his abilities, which others, by contrast, found to be exemplary. This feeling of being alone was in some respects the product of the era in which he lived; in the early nineteenth century, the lack of technology and efficient transportation made the world a very large place. Organisational hierarchy was stricter and less flexible. Social classes rarely intermingled. Yet, in a timeless way, Hornblower personally isolated himself as a leader through his feelings of unworthiness and self-doubt, and constant need to prove to himself and his officers and crew that he could do his job. Hornblower was isolated both externally and internally.

In describing the isolation of Hornblower's command, Forester—who, to a certain extent, modelled his hero on his own self-doubt and hesitation to accept his own talents—has provided lessons for many leaders of all eras and in all contexts. Forester deliberately created a desperately insecure protagonist who lacked self-confidence, yet who managed to become an outstandingly successful naval officer.

In this respect, Forester challenges his readers to address their preconceptions of effective leadership, as Hornblower's self-confessed weaknesses can be seen as contributing to his success. His constant state of reflection and doom-saying stopped him from making overly rash decisions and effectively prevented arrogance and presumption. He broke the mould of typical overconfident, daring leaders of his era, suggesting there was no tried and true template for leadership. Nelson and Cochrane established and developed the heroic school of dashing feats, icons for everything but insecurity and doubt. This theme was also picked up by other maritime novelists, such as Patrick O'Brien in his character Jack Aubrey, explored in *Master and Commander: The Far Side of the World* (released as an award-winning film in 2003). But Forester, through Hornblower, had (previously to O'Brien) suggested that there was another way.

In the Hornblower novels, Forester shows how his hero addressed his doubts and fears and came to live with the isolation of his command, which matched the high level of self-discipline which he imposed upon himself. In the same way, Forester pushed himself hard in his research and writing, at a time when he suffered the onset of a debilitating disease. This overcoming of isolation and doubt is a theme which recurs in other novels considered in the present volume, such as Joseph Conrad's *The Secret Sharer*. It is also seen in the less colourful but also effective leadership style of an officer such as Admiral Collingwood, who carried out mopping-up operations after Trafalgar. Desperately lonely and isolated, Collingwood grew plants and kept a pet dog in his cabin, never returning to his beloved home and family, eventually dying at sea, exhausted and alone.

The theme of this short review—*Hornblower's Lament*—is thus the isolation and distance experienced by Hornblower as a leader in four different ways: firstly, through geography; secondly, through organisational hierarchy; thirdly, through social stratification; and finally through the nature of his individual personality. We will look at how Hornblower operated as a leader, dealing with this distance and isolation, his relationship with his men, and his approach to decision-making and problem-solving, based on Forester's own reflective notes in *The Hornblower Companion* (1964) and the first Hornblower novel, *The Happy Return* (1937). Written while storm clouds were gathering over Europe, Forester was harking back to a previous era while it was still broadly familiar. The approaching world war was to change everything, so Hornblower's story is both a period piece and a reflection on the challenges of leadership with continuing relevance today.

Let's set the scene. 'It was not long after dawn that Captain Hornblower came up on the quarterdeck of the *Lydia*'. The opening lines of *The Happy Return* (1937) immediately create an image of isolation. It was still slightly dark around him, while he enjoyed his customary solitary pacing of the quarterdeck; Lieutenant Bush, after seven months without touching land, 'had learned something of his captain's likes and dislikes. During this hour of the day the captain was not to be spoken to, nor his train of thought interrupted' (1937, Page 5).

Geographical isolation

The novel is set the early nineteenth century, and what strikes the modern reader is the lack of communications technology and therefore the infrequent contact with higher authority. As in the case of the early colonial trading companies, the man in charge was on his own, and was almost completely empowered to do whatever he thought appropriate in interpreting his standing orders, on his own judgement. However, this isolation could be rudely interrupted. When a ship made landfall or encountered another vessel, perhaps after an interval of weeks or even months, its captain would be suddenly presented with new information, whether from newspapers or letters, telling him of perhaps dramatic turns in world events. This might necessitate instant decision-making, without the benefit of consulting a higher-ranking officer and sharing the responsibility—and with the fear of court martial, dismissal and penniless joblessness as the result of making a wrong decision. The right sort of person throve under such circumstances, and enjoyed the thrill of uncertainty. The wrong sort of commander went under, unable to cope with the pressure.

The perception of 'distance' in the early nineteenth century may be evidenced by the terms of the Treaty of Ghent between the USA and England, signed in December 1814. For example, in Article Two, the definition of when the war would officially and legally end was addressed. In the North Atlantic, this would be 12 days after the ratification of the treaty; it would be 40 days for the Baltic; and up to 120 days for distant parts of the Pacific. It was expected that it would take this long for the news to spread and for compliance. So if Hornblower captured a ship off Java 119 days after the ratification of the treaty, then it was his prize; if it was 121 days after, then he would have had to hand it back (Forester, 1964, Page 81–2). We can thus surmise that it was assumed that it would take this long for the news of the treaty to spread, to the extent that this fact had to be built into the treaty terms. This would be inconceivable in modern times, now that everything is instantaneous. But in the early nineteenth century it took months for even the most momentous news to spread...

With news taking so long to travel there was always a need to find out from the shore what was happening. During this period of European war, however, alliances frequently changed, and the captain of a lone ship might be the last to know which side he was on. Any strange ship approaching—even a small lugger—made Hornblower suspicious, and he would run up the colours, and immediately clear for action. Friend or foe? This could vary from day to day. When Spain was announced as the new ally of England, Hornblower, always distrusting and envisaging the worst possible scenario, didn't believe it. Was it a ruse to lure him into a 'safe' port but then turn on him and capture his ship? Without official confirmation from home (and given that such 'confirmation' could be fabricated), the weight of responsibility on the lone captain was heavy indeed.

The physical isolation of not knowing the ship's exact location was extreme, with Hornblower relying on his navigation skills alone, making daytime and lunar observations and calculating daily speeds and nautical miles covered. Like many officers at that time, he was not yet convinced that the marine chronometer was still accurate every day, minute-by-minute, after seven months at sea. There was a moment when Hornblower knew that the Pacific coast of Central America must be appearing on the horizon soon, but he could not know exactly when. The isolation of uncertainty was especially an area for concern, particularly for Hornblower, who wanted to appear infallible to his officers and crew. 'This Man Alone—the captain of a ship, and more especially of a ship of war, was very much alone in the days before radiotelegraphy' (Forester, 1964, Page 82).

Hornblower realised the impact on world geography and distance of the opening of the Panama Canal, which would attract many ships. In the nineteenth century the region was isolated from Europe by a much greater perception and reality of distance than now. It was not just distance: the challenge of storms and rocks involved in rounding Cape Horn in a sailing ship posed a massive barrier. For most of the novel, Hornblower was operating alone in the Pacific, an alien sea far from home, with no friendly ships or ports.

In this story, Forester deliberately created Hornblower as a frigate captain, and thus put him in a much more isolated position than he would have been in a ship of the line in a fleet. Hornblower was thus not in a squadron or unit, but operating alone, on a secret and dangerous mission, the details of which only he knew. He was forced to sit in his cabin on his own to read his orders, and could open them only in the middle of the ocean; and he was obliged to stay out of sight of land for the purposes of maintaining secrecy.

Hornblower was thus forced to use his authority when far from home without confirmation from anyone else. For example, he was required to give an 11-gun salute to the new rebel vice admiral, appointed by the crazed South American dictator el Supremo. Hornblower still believed in the rituals of home, and resented giving this ragged guerrilla fighter the same salute as he would give to his great hero Nelson. Meanwhile, el Supremo himself wanted and expected a 23-gun salute—more than Hornblower's King! But without any support, on an individual basis, it was necessary to make decisions on giving orders which must be instantly obeyed.

El Supremo's admiral was in the same position, having to exert his authority over the captured Spanish crew. His objective was to take over as their legitimate leader, and he required them to swear allegiance to el Supremo. In a symbolic gesture of his new leadership, the rebel admiral threw overboard the ship's statue of the Virgin and Child. After another symbolic shooting of a dissenting young boy sailor, the crew members accepted a new leader through fear and the promise of freedom. Hornblower berated himself for his failure to prevent further cruelty, but argued in his own defence that in such an isolated situation, the relationship of master and slave was appropriate: el Supremo *had* to use extreme measures to enforce his authority.[1] When, later in the novel, the roles are reversed and el Supremo is captured and enslaved, Hornblower finds himself disturbed and tormented. Maintaining authority while isolated was clearly challenging.

Yet, on the plus side, the geographical isolation of a sailing ship in an enemy ocean far from home gave the captain and crew a feeling of independence from the land and a sense of self-sufficiency. When his ship was again full of stores, such as water, victuals and supplies of all kinds, Hornblower was again free of the land with all its uncertainties. Forester, reflecting on his creation of the 'Man Alone', saw this situation as one of the few occasions when Hornblower would allow himself a small measure of happiness and contentment.

Organisational isolation

Especially on a small vessel, the captain of a ship had to preserve a distance from the men to maintain his authority. This requirement was compounded in Hornblower's situation of operating independently, lacking the support of a more senior officer nearby. As the captain of a frigate, Hornblower was more isolated than in a bigger ship operating as part of a fleet, with an admiral within hailing distance. Significantly, Forester puts him in a ship big enough to be important—a frigate, not a sloop—reflecting his seniority in the pecking order of captains. Forester wanted his hero to reflect his own self-doubt and lack of confidence, but to show that finally he could triumph over these afflictions. Hornblower, while keeping a distance from his crew, had to earn their respect in the small, confined world of the *Lydia*. At the same time, he had to encourage their willingness to risk everything and their enthusiasm, not just their blind loyalty.

As we have seen, Hornblower's ship had to be self-sufficient for her dangerous mission; however, during the first chapters of the novel *The Happy Return* she was running out of food, water, the scurvy-preventing lime juice, tobacco, alcoholic spirits and fuel for the galley. Hornblower feared that in a state of privation, his authority over his men would become increasingly precarious. Among all isolated captains, there was a fear of mutiny, such as in the infamous mutiny on the *Bounty* in 1789, when Captain Bligh and his supporters were cast adrift in the middle of the Pacific in an open boat. Hornblower was constantly tortured by such fears. He had a few officers of varying ability, and many crew members, some of whom had been pressed against their will from shore jobs, and many of whom were petty criminals. In having to keep authority, he also had to make sure they were busy, keeping their minds off their hunger and thirst while he eked out the few remaining supplies, and training them in seamanship and gunnery for the day, not long far off, when they would encounter the enemy.

Throughout the novel, Hornblower was plagued by fear, disgust and an inability to be as tough as he thought he should be. Witnessing the punishment of a sailor by flogging, a frequent event on any man-of-war, he felt physically sick. The offending crew member was given two dozen lashes, and Hornblower 'was ashamed of the fact that he looked upon punishment as a beastly business, that he hated ordering it and dreaded witnessing it' (1937, Page 13). Hornblower 'was sick with disgust at himself at neither being strong enough to stop it nor ingenious enough to devise a way out of the dilemma Lieutenant Bush's decision [to flog the man for spitting on the deck] had forced him into' (1937, Page 14). At the same time, he had to hide this aversion from the others because they might see it as weak and inappropriate, and it would negatively impact the strength of his authority as leader.

When the *Lydia* finally sighted land after seven months at sea, Hornblower immediately wanted to rush up on deck. Like everyone else, he was wildly excited at the thought of new adventures on a new continent. But he knew he must 'appear in the eyes of his officers and crew to be a man of complete self-confidence and imperturbability—and this was only partially to gratify himself. The more respect in which a captain was held, the better for his ship' (1937, Page 15). Hornblower could show no emotions. This was all part of the distance of hierarchy within the navy's chain of command, expected and required.

Hornblower had made a perfect landfall after eleven weeks out of sight of land: a triumph of navigation and seamanship. But Hornblower is so isolated in his position as captain that he will not take any credit for it from his officers and men, as this would appear a sign of weakness.

Nelson and Hornblower

This is the way Hornblower sees it, and we may contrast this perception with that of Nelson's constant and public 'self-aggrandisement' in his route to stardom. Hornblower's self-doubt means that he cannot enjoy his success even for a moment, but he must keep pushing himself on to the next goal. Nelson sought (successfully) to gain acknowledgement of his achievements by publicising them: he gained public recognition through the publication of his dispatches and letters to the admiralty (and as part of his public persona in general, in what was later to be called the 'cult of the personality'. Hornblower would never have sought public recognition,[2] for he would have feared compounding the risks of failure by exposing himself to greater scrutiny.

So, while the crew was excitedly on the *Lydia*'s deck chattering and looking at the land for the first time for several months, Hornblower was not basking in self-satisfied glory. 'Hornblower realized that a stern cold-blooded disciplinarian would take exception to this perfectly natural behavior, and so he did the same. "What's all this?" he snapped. "Has no one in this ship anything to do?"' (1937, Page 17).

Hornblower had trained himself to say 'ha-h'm', a usefully neutral expression instead of something more conversational. While all his officers were eager to know what was happening, he couldn't tell them, due to the hierarchy of the ship, the secret nature of his mission and his own self-imposed reticence. Hornblower decided he wanted to climb up a mast to get a better view of the land ahead; but he couldn't go through 'the lubbers' hole': the easy way up the mast. He had to go the difficult way, as all the crew members were watching him. He even felt guilty for replying to questions from his officers, thinking he should pretend to ignore them—engaging in conversation being too much of a sign of intimacy and familiarity. All he did was to send the hands to dinner half an hour earlier. This effectively sent out the message that something unusual was happening, but he couldn't, or he wouldn't, say anything more.

Hornblower's task in entering Pacific waters was to try to help start a rebellion in South America against the Spanish. He had to meet and ally with the dictator—the el Supremo referred to above—and develop commercial treaties with him to encourage trade with Britain. Hornblower's orders also indicated the presence of the Spanish two-decker *Natividad,* which posed an immediate threat to his mission. He must 'sink, burn or capture' it, explained the admiralty orders, which were typically demanding, and indeed barely possible. The admiralty, in sending the *Lydia,* had ordered a small frigate of only 36 guns to attack a 50-gun ship. With the arrogance of post-Trafalgar naval supremacy, they assumed Hornblower would be successful. If he failed, he would be court-martialled. If he succeeded, this was only what was expected. The enormity of his task made Hornblower feel even more isolated.

On reaching land, Hornblower's first priority was to think of the needs of his ship. He needed water and victuals for another long voyage. By trading weapons and ammunition for stores with el Supremo, he could enable the ship to be isolated and cope with distance for more months if necessary. Moreover, his ability to provide food, rum and tobacco for his men would be seen as a measure of success in their eyes, and make his job easier. Since he could not share privileged information with them, some of his actions must be judged arbitrary or needlessly cruel. For example, as a consequence of his secret orders, Hornblower had to be strict when his men tried to rescue a tortured local prisoner. Leaders have priorities that cannot always be shared with their followers, whether in the nineteenth-century Royal Navy or today.

The approach of the Natividad

When Hornblower learned that the *Natividad* was approaching, he knew that he would have to attack it. When he was about to fight a battle, Hornblower practised a tradition of having dinner and playing cards with his officers. Four hours before he knew the fight would start he was pacing in his cabin; but 'the iron-nerved captain of his dreams would not allow himself to work himself into this sort of fever, even though his professional reputation was to be at stake in four hours' time. He must show the ship that he, too, could face uncertainty with indifference' (1937, Page 57). So, 'Hornblower compelled himself to play the courtly host, while every word he uttered was designed to increase his reputation for imperturbability' (1937, Page 58).

Hornblower would not admit to his young midshipmen that, even when the ship was short of food, he could not bear to eat the rats running around the decks. So he lied, and told them that when he was younger, he happily ate rats. 'This little human touch had won their hearts completely, as Hornblower had known it would' (1937, Page 59). Hornblower went on to talk of 'our prisoners' and 'our victories': 'The strict cold captain, the stern disciplinarian, had for a moment revealed human characteristics and had admitted his inferiors to his fellowship. Any one of the three junior officers would at that moment have laid down his life for his captain' (1937, Page 59).

This warmth was combined with the mounting tension of the enemy ship being only a couple of hours away. Hornblower then gave them an unwelcome lecture on how to play whist creating the legend of his coolness under imminent fire. The young officers squirmed with frustration at trying to play cards, but they were full of admiration for their cool captain.

Hornblower's tactic was to lead *Lydia* out of the darkness of night to confront the *Natividad,* taking advantage of the discipline and agility of the smaller ship, while the latter ship was completely unprepared and could be taken by surprise. Boarded by boat's crews from the *Lydia,* the larger ship was taken as a prize. But Hornblower never congratulated himself in capturing a ship nearly twice the size without losing a man. Hornblower's humanitarian act of stopping the officers of the *Natividad* from being executed was not out of kindness but because there would be a riot among his crew, who saw such acts as barbaric and foreign. Again, in a state of isolation, he had to make all decisions himself, above all to preserve his authority. Untypically, Hornblower shed tears with the burial of Gerard, one of his officers badly wounded in the fight with the *Natividad,* as he read out the funeral service. But Hornblower's steely and cool exterior meant that when he did show his emotional interior, he didn't lose his authority: his hint of humanity actually strengthened his role as a leader not to be questioned.

Sharing command?

Realising he had to sacrifice prize money for continued co-operation with El Supremo, Hornblower let him have the *Natividad,* and even invited el Supremo on board the *Lydia,* ordering his men to show courtesy and threatening to flog any man who laughed at the appearance of the mad dictator. Hornblower was concerned that his men should not think that he was following el Supremo's orders. While loading the rebel soldiers on board the ships to attack the shore bases, he could not allow anyone else to usurp his leadership role in the eyes of his men. Hornblower was secretly glad to see the back of el Supremo. 'He was his own master again, free to walk his own quarterdeck undisturbed' (1937, Page 83), smiling to himself but carefully avoiding letting his crew see that he was happy.

Social isolation

Traditionally naval officers were of a higher social level and would not mingle with the lower orders; this made life more difficult for Hornblower because he was not an aristocrat, and socially only marginally above some of his officers.[3] This is highlighted by his relationship with Lady Barbara Wellesley, in the romantic finale of *The Happy Return*. Forester created a sister for the Duke of Wellington to have an affair with Hornblower and reveal another aspect of his torment and isolation.

He was not blue-blooded—he had been promoted due to merit, not influence—and he was entrusted with a special mission, so he was exciting and attractive to her, even if not well-born. Hornblower handled the beginning of their affair very badly. He was overcome by remorse that he was married already, to the lowly and awkward daughter of his landlady in his boarding house; and his perception of his lower status created endless difficulties in his relationship with Lady Barbara. When she came on board as a passenger on the *Lydia,* she threatened Hornblower's isolation, but gradually brought him out of his shell, despite himself. He was impressed at how good she was at handling others, when he had few social graces; and he could cope with the death and wounding of many of his officers and crew with her there to help care for them.

Hornblower's personality, created by Forester to reflect aspects of the author himself, compounded Hornblower's isolation of command. He was introverted, self-doubting, fearful of failure and hated the thought of seasickness, drowning and wounds. The perception of his lack of aristocratic connections, his social awkwardness and lack of experience and confidence with women compounded his perception of distance and isolation.

The Man Alone

Forester described his hero in terms of '... the situation of the man who has to make unaided decisions. The man alone; he may have technical help, he may even have friends, but as regards the crisis he is facing he can only act on his own judgment, and in case of failure he has only himself to blame... 'Hornblower was to be the Man Alone that I had sought...' (Forester, 1964, Page 82).

> Hornblower's other struggle (than war) would go on as long as he was to live, for it was the struggle with himself. He was (destined) to be self-critical. Just as no man is supposed to be a hero to his own valet, so Hornblower could not be a hero to his own self. He would be too cynical about his own motives, too aware of his own weaknesses, ever to know content; and he would have to be a man of considerable character so that, even though despairing, or even hopeless, he could maintain this struggle with himself and not subside into self-satisfaction or humility.
>
> (Forester, 1964, Page 88)

Perceptive and imaginative, Hornblower saw possibilities, but often in a negative way. He had marked ability, and was highly competent. 'He must also have the quality of leadership—that would develop out of his perceptiveness and sensitivity; it would be the kind of leadership that owes much to tact and little to animal spirits' (Forester, 1964, Page 89). Forester presents Hornblower as a contradiction in terms. Gangling and awkward, Hornblower's appearance was in contrast with his mental ability; an accomplished mathematician, he was good at card games, and could make a living off playing poker; but he was also shy and reserved socially. Even his name made him more self-conscious. Forester gave him a slightly grotesque surname, unusual and almost unpronounceable by foreigners, and his first name Horatio was more from Shakespeare's Hamlet than from Nelson. The natural cross-grainedness of Forester was matched in Hornblower.

Hornblower's lament

In summary, Hornblower wanted to come over as cool, reticent and distant. He chose a servant of 'gratifyingly few words', for 'he had to guard against his besetting sin of garrulity even with servants' (1937, Page 11). He made a perfect landfall; but 'it was Hornblower's nature to find no pleasure in things he could do; his ambition was always yearning after the impossible, to appear a strong silent capable man, unmoved by emotion' (1937, Page 21). When he escaped from French imprisonment with his two shipmates down the *Loire* 'Hornblower was happier at this time than a life of action and hardship had ever allowed him to be so far. He was still the Man Alone, but he was experiencing the comradeship and personal intimacy which—partly through his own faults of personality—had so far evaded him' (Forester, 1964, Page 103).

Was this the real Hornblower, or did circumstances force him into a strait-jacket against which he struggled in vain? Is Hornblower's lament of the isolation of command something all leaders have to live with—a necessary template for leadership—or should leaders simply be themselves? What is the proper relationship between image and reality? In creating his unlikely hero, who is able to be a successful naval commander despite his inner doubts and uncertainties, Forester leaves us to make up our own minds about the true nature of leadership.

Notes

1. We may compare his situation with that of Cyrus the Great, examined by Lynette Mitchell elsewhere in this volume, who sought to achieve the willing obedience of his followers. Bribery may also be available to the tyrant, as well as punishment or threats.

2. This is primarily a study of Captain Hornblower, a fictional creation, and not of Admiral Nelson, a real-life national hero. The barrier between fact and fiction is crossed in that Hornblower has views on Nelson, as any naval officer would have done at the time. (Nelson, naturally, cannot have had views on Hornblower: a gap to be regretted perhaps, and an opportunity for a future novelist.) The reader is directed to the following text for a study of Nelson's style of leadership and its relevance today:

    Nelson's Way: Leadership Lessons from the Great Commander
    Stephanie Jones and Jonathan Gosling
    Nicholas Brealey, London, 2005

    We may note that Nelson's talent for self-publicity is a characteristic of many successful leaders, and a necessary but not a sufficient part of their repertoire. It is insufficient because, unless you are a 'celebrity' for its own sake, you must first do something about which to spin the legend. That something need not be what it claims to be; and its actualisation may be more symbolic than real. Compare Mussolini's 'march' on Rome, which he completed by taxi. Even a widely respected leader such as Gandhi recognised the need to publicise his achievements, and his campaign for civil disobedience was a (successful) move to capture the high moral ground from British imperialism, in part by provoking its officials into overreaction. One of British imperialism's later officials was to reflect bitterly on his experiences in his essay 'Shooting an elephant': an early piece by George Orwell.

    The really successful leader may be someone who apparently avoids publicity, while making sure that people know of his achievements: this is sometimes known as backing into the limelight. A variation was practised by T E Lawrence, who sought anonymity after his wartime achievements in

Arabia by adopting a new life and identity as aircraftman Ross. At the same time, he kept up with his old friends, who remained the leading figures of the day, so that his eventual unmasking would be unavoidable. Whether or not Lawrence/Ross (and later Shaw) intended to be unmasked is an aspect of his psychology which is beyond the scope of this volume to explore further. However, pretending to hide while hoping to be discovered is as old as hide-and-seek.

3. Nelson was the son of a country parson, a convenient and comfortable social location. The Church of England is part of the establishment—indeed, it might be argued that it *is* the establishment—but its clergymen and women are not over-endowed with status, although no-one would suggest that they sat below the salt.

Bibliography

Forester, C.S. (1937) *The Happy Return*. London: Michael Joseph.

Forester, C.S. (1938) *A Ship of the Line*. London: Michael Joseph.

Forester, C.S. (1938) *Flying Colours*. London: Michael Joseph.

Forester, C.S. (1964) *The Hornblower Companion*. London: Michael Joseph.

4
Leadership and Monomania: Herman Melville's *Moby-Dick*

Burkard Sievers

> All my means are sane—my motive and my object mad.
>
> God keep me from completing anything. This...is but a draught—nay, but the draught of a draught.
>
> (Melville, 1851/1967, Page 128)
>
> *Moby-Dick*, an apparently simple tale of whaling—will turn out to be a very challenging read indeed. Our thinking about whaling will never be the same again. Our minds have been pushed to think in a different manner, processed by an object (a novel) which, when encountered, will change our mental life.
>
> (Bollas, 2009, 85f.)

Prescript

This paper has turned out to be a whale of a paper and is at the same time 'but a draught—nay, but the draught of a draught' (Melville, 1851/1967, Page 128). Nevertheless, as Joseph Conrad (1920) once replied to the critics of his novel *Chance*, it seems that I am in good company:

> No doubt that by selecting a certain method and taking great pains the whole story might have been written out on a cigarette paper. For that mater, the whole history of mankind could be written thus if only approached with sufficient detachment. The history of men on this earth since the beginning of ages may be rescued in one phrase of infinite poignancy: They were born, they suffered, they died...Yet it is a great talent. But in the infinitely minute stories about men

and women it is my lot on earth to narrate I am not capable of such detachment.

(Preface, *Chance*, Page i)

Introduction

Herman Melville chose the sea as the centre of many of his writings based on his varied experiences during his naval career. It thus is no surprise that captains of merchant ships, whalers and man-of-wars were protagonists in several of his novels and short stories—for example, *Redburn* (Melville, 1849/1969), *White-Jacket* (Melville, 1850/1990), *Moby-Dick* (Melville, 1851/1967), *Benito Cereno* (Melville, 1856/1993) and *Billy Budd* (Melville, 1924/1962). While the portraits of some of them, in particular that of Captain Vere, the commander of the *Rights-of-Man*, in *Billy Budd*, were directly drawn from Melville's experience at sea, Ahab, the captain of the *Pequod* in *Moby-Dick*, is a fictional character.

Nowadays, the percentage of people who have read an abridged version of *Moby-Dick* is far higher than those who have worked through the entire book (cf. Kruse, 1976, Page 24). For this reason, 'people who have never seen a copy of *Moby-Dick* know who Captain Ahab is and use the chase of the great white whale as a metaphor for the obsessive pursuit of irrational goals' (Brodhead, 1986, 18f.). *Moby-Dick*, the novel as well as the whale, has been extensively used for popular literature and culture; Ahab and the White Whale have been protagonists in an almost endless succession of movies, comics, music, radio dramas, children's books and science-fiction—not to mention an endless number of restaurants, hotels, oceanfront lodges, marinas, etc. which call themselves 'Moby Dick' or 'The White Whale'.[1]

In addition to almost endless interpretations of this novel, *Moby-Dick* may be taken as 'a study of labour conditions and of labour problems in a much-neglected corner of American economic history' (Hohman, 1928/1974, Page VIII). It is a story about work, a multiracial proletariat, leadership, political order and rebellion, slavery and social issues (Rogin, 1985, Page 114). *Moby-Dick* is not least an industrial saga (Hall, 1950, Page 226), reflecting the early development of US industrialisation and the rise of the capitalist worldview through the middle of the nineteenth century.

In both common vernacular and in much of psychology Herman Melville's (1851/1967)[2] *Moby-Dick* has been broadly reduced and simplified to primarily the story of a single person; Captain Ahab is portrayed as a narcissist (for example, Kohut, 1972; Dyer, 1994; Adamson, 1997) and pathologised as a madman. From this perspective, he is seen as a leader who ultimately ruins himself, the crew and the *Pequod*. It thus is no surprise that Hitler (cf. Delbanco, 2005, Pages 12, 165, 175) or even Lyndon Johnson or George W. Bush, former US presidents, have been compared to Ahab (Shaw, 1993, Page 68; Kimaid, 2005; Sexton, 2005).

Such a reduction and simplification, however, does justice neither to the novel nor its author. Not only does it lose sight of Melville's intentions, the immense complexity of the novel and the manifold possible readings and levels of interpretation (cf. Mumford, 1926, Page 149; Gleim, 1962, Pages 2, 9), it also neglects the fact that *Moby-Dick* is—above all—a saga of human civilisation, which illuminates the deep conflicts in America regarding its young democracy and the serious threat that it would split apart as a nation.

While aware that *Moby-Dick* is a fictional story mirroring Melville's inner world and his experience of the outer one, my primary perspective in this paper is to regard the novel from a socioanalytic and systemic perspective (cf. Bain, 1999). The main focus will thus be on the unconscious dynamics aboard the whaler with special emphasis on leadership and followership. It is not surprising that leadership aboard the *Pequod*, Captain Ahab's in particular, has been a prominent topic, given the almost countless themes and issues which Melville's novel invites one to explore. As Mumford (1929, Page 194) once stated: 'each man will read into Moby Dick the drama of his own experience and that of his contemporaries'. This is equally true for a wide range of different readings of leadership (and management) in *Moby-Dick* (cf. Warner, 2008, 17f.).

A socioanalytic perspective of the novel, rooted in psychoanalysis and systemic thinking, recognises that, for Melville, the *Pequod* represents, in a metaphorical sense, a 'whole world of humanity in microcosm' (Hohman, 1928/1974, 51f.), 'a picture of world civilization' (James, 1953, Page 150), 'a perfectly ordered and isolated shipboard society . . . [in which] society (the traditional dominion of the novel) and the sea (subject of romance) join together in diabolic harmony' (Rogin, 1985, Page 129).

The novel, like the vessel, is embedded in at least a double scape—the sea and the 'high and mighty business of whaling' (Page 99), that is, the American whaling industry during its Golden Age (cf. Sievers, 2009a, 2010). Both the seascape and the business-scape are significant dimensions of the fictional reality of the novel and its reflection of contemporary social, political and economic realities. Whereas the seascape stands for the uncontrollable, the uncivilised (Page 155), the incorrupt (Page 265), the unknown and the howling infinite (ibid., Page 97), the business-scape of the novel points to the rise (if not the revolution) of a new economic order, the market (Sellers, 1991/1994) and capitalist thinking. As Douglas (1977, Page 6) puts it, the years between 1820 and 1875 were in 'the midst of the transformation of the American economy into the most powerfully aggressive capitalist system in the world'.

Ahab's differentiation of sane means and mad motive and object may, at first sight, be further proof of his madness. However, when seen in the larger context of the emerging American capitalist economy during the middle of the nineteenth century and that of the whaling industry in particular, it reveals something much broader. The whaling industry was probably the very first industry to be established in New England, and its development marks the beginning of early American industrialisation and the transformation of America from an agrarian to a capitalist society. 'Much of America's culture, economy, and in fact its spirit were literally and figuratively rendered from the bodies of whales' (Dolin, 2007, Page 11).

'Between 1830 and 1860 the image of the machine, and the idea of the society founded upon machine power suddenly took hold of the public image' (Marx, 1956, Page 30; cf. Marx, 1964; Mumford, 1966). Like workers in the factories ashore since the beginning of the nineteenth century, sailors were perceived as appendices of the machine and were 'compelled . . . to objectify themselves and others as abstract labor-power' (Sellers, 1991/1994, Page 153; cf. Marx, 1956, 1964). The machine, both as a reality and metaphor, is not only a predominant object and image in early US industrialisation, it was also reflected in the exercise of authority and command aboard a whaler—both in general and in Melville's novel (see, for example, Ausband, 1975).

On a whaler, as on merchant ships and man-of-wars in the middle of the eighteenth century, authority was centred in the role of captain as a representative of the ship owners, commander and navigator, expert in whaling and superior to his mates and the crew as a whole. It, therefore, 'was essential to give the captain wide latitude in making decisions, as well as in changing plans and policies' (Hohman, 1928/1974, Page 287). While the captain still remained *the* authority aboard his vessel during the Golden Age, he had lost much of the authority, responsibility and autonomy that his earlier counterparts enjoyed. By the Golden Age, ship-owners and whaling agents had increased their demands for profit and thus their pressure on the captain. More than likely, the captains passed on this pressure to their crews. Attempting to deny his own experience of dependency and weakness, the captain projected it onto his crew and on the lower ranks, in particular. And very probably this latter group, due to their origin, low status and poor skills, were more than willing to introject it. Devilish discipline and brutality thus appeared to be the appropriate means by which the captain, both consciously and unconsciously, tried to salvage his authority, responsibility and autonomy.

A socioanalytic understanding of leadership in Melville's novel must encompass the paradoxes and tragic dimensions and focus on the unconscious dynamics of how Ahab and his crew led themselves and their vessel to ultimate chaos and downfall. Any attempt to derive leadership lessons from *Moby-Dick* and the Pequod is likely to fail without a deeper consideration of how the some 30 people aboard the whaler 'accomplished' their own destruction and that of their business, that is, the vessel. It is only from a deeper perspective on the man-made tragedy of the entire crew—from the forecastle to the quarterdeck—that a better understanding of how contemporary corporations and other social systems often consciously or unconsciously suffer from a similar fate.

The meaning of management in *Moby-Dick* and in the whaling literature of that time, does not, however, refer to the role of manager or to a group of managers in the contemporary sense; it is restricted to certain activities like, for example, 'the whole management of the ship's affairs' (Page 74). While the Captain and his mates are now and then referred to as being in command or commanders, it seems that leadership in *Moby-Dick* is explicitly mentioned only once: In Chapter 46, 'Surmises', the narrator (Page 183) states that 'Starbuck would ever be apt to fall into open relapses of rebellion against his captain's leadership'. This is not a great surprise, because contemporary management theories of motivation, management and leadership did not exist before the middle of the twentieth century (Sievers, 2009a, Page 399). Nevertheless, there can be no doubt that there are countless phenomena relating to what we now refer to as leadership, both in daily practice and in the social sciences. Discovering the actual drama of leadership (and management) inherent in *Moby-Dick* requires, however, several readings; it is often hidden behind the plot line and its spiritual and metaphysical meanings. 'Melville persistently reads history as mythology and mythology as history, and both provide the symbolic shorthand for treating his own society' (Fisher, 1966, Page 203). It thus is not surprising that, as Warner (2008, Page 4) indicates, 'a full account of these issues in *Moby-Dick* could easily threaten to reach the length of a novel itself.'

The business of revenge—a triple drama

While the *Pequod* is a whaler characterised by the means, objective, technology and crew typical for the fishery at that time, it is Ahab's business of revenge, its impact on the crew and ultimately the loss of the vessel that makes *Moby-Dick* unique as a novel. Captain Ahab's quest for vengeance on the White Whale can be seen from multiple perspectives: the drama of his childhood, the drama at work in the context of the business of whaling and the broadly hidden culture of the maritime world (cf. Linebaugh and Rediker, 2000). The drama of childhood and the drama at work are intertwined; the accident at work on the previous voyage, when Ahab was dismembered by Moby-Dick, can be seen both as a re-traumatisation of the drama of childhood and a revitalisation of the trauma of the loss of the leg (Drewermann, 2004, Page 133, 136ff.); the re-traumatisation and the revitalisation then are turned into and acted out in a drama at work (Sievers, 1995).

The 'workplace tragedy and drama' cannot, however, adequately be grasped without taking the larger cultural and socioeconomic context into account, that is, the fact that the American whaling industry had become a capitalist business in the midst of the nineteenth century. This is similarly the case for a deeper understanding of leadership in Melville's novel. It requires both insight into Ahab's 'inner world' as it is rooted in his infancy (Klein, 1959) and into the 'outer world' of the 'business of whaling' and its broader social and political implications. There is not least ample evidence from the seventeenth to the nineteenth century and 'the hidden history of the revolutionary Atlantic' in particular (Linebaugh and Rediker, 2000) that taking revenge on ship-owners, commodores, captains and slave dealers by common seamen was an incalculable social and political dynamic—and an almost permanent risk for those in command.

Ahab's 'drama of childhood', as invented by Melville, is marked by the fact that his father died before he was born and that, as an orphan, Ahab grew up as a fosterling. In 'a foolish, ignorant whim of his crazy, widowed mother, who died when he was only a twelvemonth old' (Page 77) she had named him after Ahab, the wicked son of the sixth king of Israel (1 Kings 16–22). When Ishmael, *Moby-Dick*'s narrator, refers to Ahab's namesake in a conversation with Captain Peleg, one of the ship-owners, he is warned to 'never say that on board the *Pequod*. Never say it anywhere' (Page 77). Ahab is also scarred by a 'slender rod-like mark, lividly whitish' (Page 110) 'threading its way out from among his grey hairs, and continuing right down one side of his tawny scorched face and neck, till it disappeared in his clothing' (ibid.). And unlike Starbuck, his first mate, for example, he is not a descendent of one of the elite Nantucket families.

All this may have raised deep feelings of humiliation, shame and loss which Ahab likely can neither acknowledge nor mourn. That he lost his leg by the White Whale on the previous voyage can, from this perspective, also be perceived as a re-traumatisation of these earlier losses. 'The injury inflicted on Ahab by the whale brings into focus a pervasive hostility that was already present in Ahab' (Smith, 1976, Page 20).

Ahab's vengeance, from a systemic and socioanalytic point of view, allows a further reading: as he was dismembered while hunting whales and thus pursuing the primary purpose of the business of whaling—and his profession—the loss of his leg and his subsequent quest for vengeance can also be seen in the context of the whale-fishery business and thus as a 'drama at work'. Countless whalemen were to suffer an early death either by accident, extreme weather conditions or bad health—'there is death in the business of whaling' (Page 41; cf. Hohman, 1928/1974, Page 68, cf. 183ff.; Vickers and Walsh, 2005, Page 5). Melville recounts that when 'we spoke thirty different ships, every one of which had had a death by a whale, some of them more than one, and three that had each lost a boat's crew' (Page 178).

Though Ahab's quest for vengeance apparently originates from his personal injury and loss, the enormous violence of this incident reflects the violence of the whaling industry at large, which first incarnated 'violence in the economy' (Ruggiero, 2002, Page 99). 'Killing is a duty, and duty and profit go hand in hand' (ibid., Page 100). 'Although whaling is a rationalized, collective operation, based on a strict division of labor, it remains a bloody, murderous hunt' (Marx, 1964, Page 296). While working conditions deteriorated in the later periods of the whaling industry, violence and brutality had, from its very beginning, always been at the core of the business.

The word 'brutal' is actually derived from the Latin word *brutalis*, meaning 'animal' and 'unreasonable' (derived from *brutus*, meaning 'ponderous', 'coarse'). This may well have influenced whalers to projectively identify the Leviathan with their own inner animalistic and unreasonable parts and their coarseness and ponderosity. Displacing their own 'primitive' feelings or 'drives' into the object of their hunt, whalers—as well as the whaling industry at large—felt legitimised to treat their 'victims' with the brutality with which it had been identified. 'Butchers we are' (Page 98). Projecting their own brutality on the whale and the hunt apparently was the only legitimate way brutality could be exercised and controlled—not only by the common seamen but in community with the captain and his mates.

Leadership aboard the *Pequod*—a drama in three acts

Perceived from the predominant dynamic of Ahab's attempt at winning over the crew as accomplices and collaborators for his vengeance, *Moby-Dick* can be read as a tragic drama at sea unfolding in three acts: In the 'prelude' (Chapters 1–35) Ahab's vindictiveness and megalomania and thus the potential fate of the *Pequod* is intimated but remains somehow latent and concealed. It is not before the beginning of the first act (Chapters 36–46) in Chapter 36, 'The Quarter-Deck', that Ahab reveals his secret purpose for the voyage and begins to win over the crew as allies. While the second act deals with an extensive search for Moby-Dick, which they thought they had spotted (Chapters 47–132), the futile attempt to kill it takes place in the third act during the last three days of the chase (Chapters 133–135). Like ancient classical drama, Melville's tale at sea ends with an epilogue.

The prelude (Chapters 1–35)

Ahab is first introduced to Ishmael and Queequeg, his harpooner companion, by Captain Peleg and Captain Bildad, 'the largest owners of the vessel' and in charge of 'nearly the whole management of the ship's affairs' (Page 74), in a highly ambiguous way. He is

> a sort of sick, and yet he don't look so...He's a queer man,...but a good one....He's a grand, ungodly, god-like man, Captain Ahab;...(he's) above the common; Ahab's been in colleges, as well as 'mong the cannibals; been used to deeper wonders than the waves. (Page 76)

While both Captains are unreservedly convinced that Ahab, an experienced and competent captain, will bring in a profitable harvest, Elijah, the curious prophet, with his veiled prophecy about the fatal fate of the voyage, warns Ishmael and his companion about 'Old Thunder'.

Ahab ultimately appears on the quarter-deck for the first time some days after the *Pequod* sets sail from Nantucket. It was quite common for the captain to leave the 'management of the ship' to his mates during the first days of a voyage, delegating to them the task of setting up the vessel and instructing the crew. While Ahab stays on deck in total silence and does not communicate with any of his crew, he is perceived by Ishmael as a bronze figure of light 'with a crucifixion in his face' (Page 111) and is referred to as having 'some considering touch of humanity...in him' (Page 112).

There is a dubious contradiction between the competence and the authority of the mates aboard the *Pequod*. On the one side they are referred to as 'three better, more likely sea-officers and men, each in his own different way, [that] could not readily be found' (Page 109), 'momentous men' and as headmen of the whale boats 'captains of companies' (Page 106). On the other side, however, they are described as sitting at their captain's cabin-table with its 'nameless invisible domineerings' (Page 133), 'little children before Ahab' (Page 131). However, this strange discrepancy between being the Captain's deputies and commanding the boats—or the harpooneers, though characterised as part of 'the Captain's more inferior subalterns', the real experts during the chase of a whale—and as childish underlings at the cabin-table is specific not just to the *Pequod*. 'Ahab seemed no exception to most American whale captains' (Page 134). More often than not, captains treated their subordinates in an extremely harsh and contemptuous manner, not shrinking from ripping and swearing, cajoling and kicking; in them 'was lodged a dictatorship beyond which, while at sea, there was no earthly appeal' (Melville, 1856/1993, Page 218).

On the other hand, as Krantz and Gilmore (2009, Page 26, in reference to Jacques, 1955) indicate, the first mate in particular,

> becomes a displaced target, or receptacle, for...unwanted feelings [of the ordinary seamen] toward the captain, and typically comes to be regarded as far more insensitive and mean spirited than is the case. Through this, the sailors establish and maintain, unconsciously, a collective defensive system in which they are protected from painful disturbances in the relationship with the captain.

Feelings, fantasies and rumours about Ahab, his insanity, vindictive mind and the ultimate purpose of the *Pequod*'s voyage swirl around the ship once it leaves Nantucket. Many of the crew are apprehensive that something might be wrong, obscure and dubious both with the Captain and the voyage, and have mixed feelings about what the Captain is up to. While all of them expect to be paid their lay at the end of the voyage, that is, their share of the profit negotiated at the beginning, several have a funny feeling about the Captain, which, though it is officially kept secret, is shared informally in private conversations among crew members on several occasions. Most seem to play down their hunches and those of others, because taking them seriously would increase their unconscious mortal anxieties already endemic in the business of whaling.

Act 1: the first part of the voyage (Chapters 36–46)

At the beginning of the first act—Chapter 36, 'The Quarter-Deck'—Ahab suddenly commands Starbuck to assemble the crew on deck so that he may address it for the very first time. He leaves the crew in no doubt that 'with the mad secret of his unabated rage bolted up and keyed in him, [he] . . . had purposely sailed upon the present voyage with the one only and all-engrossing object of hunting the White Whale' (Page 162). In order to confirm this hitherto hidden intent, Ahab nails a Spanish gold doubloon on the main-mast as a reward for the one who first sites Moby-Dick. '[T]his is what ye have shipped for, men! to chase that white whale on both sides of land, and over all sides of earth, till he spouts black blood and rolls fin out' (Page 143).

Ahab is aware that his private objective contradicts the assignment of the Nantucket ship-owners and thus violates the crew members' contract. In order to win over his subordinates as allies and accomplices for his mad object, he knows he has to make a special effort to win (what contemporary management rhetoric would call) their 'commitment'. Facing a greater risk than the normal whale captain in making his crew subordinates to his command, he must somehow manage the primary risk (Hirschhorn, 1999) of this voyage, that is, that the crew may revolt or even mutiny against his betrayal. In the language of psychodynamics, Ahab, therefore, has to create additional containment and social defences sufficient to help him and the crew cope with the extreme anxieties raised by his vindictiveness, which exceed by far those of a murderous hunt under normal conditions. Therefore, 'at the head of a crew . . . chiefly made up of mongrel renegades, and castaways, and cannibals—morally enfeebled also', Ahab had good reason to be afraid of the crew's resistance; referring to Starbuck, his first mate, he 'thought to find one stubborn, at the least' (Page 147).

Ahab revives the 'noble custom of the fisherman fathers' (Page 145) and conspiracy rituals not uncommon for maritime buccaneers and pirates of the time (cf. Linebaugh and Rediker, 1990, 2000; Haude, 2008), and in so doing, he pursues his fantasy of making the crew 'one and all with [him] . . . , in this matter of the whale . . .—that inscrutable thing' (Page 144). To the extent that Ahab's image of leadership is led by the desperate desire for the 'incorporation of the others', it suggests an illusion of oneness as, for example, described by Turquet (1974) as a basic assumption in social systems. Unlike the engraving on the cover of Thomas Hobbes' (1651/1996) book *Leviathan*, which reveals a sovereign whose body consists of the people who have agreed to the social contract, Ahab uses the machine metaphor—'my one cogged circle fits into all their various wheels, and they revolve' (Page 147)—and refers to hills of powder for which he himself is the match. Ironically, in order to set the powder on fire, one unavoidably burns oneself. With the image of the machine (and that of the iron rails of the railway) Melville refers to the predominant metaphor—and thinking—of American industrialisation during the first half of the nineteenth century (cf. Marx, 1956, Page 30, 1964; Mumford, 1966).

The crew's obedience and abdication of responsibility influence Ahab not to feel much fear and suspicion towards them. These concerns, however, almost immediately prove to be correct when Starbuck—'no crusader after perils' and 'uncommonly conscientious for a seaman, and endued with a deep natural reverence' (Page 103)—indignantly cuts Ahab short the very moment he declares his unambiguous betrayal of the ship-owners:

> I came here to hunt whales, not my commander's vengeance. How many barrels will thy vengeance yield thee even if thou gettest it, Captain Ahab? It will not fetch thee much in our Nantucket market. (Page 143)

Starbuck, identifying with the ship-owners and reminding Ahab of the actual primary task of the voyage, attempts to re-establish legal authority and power. After a long dispute with the Captain, however, he feels defeated and submits to his compelling will and command. As a matter of fact, Starbuck's monologue after this defeat is a frightening and at the same time brilliant example of how Melville senses the internal conflict, the ambiguity, the feeling of hopelessness and despair and the loss of courage of a leader/manager in a hopeless subordinate middle position vis-à-vis a tyrannical commander.

Ahab is convinced that he has brought Starbuck to heel—'Starbuck now is mine; cannot oppose me now, without rebellion' (Page 144). Starbuck, earlier described as a man who 'cannot withstand those more terrific, because more spiritual terrors, which sometimes menace you from the concentrating brow of an enraged and mighty man' (Page 104), is still hopeful, even after his desperate defeat in the confrontation with Ahab; 'with the soft feeling of the human' in him, he resolves to fight the 'grim, phantom futures' (Page 148).

As it becomes obvious in the following episode, when Ahab calls on his three mates to cross their lances before him, they 'quailed before his strong, sustained, and mystic aspect. Stubb and Flask looked sideways from him; the honest eye of Starbuck fell downright' (Page 146). Apparently unconsciously unnerved by the reaction of his mates, Ahab subsequently subjugates the harpooneers in an absolutely diabolic manner: 'I do not order ye; ye will it' (Page 146). By urging the mates and the harpooners to drink 'the fiery waters from the pewter', Ahab makes them 'parties to this indissoluble league . . . . Death to Moby Dick! God hunt us all, if we do not hunt Moby Dick to his death!' (Page 146). The Captain has already been referred to on several occasions in the novel as 'Old Thunder' (Page 86), 'the absolute dictator' (Page 90) or 'a Khan of the plank, and a king of the sea, and a great lord of Leviathans' (Page 114). He ultimately shows these aspects in a most uncanny and awful way. The collusion over the secret about Ahab and the real purpose of the voyage now becomes manifest as an oath taken and sealed by everyone on the vessel.

At the end of this scene Ahab is astonished and relieved at 'succeeding that wild ratification of his purpose with the crew' (Page 171). Regarding the first night with the crew on the quarter-deck as a major success, Ahab denies or ignores the noticeable reservations by his mates indicated above. It appears that Ishmael, on behalf of the crew, is able to express the ambivalence towards what happened on the quarter-deck. While, on the one side, he makes 'Ahab's quenchless feud' (Page 155) his own, he also asks himself how

such a crew so officered, seemed specially picked and packed by some infernal fatality to help him to his monomaniac revenge. How it was that they so aboundingly responded to the old man's ire—by what evil magic their souls were possessed, that at times his hate seemed almost theirs. (Page 162)

To answer these questions 'would be to dive deeper than Ishmael can go' (Page 162). Ishmael refers instead to 'the subterranean miner that works in us all' (Page 162), which can be seen as an example of Melville's proto-psychoanalytic perspective (Ohlmeier, 2008; cf. Murray, 1929, Page 526, 1949, Page XXVI; Halverson, 1963, Page 436), as he often refers to the unconscious at a time long before psychoanalysis existed as a field of study.

While the White Whale for most of the crew had been a nebulous, phantom-like creature up to then, once it is made out as being Moby-Dick, the 'inscrutable thing' (Page 144) towards which

Ahab decided to take vengeance for his lost leg, the whale turns into a disastrous, incomprehensible object, the incarnation of a panic, striking 'half-formed foetal suggestions of supernatural agencies' (Page 156); 'not only ubiquitous, but immortal (for immortality is but ubiquity in time)' (Page 158). 'All evil, to crazy Ahab, were visibly personified, and made practically assailable in Moby-Dick' (Page 160).

Ahab's loss of his leg to Moby-Dick did not only make him a cripple; it also deprived him of a part of his psychic life. These losses are akin to what Bollas (1987, 157ff.) refers to as 'extractive introjection', which 'occurs when one person steals . . . an element of another individual's psychic life'. This extraction by the whale is not only the most severe defeat Ahab has ever experienced but would have unconsciously been a catastrophic reminder of his earlier losses and injuries. Ahab 'is consumed with one unachieved revengeful desire' (Page 176) and works himself up to rage and monomania in which 'the mind broods over one *idea* and cannot be reasoned out of it' (Chief Justice Lemual Shaw of the Supreme Judicial Court of Massachusetts [and later father-in-law of Melville], quoted in Smith, 1976). Moby-Dick becomes an 'internal bad object' for Ahab—'thy thoughts have created a creature in thee' (Page 175).

In psychoanalytic theory, an 'internal object refers to the mental representation that results from introjection, incorporation, or internalization of the relationship to an external object' (Benavides, n.d.). 'Internal objects are phantoms, that is, they are images occurring in phantasies which are reacted to as "real"' (Rycroft, 1968/1995, 113f.). While Ahab's madness and monomania are not least triggered by his accident at work on the previous voyage, they have, during the 'prelude' of the novel, a more individual quality. Chapter 44, 'The Chart', contains an impressive description of Ahab's dreadful inner struggle with his internal object.

Monomania as a 'term, and with it the notion of a disease with specific symptoms' (Smith, 1976, Page 16), only became current at Melville's time. It appears to be characterised by a fundamental split of the personality. While the sane part of the person or the mind retains its original vigour and soundness, the insane part is perverted and fixed to a certain object and/or part of reality. This is obvious with Ahab, who, despite his vindictive obsession, retains his capacity and competence as a captain in following the trail of Moby-Dick. It seems that the distinction between sane and insane parts of a person concomitant with monomania somehow anticipates the thinking of British psychoanalyst Bion (1957), who postulated a differentiation between psychotic and non-psychotic parts of the personality.

In applying this differentiation of parts of the *personality* to *social* systems, one may presume that the psychosocial dynamic of an organisation can be psychotic as well as a non-psychotic. As with persons, the non-psychotic parts of an organisation usually exist in tandem with its psychotic parts. The psychotic organisation refers to that part of the social system that induces in its role holders—either temporarily or permanently—psychotic thinking. When organisational role holders are unconsciously demanded to mobilise their personal psychotic parts, they lose their capacity to think. As a result, they tend to reduce and distort organisational reality according to their unconscious anxieties and fantasies. To the extent that the thinking in an organisation becomes psychotic, its role holders will incline to a hatred of thinking (Bion, 1959/1967; Lawrence, 1998a, 2000; Sievers, 1999a, 2006). A most striking example of this hatred of thinking occurs when Ahab, who, on the third and final day of the chase, shortly before his death and the sinking of the *Pequod*, confirms towards Starbuck: 'Ahab never thinks; he only feels, feels, feels; *that's* tingling enough for mortal man! to think's audacity' (Page 460).

Not least due to the permanent risk of an early death, life on a 'normal' whaler was characterised on a daily basis by psychotic anxieties. The captain and his mates were usually able to contain them, more often than not with brutality and violence. Once the voyage progressed, the original primary task of the *Pequod*—that is, 'extracting economic value from the whale' (Marx, 1964, Page 306)—is substituted with the goal of killing Moby-Dick. At this juncture the level of psychotic anxiety aboard increases considerably and, on occasions, escalates even further, particularly towards the end of the novel.

Excessive projective identification by which evil and aggression are placed outside the organisation is a further dynamic typical of an organisational psychotic state of mind. Once the White Whale turns into the monstrous phantom Moby-Dick and thus becomes the incarnation of all evil and mortal threat, Ahab and most of the crew become consumed by fear of their own projections. Though Ahab, particularly in the quarter-deck scene, may have thought to provide some containment by social defence, which he engineered with various rituals and the oath on the death of Moby-Dick, he himself, in the course of the chase for his dismemberer, increasingly becomes a further source of immeasurable anxiety for most of the crew. As Ahab no longer appears as a reliable captain, due to his apparent madness and monomania, which he himself projects onto Moby-Dick—'The White Whale swam before him as a monomaniac incarnation of all those malicious agencies which some deep men feel eating in them' (Page 160)—he not only becomes a recipient of the mortal anxiety projected onto him but also of the split-off madness and irresponsibility of crew members. As Captain and crew mutually collude in the psychotic dynamic, Ahab's personal monomania increasingly turns into a social one. In a sense, the social dynamic aboard the *Pequod* appears to resemble a madhouse—not so different from the one Melville (1856/1993) described a few years later on the *San Dominick* in *Benito Cereno*.

Though Ahab thought he had won the crew over to his side when he assembled it around him on the quarter-deck, he is apparently full of doubt as to whether he actually did succeed in winning over his subordinates to his conspiracy. Chapter 46 shows that he is still full of concerns that 'his crew ... could refuse all further obedience to him, and even violently wrest from him the command' (Page 184). 'Ahab must of course have been most anxious to protect himself' (Page 184). Knowing that, his

> chief mate, in his soul, abhorred his captain's quest, and could he, would joyfully disintegrate himself from it, or even frustrate it .... [Starbuck thus] would ever be apt to fall into open relapses of rebellion against the captain's leadership, unless some ordinary, prudential, circumstantial influences were brought to bear upon him. (Page 183)

In his thoughts about adequate tools to maintain and regain the crew's support, Ahab sounds very much like a contemporary human resources manager who, either naïvely or cynically, contemplates how to increase the motivation of his employees (cf. Sievers, 1986). He is convinced that

> all sailors of all sorts are more or less capricious and unreliable ... [and] that when they stood their long night watches, his officers and men must have some nearer things to think of than Moby Dick. (Page 183)

Being aware that 'having impulsively ... and perhaps somewhat prematurely revealed the prime but private purpose of the Pequod's voyage' (Page 184) and trying to protect himself against 'even the barely hinted imputation of usurpation, and the possible consequences of such a suppressed impression gaining ground' (Page 184), Ahab, in his 'heed-ful, closely calculating attention to every minute atmospheric influence' (Page 184), decides 'that the full terror of the voyage must be kept withdrawn into the obscure background' (Page 183).

Ahab saw that he must still in a good degree continue true to the natural, nominal purpose of the *Pequod*'s voyage; observe all customary usages; and not only that, but force himself to evince all his well-known passionate interest in the general pursuit of his profession (Page 184).

Act 2: in search of vengeance (Chapters 47–132)

While the first act can be seen as preparation for the chase of Moby-Dick and the establishment of the psychotic organisation required for it, the second act relates Ahab's desperate quest for Moby-Dick through the world's oceans. It further reveals Ahab's obsession, determination, increasing impatience and occasional 'deep helpless sadness' (Page 203). He leaves no doubt that he is uncompromisingly pursuing his 'mad motive and object'. Eventually he reconfirms how he had already described himself on an earlier occasion: 'They think me mad...; but I'm demoniac, I am madness maddened!' (Page 147).

While up to now the *Pequod* has sailed isolated on her voyage through the oceans, she now, in the second act, meets nine whalers. With the exception of one ship from France and another from London, all the others sailed from Nantucket. Though it was common practice for 'whaling-vessels when meeting each other in foreign seas' (Page 204), often after weeks if not months of isolation, to have a 'Gam' (that is, the crews visiting one another and 'socialising', exchanging news and letters), Ahab 'cared not to consort...with any stranger captain, except he could contribute some of that information he so absorbingly sought' (ibid.). The information he receives from these ships is, with three excep-tions, rather limited; he is torn between hopelessness and an increasing certainty of being on the right course.

Meeting Captain Boomer, the Commander of the *Samuel Enderby*, of London, who had lost an arm by the White Whale on a previous voy-age, must have been the most disappointing of these meetings. While Ahab is confident that he has found a companion in misfortune and thus an ally in his hunt for Moby-Dick, Captain Boomer has accepted his fate without resentment or the desire for revenge. The *Rachel* reveals a most tragic story; two of Captain Gardiner's sons were lost at sea while hunting Moby-Dick the previous night. While Stubb, the second mate, is convinced that the *Pequod* must help, following the unwritten rules of the whaling business, Ahab, in his 'iciness', apathetically refuses the other Captain's request for help in searching for his missing boys. With 'unconditional and utter rejection' (Page 435), he orders the still beseeching captain to leave the *Pequod* immediately. Captain Gardiner's loss of his sons by the White Whale is but further proof for Ahab that he is drawing nearer to his object of vengeance. The next ship, the *Delight*, confronts Ahab and his crew with a most dreadful picture. Not only has Moby-Dick destroyed a whale-boat the previous day, but it has also killed five crew members. While this devastating incident convinces her captain that the White Whale can not be conquered with normal means, Ahab, holding out 'Perth's levelled iron ... tempered in blood, and tempered by lightning' (Page 441), boasts that this harpoon will kill it. Though the more recent fate of these three ships—and not least Fedallah's prophecy of the *Pequod's* final catastrophe (Chapter 117)— certainly would have raised premonitions both for Ahab and the crew, they repudiate the 'forebodings as to things to come' (Page 408).

Ahab, in all these meetings, and especially in the three ones mentioned here, remains unimpressed and continues to pursue his obsession of vengeance. There are two meetings in particular, however—the one with the *Town-Ho* and the other with the *Jeroboam*—that could have offered the crew different possibilities for its role other than that as followers.

During the meeting with the *Town-Ho*, the crew is told a story from the ship's recent past, which is only shared in secrecy. It is the story of a whaling captain who failed in his role and authority in a desperate attempt to overpower a crew that was rebelling and nearly mutinying against the brutal violence of the captain.

The *Town-Ho* tale suggests a different fate for the *Pequod's* crew, were it to disobey its captain and revolt against him. The crew must unconsciously sense Ahab's deep fear of eventually losing his men's loyalty and support. This becomes evident when Ahab—and some other crew members, not least Fedallah and his tiger-yellow men—are not told the *Town-Ho* secret and the critical fact that, on a previous voyage, the ship lost a mate hunting for Moby-Dick.

The *Pequod* next meets the *Jeroboam*, whose captain, Mayhew, had once been stripped of his power and authority by one of his crew members, apparently a madman, who 'announced himself as the archangel Gabriel, and commanded the captain to jump overboard' (Page 266). Gabriel was supported by the *Jeroboam's* crew, and the captain eventually had no other choice than to keep Gabriel in 'complete freedom' (Page 267) with the consequence that 'the sailors, mostly poor devils', obeyed 'his instructions, sometimes rendering him personal homage, as to a god' (Page 267). After the ship had lost its first mate to Moby-Dick,

'Gabriel called off the terror-stricken crew from further hunting on the whale.... [and Moby-Dick since] became a nameless terror to the ship' (Page 268). It thus is not too much of a surprise 'that after this interlude, the seamen [on the *Pequod*] resumed their work..., many strange things hinted in reference to this wild affair' (Page 270). Not only had they met another madman who, as an ordinary sailor, took command of a vessel and successfully stopped the hunt for Moby-Dick, they were also confronted with their own impotence, despair and shame for not being able to put their captain off his megalomaniac obsession in 'route to his vengeance' (Page 321).

In a sense, the series of meetings with other whalers in the novel forms a foreground, while the actual drama, the ongoing quarrel about leadership and followership and who will ultimately determine the fate of the voyage and the crew, takes place 'behind the scenes', so to say.

Starbuck, already described as Ahab's main opponent in the first act and someone who 'would ever be apt to fall into open relapses of rebellion against his captain's leadership' (Page 183), remains the main character to seriously question Ahab; 'almost the only one man who had ever ventured to oppose him with anything in the slightest degree approaching to decision' (Page 440).

Ahab and Starbuck were in grave dispute over the original primary task of the voyage almost from the beginning. Both are in a collusion of contempt (cf. Sievers, 1994a, Pages 74–82; Pelzer, 2005): Ahab is quite aware that Starbuck disapproves of his purpose for the voyage, and Starbuck knows that Ahab disapproves of his criticism. Though Ahab has earlier decided to foster hunting and catching sperm whales in order to 'motivate' his men and not least to avoid the appearance that he would intentionally offend against the Nantucket owners, Starbuck, from experience, has every reason not to trust his Captain. Despite Ahab's mendacious attempt to outwardly integrate the two tasks, his private one and the one he has agreed on in his shipping contract, the two tasks—and thus leadership and management (Krantz and Gilmore, 2009)—actually are split. The split leaves Ahab as the commander of his vengeance and Starbuck as the one who, in his loyalty to the shipowners, and not least due to his own personal interest, regards himself as being responsible for covering costs, gaining a reasonable profit and paying the seamen their lay, that is, the percentage of the ship's earnings, to which they have contracted: 'I came here to hunt whales, not my commander's vengeance' (Page 143).

Starbuck's distrust of his Captain is clearly reconfirmed when he goes to Ahab's cabin to report that 'the casks below must have sprung a bad leak' (Page 392) when the ship was pumped. Ahab gives the intruder short shrift and orders him back on deck. Despite Starbuck's persistent attempts to convince the Captain of his duties and responsibilities as first mate, Ahab, full of rage and impatience, eventually threatens Starbuck with a loaded musket and makes clear to him: 'There is one God that is Lord over the earth, and one Captain that is lord over the *Pequod.—*On deck!' (Page 394). It is an open question as to whether, when Ahab shortly thereafter goes on deck and orders the sails lowered and the leaks repaired, that 'may have been a flash of honesty in him; or mere prudential policy' (Page 394, cf. 182ff.).

Aside from various similar episodes and incidents in which Starbuck is contemptuously treated by Ahab, the conflict re-escalates during a typhoon following several months of extensive but futile searches for Moby-Dick (Chapter 123, 'The Musket'). Knocking at the Captain's cabin door and finding him sleeping, Starbuck sees the loaded musket in the rack, the very musket that Ahab had pointed at him in the scene above. Filled with the shame, contempt and humiliation he has endured for months, if not years, at the hands of his Captain, he is convinced that Ahab will ultimately kill the 'thirty men and more'. Starbuck becomes preoccupied by thoughts of saving the crew and the ship by shooting the tyrant dead. Weighing up his motives and reservations in an internal agonising monologue, he ultimately dismisses the alternative idea to imprison Ahab. It seems that any plan to kill Ahab has to be displaced onto Moby-Dick (Stein, 2009)—'Seldom in world literature has the problem of tyrannicide been raised more forcefully than in this scene' (Drewermann, 2004, Page 278).

Ahab regards his subordinates as mere tools, which can be engineered by means of 'motivation' or overcome by seduction, power and violence. In addition, he has a deep inclination towards magic and magical thinking, as demonstrated by a belief in his supernatural power over the crew and his personal thoughts regarding the cosmos and its forces. This thinking is governed by an 'omnipotence of thoughts' (Freud, 1912–13, Page 374, note 2; 1919, Page 263, note 2; cf. Winnicott, 1935/1975, Page 132). Action that is guided by magic as a modality of thinking is oriented towards preventing catastrophe; it is a manic defence that is an expression of psychotic thinking.

Although Ahab seems at times to be convinced that he has subjugated the crew to his will, he again and again is aware of his ambivalence and is increasingly in doubt as to whether he can actually rely on them. In a sense this mirrors the contradictory feelings among the crew. While on some occasions they are sure of his leadership or seduced by his magic, at other times, they are seriously distrustful, doubtful, hopeless, if not in despair, and full of dread about the possible tragic outcome of the voyage. This becomes clear, for example, in the first scene of this act—Chapter 47, 'The Mat-Maker'—when Fedallah, the Parsee, and his tiger-yellow Manilla men appear on deck for the first time. Ahab is suddenly 'surrounded by five dusky phantoms that seemed fresh formed out of air' (Page 187), and the crew is shocked by their sudden appearance.

Panic-stricken as the crew is when the St Elmo's fire covers the masts, they can only make 'a half mutinous cry' (Page 418) before Ahab speaks like a tyrannical demon, exhorting the crew to stick to their oaths to hunt the White Whale. To demonstrate to the crew that he can master supernatural forces in a magical way, he extinguishes the flames of the corposants with one blast of his breath—symbolic of his intention to blow out the last fear aboard the *Pequod*. But the opposite occurs: 'at those last words of Ahab's many of the mariners did run from him in a terror of dismay' (Page 418). And when shortly afterwards Starbuck approaches Ahab to make arrangements to rescue the ship from the tempest, Ahab, full of contempt, leaves no doubt that he regards him and probably most of the crew as cowards. The crew watches Ahab trampling and destroying the quadrant, 'awestruck by the aspect of their commander, the seamen clustered together on the forecastle' (Page 412), until Ahab shouts out an order to change the ship's course. When, some time later, Ahab replaces the turning needle of the compass by his own construction (Chapter 124) 'their fear of Ahab was greater than their fear of Fate' (Page 424).

Once Ahab 'found himself hard by the very latitude and longitude where his tormenting wound had been inflicted' (Page 437), 'now it was there lurked a something in the old man's eyes, which it was hardly sufferable for feeble souls to see' (Page 437). 'Ahab's purpose now... domineered above [the crew] ... so, that all their bodings, doubts, misgivings, fears, were fain to hide beneath their souls' (Page 437).

Though Ahab remains the tyrannical commander of the *Pequod* until it sinks, Fedallah, the Parsee, becomes more than just the leader of the tiger-yellow Manilla men; in a sense, he more and more becomes Ahab's alter ego. The symbiotic relationship between Ahab and Fedallah—which Ishmael describes thus: 'in the Parsee Ahab saw his forethrown shadow, in Ahab the Parsee his abandoned substance.... Both seemed yoked together, and an unseen tyrant driving them' (Page 439)—must have appeared as a frightening enigma to the crew.

There are various prophecies in the novel that predict the catastrophic and tragic end of the *Pequod*'s voyage. Elijah warned Ishmael and Queequeg before the ship set sail. Gabriel, the Shaker prophet on the *Jeroboam*, predicted that Ahab would soon follow her first mate to the bottom of the sea. And Fedallah, in his most elaborate prophecy, even describes the circumstances of the Captain's death (Chapter 117). Ahab, guided by his wishful thinking, deals with these dire predictions and prophecies by misinterpreting them. This is further evidence of his inadequacy in coping with reality. He remains caught in psychotic thinking till the very end. Unable to grasp the meaning of Fedallah's enigmatic and concealed prophecies until shortly before his death, Ahab instead confirms them, one after another, as becomes obvious during the next three and last days of the hunt.

At the end of the 'second act', the ship is in an almost hopeless state. Captain Ahab, the *Pequod*'s commander, is still desperately determined to bring his vindictive object to a successful end. He is apparently closer than ever to facing his dismemberer, after an almost endless voyage, but he is extremely torn in his inner world—and extremely lonely. He is no longer certain whether he himself is the master of his mind or whether he is being driven by supernatural forces, be they God or the devil. Helpless in the face of his mates and crew, whom he no longer trusts, totally uncertain as to whether they still are his collaborators, much less his allies, he and the Parsee are in awe of each other and mutually estranged. By now Ahab is probably aware that he will not survive the final battle. As the crew realises that their Captain's mind cannot be changed to end the chase for the White Whale, they seem to surrender to their fate in hopelessness, resignation and despair. With the exception of the chief-mate, they have long ago given up their responsibility both for themselves and for the primary task of the voyage. Like helpless children, they have surrendered to what is demanded of them by the commander of their ship. The *Pequod*, with its captain and crew, is thus in a state very unlikely to win the upcoming battle.

Act 3: the chase—first to third day (Chapters 133–135)

Ahab scents a whale at night and realises by dawn that it is Moby-Dick, so the first day of the longed-for chase begins. Ahab orders three whale boats into the water, with the one he commands as 'heading the onset', and tells Starbuck to 'stay on board, and keep the ship' (Page 446). Ahab attempts vainly to steer the boat so as not to be seen by the surfacing whale, but eventually 'the White Whale ... shook the slight cedar as a mildly cruel cat her mouse' (Page 449). 'Monomaniac Ahab, furious with this tantalizing vicinity of his foe' (Page 229) tries with his own hands to wrench the boat from Moby-Dick's grip, but cannot prevent the boat from being destroyed: Ahab 'fell flat-faced upon the sea' (Page 449). Being 'too much of a cripple to swim' (Page 450) he almost drowns. He still stays in command, however, and orders the *Pequod*: 'Sail on the whale!—Drive him off!' (Page 450).

Dragged into Stubb's boat with blood-shot, blinded eyes, the white brine caking in his wrinkles; the long tension of Ahab's bodily strength did crack, and helplessly he yielded to his body's doom: for a time, lying all crushed in the bottom of Stubb's boat, like one trodden under foot of herds of elephants. Far inland, nameless wails came from him, as desolate sounds from out ravines (450f.).

No sooner has Ahab recovered that he asks whether his harpoon is safe. Only then, after Stubb shows it to him, does he ask whether the five men of his boat crew are safe.

Moby-Dick prevails the second day as well, and—as Ahab still believes in his destiny to confront him—he continues to take control of the chase. When Stubb expresses his conviction that Ahab will be successful up to the bloody end, he

> did but speak out for well nigh all that crew. The frenzies of the chase had by this time worked them bubblingly up, like old wine worked anew. Whatever pale fears and forebodings some of them might have felt before; these were not only now kept out of sight through the growing awe of Ahab, but they were broken up, and on all sides routed. (Page 454)

Since the quarter-deck scene at the beginning of the first act, Ahab has pursued his fantasy of making the crew 'one and all with [him]..., in this matter of the whale...—that inscrutable thing' (Page 144). Though meanwhile he had ample reason to doubt that his fantasy would ever come true, now, at the beginning of the second day of the chase, it is confirmed:

> They were one man, not thirty. For as the one ship that held them all; though it was put together of all contrasting things... all varieties were welded into oneness, and were all directed to that fatal goal which Ahab their one lord and keel did point to. (Page 454f.)

Soon 'the triumphant halloo of thirty buckskin lungs was heard... [when] Moby Dick bodily burst into view!' (Page 455). Taking a spare boat, Ahab again gives the ship's command to Starbuck. When all three boats reach the whale, Moby-Dick 'irresistibly dragged the more involved boats of Stubb and Flask towards his flukes; dashed them together like two rolling husks on a surf-beaten beach' (Page 457). Pouncing on

> Ahab's yet unstricken boat . . . the White Whale dashed his broad fore-head against its bottom, and sent it, turning over and over, into the air; till it fell again . . . and Ahab and his men struggled out from under it, like seals from a sea-side cave. (Ibid.)

Though Ahab's 'ivory leg had been snapped off' (Page 458), he must reassure himself that he is ultimately invulnerable: 'Nor white whale, nor man, nor fiend, can so much as graze old Ahab in his own proper and inaccessible being' (ibid.).

'Upon mustering the company' (ibid.), it is clear that Fedallah, the Parsee, is missing and cannot be found anywhere on the ship. When Stubb relates—'caught among the tangles of your line—I thought I saw him dragging under' (ibid.)—it is obvious that Fedallah has been lost at sea and that his prophecy that he would go before Ahab had come true. As Ahab orders 'all hands to the rigging of the boats' (Page 458), Starbuck again tries to calm him down and to make him give up his mad intent. But again Ahab refuses; instead he reconfirms his own authority as given to him by a higher commander:

> Ahab is for ever Ahab, man. This whole act's immutably decreed. 'Twas rehearsed by thee and me a billion years before this ocean rolled. Fool! I am the Fates' lieutenant; I act under orders. Look thou, underling! that thou obeyest mine. (Page 459)

Ahab, who ridiculed God again and again during the voyage and claimed divine powers for himself, in a curious, self-negating and, at the same time, self-contemptuous way, by psychotic thinking differentiates himself as a mortal man from the immortal God:

> Here's food for thought, had Ahab time to think, but Ahab never thinks; he only feels, feels, feels; *that's* tingling enough for mortal man! to think's audacity. God only has the right and privilege. Thinking is, or ought to be, a coolness and a calmness; and our poor hearts throb, and our poor brains beat too much for that. (Page 460)

Meanwhile he becomes convinced that Moby-Dick is chasing him— 'Aye, he's chasing me *now*; not I, *him*—that's bad; I might have known it, too. Fool!' (Page 461). He again is the first one to spot the whale on the third day. When leaving the ship for his boat, Ahab recognises that Fedallah's prediction regarding the circumstances of their deaths was partly correct and shares the foreboding of his own immanent death with Starbuck. In a most touching scene, Ahab and Starbuck shake hands with one another. Just before Ahab leaves, he asks Starbuck again to 'stand with the crew!', while Starbuck, in tears, tries to persuade him otherwise: 'Oh, my captain, my captain!—noble heart—go not— go not!—see, it's a brave man that weeps; how great the agony of the persuasion then!' (Page 462f.).

'Maddened by yesterday's fresh irons that corroded in him, Moby Dick seemed combinedly possessed by all the angels that fell from heaven' (Page 464). The White Whale starts by severely damaging two of the boats, leaving Ahab's and his crew's mainly intact. When the whale rises again to the surface, much to Ahab's horror, he carries the 'the half torn body of the Parsee...; his sable raiment frayed to shreds; his distended eyes turned full upon old Ahab' (Page 464). Ahab realises then that another of Fedallah's prophecies has come true. Warning his boat crew that he would harpoon 'the first thing that but offers to jump from this boat I stand in' (Page 465), Ahab reconfirms his image of leadership as oneness. This time, however, in a most drastic and excessive manner, he strips from his men their individual identity, by turning them into his own bodily members: 'Ye are not other men, but my arms and legs; and so obey me' (Page 465).

After Ahab gives the order that the *Pequod* is to follow the whale and his boat, he approaches the ship. ' "Oh! Ahab", cries Starbuck, "not too late is it, even now, the third day, to desist. See! Moby Dick seeks thee not. It is thou, thou, that madly seekest him!" ' (Page 465).

Only later, when the whale is close to Ahab's boat, has he 'darted his fierce iron, and his far fiercer curse into the hated whale' (Page 466), who 'spasmodically rolled his nigh flank against the bow, and, without staving a hole in it, ... suddenly canted the boat over' (Page 466). Three of the oarsmen are flung out and only two are able to hurl 'themselves bodily inboard again'.

Soon after, Moby-Dick heads for the *Pequod*.

> Retribution, swift vengeance, eternal malice were in his whole aspect, and spite of all that mortal man could do, the solid white buttress of

his forehead smote the ship's starboard bow, till men and timbers reeled. (Page 468)

Though Ahab is in great despair about the loss of his ship and fully aware that he will soon die, he is still caught in his vindictive obsession and throws his harpoon into his dismemberer. Denying that Moby-Dick has conquered him, he is convinced he can be killed but not defeated:

> Death-glorious ship! must ye then perish, and without me? Am I cut off from the last fond pride of meanest shipwrecked captains? Oh, lonely death on lonely life! Oh, now I feel my topmost greatness lies in my topmost grief.... Towards thee I roll, thou all-destroying but unconquering whale; to the last I grapple with thee; from hell's heart I stab at thee; for hate's sake I spit my last breath at thee.... *Thus*, I give up the spear! (Page 468)
>   The harpoon was darted; the stricken whale flew forward; with igniting velocity the line ran through the grooves;—ran foul. Ahab stooped to clear it; he did clear it; but the flying turn caught him round the neck, and voicelessly as Turkish mutes bowstring their victim, he was shot out of the boat, ere the crew knew he was gone. (Ibid.)

Epilogue

This brief epilogue was added after the first British printing of *Moby-Dick* (Boies, 1963). It shows that Ishmael, the narrator, survives the wreck only because he took Fedallah's place as Ahab's bowsman, after his death. Ishmael escapes the vortex of the sinking ship and, after a whole day and night of floating and clinging to the buoy formed by Queequeg's coffin, is miraculously rescued by the *Rachel* 'that in her retracting search after her missing children, only found another orphan' (Page 470).

Conclusion

The sailors whom Melville met during his voyages probably shared the fate of the majority of those working at the peak of the whaling industry (that is, their existence a wreck after a three or four years' whaling voyage). Unlike them, Melville was able to creatively transcend both his own suffering and the pain and hardship that he witnessed on these voyages (cf. Dejours, 1990). Working through his own experience was a prerequisite for writing a tragic drama, a tragedy in which all main characters suffer obsession, vengeance, madness, enormous brutality and—with the exception of Ishmael—an early, unexpected death. *Moby-Dick* thus is a drama of a failed search for vengeance; 'the story of a man who was himself destroyed in his efforts to destroy evil' (Myers, 1956, Page 75). And like the ancient classic drama, it is not primarily the drama of an individual protagonist or a group, but, like *Oedipus Rex*, *King Lear* or *Waiting for Godot*, a drama of the polis—in this particular case, the drama of a crew and an organisation. This drama's protagonist is Captain Ahab, and Melville tells the tale of his vengeance and how he submits the crew to his will until he finally destroys them all in an unsuccessful chase of a 'monster', Moby-Dick.

From a more general point of view, however, this novel is also the story of the decline and death of an organisation. It is certainly no coincidence that Melville gave the doomed ship the same name as 'a celebrated tribe of Massachusetts Indians, now extinct as the ancient Medes' (Page 67; cf. Rogin, 1985, 122ff.). Like later novels, for example, Emile Zola's (1891/1994) *L'Argent*, Joseph Conrad's (1913) *Chance* or Thomas Mann's (1901/1993) *Buddenbrooks*, it is the story of the collapse of an enterprise and addresses a topic that, despite its normality and frequency, is not broadly studied in economics or the social sciences (cf. Horst, 2009).

Madness in organisations has been the primary focus of my research for more than a decade (Sievers, 1999a, b, 2003a, b, 2006, 2008), and the White Whale has been swimming around in my study for more than 15 years (Sievers, 1994b, 2009a, b, 2010). What struck me most in (re-) thinking *Moby-Dick* from the socioanalytic perspective chosen here was the extent to which Captain Ahab's incredible and relentless pursuit of vengeance not only predominates his psyche but how, in a most diabolic way, he succeeds in winning over virtually his whole crew as allies of his business of revenge (Sievers, 1994b; Sievers and Mersky, 2004, 2006).

Ahab's betrayal of the ship-owners and his betrayal of his mates and the crew began before the *Pequod* set sail from Nantucket, when he hired the Manila crew as support and reinforcement for the hidden purpose of the voyage. He thus keeps Fedallah and his tiger-yellow men hidden under deck, in the underground 'unconscious', so to say, for quite some time.

Unable to acknowledge and mourn his own experience of shame, injury and loss, Captain Ahab turns his personal revenge for an accident at work into the primary task of the *Pequod*. In so doing, he displaces his personal experience and suffering into the role of captain and the crew at large. Driven by his 'mad motive and object', he enacts his individual fate at work as a social drama. In so doing, he substitutes the primary task of the whaler given by its ship-owners—that is, extracting value from the whale—into a search for personal vengeance.

Substituting an organisation's primary task with a secondary one is more often than not an expression of task hatred. The hatred of task, as Jane Chapman (2003) elaborates, is an expression of task corruption. Task corruption happens if 'the change in the nature of the task... [is] destructively motivated, whether at the conscious or the unconscious level' (ibid., Page 46). Task simulation

> is where the system or individual adopts the appearance of task engagement precisely in order to avoid task engagement.... The corruption derives from the destructive intent: not only is real task killed off and system energies devoted to the appearance of the tasks being done, but task values are subverted and task power becomes abusive. Simulating organisations, i.e. those which behave as if they are a system engaged in a real task in order to avoid becoming a system engaged in a real task, are characterised by poor morale, low system energy, ... questionable ethics, and high levels of conflict.
>
> (Ibid., 46f.)

In this sense, Ahab can be regarded as the captain of a simulating organisation, driven by his manic defence against shame and loss. To the extent that the crew increasingly submits itself to his corruption of the primary task and, with very few exceptions, does not dissent (Stein, 2007), the mates and the ordinary seamen form a collusion of perversity with the captain as they take part in the corruption and endorse it. Ahab's corruption thus becomes a social and organisational one in which the whole crew both unconsciously and consciously takes part.

Corruption is often the bedfellow of perversion—'perverse dynamics eventually lead to corrupt behaviours within the system [and] corruption builds on an underlying social fabric of perversity' (Long, 2008, 2f.). This can be fostered, if not created, by psychotic processes, which 'for the most part, [are] collusively produced' (Lawrence, 1998a, Page 66).

One might further assume that Captain Peleg and Bildad, the *Pequod*'s Nantucket ship-owners, unconsciously contribute to this corruption. Despite Peleg's concerns about Ahab's 'character', the two Captains nevertheless delegate to him the primary task of the voyage and the role of captain. They thus make themselves unconscious participants in this perverse system, with the loss of 'some thousands of [their] hard earned dollars' (Page 96) invested in the vessel and its fateful voyage. Had they

> half dreamed of what was lurking in him then, how soon would their aghast and righteous souls have wrenched the ship from such a fiendish man! They were bent on profitable cruises, the profit to be counted down in dollars from the mint. [Ahab] ... was intent on an audacious, immitigable, and supernatural revenge. (Page 162)

The collusion of corruption serves not least to create and maintain Ahab's hubris (Gabriel, 1998) that ultimately leads to the downfall of the crew and the vessel. His merciless quest for vengeance determined the business aboard the *Pequod* and reflected the 'rationality' of the 'capitalist spirit' of the industry and time. In this industry, 'oil is always clearly more valuable than men' (Hall, 1950, Page 224), and executing vengeance and thus the annihilation of the White Whale become 'clearly more valuable than men'—for Ahab and eventually for his crew too. It is not least this notion of 'capitalist vengeance' that seems to have survived into the contemporary world of business—and warfare (cf. Sievers, 2003a).

The corrupt organisation creates a totalitarian regime that fosters naval miasma. The concept of miasma has been recently introduced into organisational theory by Yiannis Gabriel. It 'describes a contagious state of pollution, material, psychological and spiritual, that affects all who work in particular organizations' (Gabriel, 2008, Page 52). Howard Stein (2008), building on Gabriel's concept, offers the 'inconsolable organisation' as

> a state of affect paralysis in the face of massive, often sustained, loss that cannot be mourned.... When organizational loss is not acknowledged, and mourning is proscribed, inconsolable grief and miasma follow.
>
> (Ibid., Page 91)

Ahab's vindictive obsession results from his inability to mourn the loss of his leg and thus of his inviolability as an integral part of his identity and soul. As Bollas (1987, Page 166) puts it, retaliation is 'an unconscious act intended to recover the lost part of the self by violent intrusion into the other—to recover what has been stolen from oneself'. During the voyage, the Captain's individual loss becomes an organisational one that fosters paralysis and a psychotic dynamic. This obsession was 'yielding up all his thoughts and fancies to his one supreme purpose; that purpose . . . forced itself . . . into a kind of self-assumed, independent being of its own' (Page 175).

Moby-Dick, the novel, is above all about Melville and his time—and not primarily about a character or 'a reality'. It was written at a time of great socioeconomic and technical upheaval in America, when society was beginning to control nature and the elements through expanded textile and steel industries, technological innovations of the steam engine and the building of canal and railway systems. As whaling was the industry that first incarnated 'violence in the economy' (Ruggiero, 2002, Page 99), the fate of the *Pequod*, at a time when the whaling industry was approaching its end, 'symbolizes, and sets the pattern for, a new economic order in which nature is systematically exploited for profit' (ibid.) as were men in their working roles. Hall's (1950, Page 224) point regarding the capitalist rationality of the whaling industry during the middle of the nineteenth century—that is, that 'oil is always clearly more valuable than men'—is the rationality that increasingly took place in the above mentioned onshore industries. This may, among other factors, have contributed to the fact that such a great story could not be acknowledged at the time of its publication; thus it is not too much of a surprise that the Melville revival and that of *Moby-Dick*, in particular did not begin before the end of the First World War (Van Doren, 1921; Mumford, 1929).

Mathiessen (1941; quoted in Shaw, 1993, Page 63) suggested that Ahab's 'career is prophetic of many others in the history of later nineteenth-century America'. 'But if Melville had been 'prophetic' of what was to come, Mathiessen added, it was 'without deliberately intending it' (Shaw, ibid.). With this proviso in mind, Ahab appears prophetic to this day in that his megalomania can be seen as a metaphor for 'rational madness' (Lawrence, 1995; cf. 1998b), 'madness of normality' (Gruen, 1987, Page 20), 'madness in normality' (Hoggett, 1992, Page 73), 'pseudo-normality' (McDougall, 1974, Page 444) or 'surface sanity' (LaBier, 1986, Page 62) in contemporary organisations and corporations in particular. It is the rational madness to which Ahab is devoted in his self-description: 'All my means are sane, my motive and my object mad' (Page 161).

Karl Marx (1867, Page 39) regarded 'the madness of bourgeois economy' as the major source of 'the secret of profit making' (Misik, 1997, Page 140). He was mainly concerned with the madness resulting from the contradiction between subjectively rational economic strategies, which proved to be irrational in the context of the larger economy. Management in contemporary organisations often seems to be unconsciously inclined to disguise madness by making it appear normal (Gruen, 1987, Page 24). Such a 'pathological' notion of normality serves to cover the anxiety of the chaos inescapably connected with the traumatic impact of change, when organisations are being deconstructed (Jacobsen, 1959, Page 587; Lawrence, 1995, cf. 1998b).

In so far as the voyage of the *Pequod* 'is an industrial enterprise bossed by Ahab, the nineteenth century type of the manager of an absentee-owned plant' (Chase, 1949, Page 101), Ahab

is the American cultural image: the captain of industry and of his soul; the exploiter of nature who severs his own attachment to nature and exploits himself out of existence; the good progressive American; the master of the most beautifully contrived machine of his time; the builder of new worlds whose ultimate spiritual superficiality drives him first to assume an uneasy kingship and a blind, destructive motive of revenge, and then gradually reduces him to a pure, abstract fury on whose inhuman power he rides off into eternity, leaving nothing behind but disaster for the races of the world and an ambiguous memory of the American flair which accompanied the disaster and was the only hint of moral meaning or of solace for the future or for the dead at the bottom of the Pacific.

(Ibid., Page 43)

And this cultural image seems to broadly prevail in the present:

Moby Dick is both a cultural metaphor and social cynosure. Ahab resonates with us because he is a cultural-historical type, one that extends far beyond the mid-19th century New England. Ahab foreshadows the economic and political 'bossism' in American cities, a leadership that continues to fascinate and lure Americans to this day (e.g. CEOs as Jack Welch, Dennis Kozlowski, Albert Dunlap etc.).

(Stein, 2009)

Melville, with impressive clarity, shows how Ahab succeeded in manifold ways—by seduction, dependency, contempt, madness, monomaniac vengeance, magic and not least by feigned powerlessness—to bring his crew to heel for his vengeance and weld it together.

They were one man, not thirty … all the individualities of the crew, this man's valor, that man's fear; guilt and guiltlessness, all varieties were welded into oneness, and were all directed to that fatal goal which Ahab their one lord and keel did point to. (454f.)

That a captain obsessed by the madness of taking personal revenge is entrusted to lead an enterprise into disaster apparently is not just fiction but, at the same time, serves as a striking metaphor for the present business world.

This epic of world literature neither gives instructions for sailors nor is it a textbook on leadership. *Moby-Dick* is a drama of human delusions of grandeur, the desire for godliness and immortality and a metaphor for how we as leaders and followers may destroy ourselves and others if we are not able to acknowledge, mourn and recover from the losses, injuries and humiliations of our inner world other than by projecting them onto the outer world and retaliating against those who appear to be threatening and annihilating persecutors.

To the extent that organisations are solely devoted to the maximisation of profits or the optimisation of shareholder value, seek (unrestricted) growth and immortality and sacrifice doubts, not-knowing and reservations to the esprit de corps, they are betraying—like Ahab and his crew—not only the essential tasks of the organisation or the enterprise but are also losing sight of the meaning of work and the social relatedness of leaders and followers. They are likely to become corrupt organisations in which leaders and followers are in a collusion of hatred of the primary task.

Acknowledgements

I am grateful to Howard F. Stein for his thoughts on a previous version of this chapter and to Rose Mersky for her enormous help in editing it.

Notes

1. Readers not familiar with the novel may want to refer to either of these links for plot summaries:
   http://www.sparknotes.com/lit/mobydick/summary.html
   http://en.wikipedia.org/wiki/Moby-Dick#Plot
   http://www.studyworld.com/studyworld_studynotes/jnotes/MobyDick/PlotSummary.html (27/12/2009)
2. All references to Herman Melville's (1851/1967) *Moby Dick* are indicated by page numbers; they are taken from *Moby-Dick*. Ed. by Harrison Hayford & Hershel Parker. New York: Norton, 1967; a Norton Critical Edition.

References

Adamson, Joseph (1997): Melville, Shame, and the Evil Eye: A Psychoanalytic Reading. New York: State University of New York.

Ausband, Stephen C. (1975): The Whale and the Machine: An Approach to Moby-Dick. American Literature 47, 2, 197–211.

Bain, Alastair (1999): On Socio-Analysis. Socio-Analysis 1, 1, 1–17.

Benavides, Marie Eugénie Julian Muzzo (n.d.): Internal Object. http://www.answers.com/topic/internal-object (9/20/2009).

Bion, Wilfred R. (1957): Differentiation of the Psychotic from the Non-psychotic Personalities. International Journal of Psycho-Analysis 38, 3–4, 266–75; again in: Elizabeth Bott Spillius (ed.) (1988): Melanie Klein Today. Developments in Theory and Practice. Vol. I: Mainly Theory. London: Routledge, 61–78.

Bion, Wilfred R. (1959/1967): Attacks on Linking. In: Second Thoughts. London: Heinemann, 93–109.

Boies, J. J. (1963): The Whale Without Epilogue. Modern Language Quarterly 24, 2, 172–6.

Bollas, Christopher (1987): The Shadow of the Object. Psychoanalysis of the Unthought Known. New York: Columbia University Press.

Bollas, Christopher (2009): The Evocative Object World. Hove, East Sussex: Routledge.

Brodhead, Richard H. (1986): Trying All Things: An Introduction to Moby-Dick. In: R. H. Broadhead (ed.), New Essays on Moby-Dick. Cambridge: Cambridge University Press, 1–21.

Chapman, Jane (2003): Hatred and the Corruption of Task. Organisational and Social Dynamics, 3, 1, 40–60; first published in (1999) Socio-Analysis, 1, 2, 127–50.

Chase, Richard (1949): Herman Melville: A Critical Study. New York: Macmillan

Conrad, Joseph (1913): Chance: A Tale in Two Parts. Garden City, NY: Doubleday, Page & Co. http://www.gutenberg.lib.md.us/1/4/7/1476/1476-h/1476-h.htm (1/9/2010).

Conrad, Joseph (1920): Notes on My Book (Chance). Garden City & Toronto: Doubleday, Page & Company. ftp://sailor.gutenberg.lib.md.us/gutenberg/2/0/1/5/20150/20150-h/20150-h.htm#CHANCE (1/6/2010). The quotation from *Chance* (first published in 1913) is taken from the Introduction, page i.

Dejours, Christophe (1990): Nouveau Regard sur la Souffrance Humaine dans les Organisations. In: Jean-Francois Chanlat (ed.), L'individu dans l'organisation. Les dimensions oubliées. Quèbec: Les Presses de l'Université Laval, Edition ESKA, 687–708.

Delbanco, Andrew (2005): Melville: His World and Work. New York: A. Knopf.

Dolin, Eric Jay (2007): Leviathan: The History of Whaling. New York: W. W. Norton.

Douglas, Ann (1977): The Feminization of American Culture. New York: Alfred A. Knopf.

Drewermann, Eugen (2004): Moby Dick oder vom Ungeheuren, ein Mensch zu sein. Melvilles Roman tiefenpsychologisch gedeutet. Düsseldorf & Zürich: Walter [Moby Dick, or: On the enormity of being human: A depth psychological interpretation].

Dyer, Susan K. (1994): Narcissism in the Novels of Herman Melville. Psychiatric Quarterly 65, 15–30.

Fisher, Marvin (1966): Melville's 'Bell-Tower': A Double Thrust. American Quarterly 18, 200–7.

Freud, Sigmund (1912–13): Totem und Tabu. S.A., Vol. 9. Frankfurt: S. Fischer, 287–444; English translation: Totem and Taboo, S.E., Vol. 13. London: Hogart, 1–161.

Freud, Sigmund (1919): Das Unheimliche. S.A., Vol. 4. Frankfurt: S. Fischer, 241–74; English translation: The Uncanny. S.E., Vol. 17. London: Hogart, 219–56.

Gabriel, Yiannis (1998): The Hubris of Management. Administrative Theory and Praxis 20, 3, 257–73.

Gabriel, Yiannis (2008): Organizational Miasma, Purification and Cleansing. In: Arndt Ahlers-Niemann, Ullrich Beumer, Rose Redding Mersky & Burkard Sievers (eds), Organisationslandschaften. Sozioanalytische Gedanken und Interventionen zur normalen Verrücktheit in Organisationen/The Normal Madness in Organizations: Socioanalytic Thoughts and Interventions. Bergisch-Gladbach: Verlag Andreas Kohlhage, 52–73.

Gleim, William S. (1962): The Meaning of Moby Dick. New York: Russell & Russell.

Gruen, Arno (1987): Der Wahnsinn der Normalität. Realismus als Krankheit: eine grundlegende Theorie zur menschlichen Destruktivität. München: Kösel-Verlag, The Insanity of Normality: Understanding Human Destructiveness. Berkeley: Human Development Books, 2007.

Hall, James B. (1950): Moby Dick: Parable of a Dying System. Western Review 14, 223–6.

Halverson, John (1963): The Shadow in Moby-Dick. American Quarterly 15, 436–46.

Haude, Rüdiger (2008): Frei-Beuter. Charakter und Herkunft piratischer Demokratie im frühen 18. Jahrhundert. Zeitschrift für Geschichtswissenschaft 7–8, 593–616.

Hirschhorn, Larry (1999): The Primary Risk. Human Relations 52, 1, 5–23; again in: Burkard Sievers (ed.) (2009): Psychoanalytic Studies of Organizations. Contributions from the International Society for the Psychoanalytic Study of Organizations (ISPSO) 1983–2008. London: Karnac, 153–74.

Hobbes, Thomas (1651/1996): Leviathan or the Matter, Forme and Power of a Commonwealth Ecclesiastical and Civil. (1996): Leviathan (Norton Critical Editions), edited by Richard Flathman & David Johnston. New York: Norton.

Hoggett, Paul (1992): Partisans in an Uncertain World. The Psychoanalysis of Engagement. London: Free Association Books.

Hohman, Elmo Paul (1928/1974): The American Whaleman. A Study of Life and Labor in the Whaling Industry. New York: Longmans, Green & Co., reprint: London: Macdonald and Jane's.

Horst, Ernst (2009): Brandweinbrennerei ausgebrannt. Frankfurter Allgemeine Zeitung 15.09.09, No. 214, 32.

Jacques, Eliot (1955): Social Systems as a Defense Against Persecutory and Depressive Anxiety. In: M. Klein, P. Heimann & R. E. Money-Kyrle (eds), New Directions in Psychoanalysis. London: Tavistock Publications.

Jacobsen, Edith (1959): Depersonalization. Journal of the American Psychoanalytic Association 7, 4, 581–610.

James, C. L. R. (1953): Mariners, Renegades and Castaways. The Story of Herman Melville and the World We Live in. New York: C. L. R. James.

Kimaid, Michael (2005): Bush as Ahab. Aboard the Modern Day *Pequod*. Counterpunch, Weekend edition May 28/30. http://www.counterpunch.org/kimaid05282005.html (7/18/2010).

Klein, Melanie (1959): Our Adult World and its Roots in Infancy. Human Relations 12, S. 291–303; again in: Melanie Klein (1988): Envy and Gratitude and Other Works 1946–1963. London: Virago Press, 247–63.

Kohut, Heinz (1972): Thoughts on Narcissism and Narcissistic Rage. Psychoanalytic Study of the Child 27, 360–400.

Krantz, James & Thomas N. Gilmore (2009): The Splitting of Leadership and Management as a Social Defence. In: Burkard Sievers (ed.), Psychoanalytic Studies of Organizations: Contributions from the International Society for the Psychoanalytic Study of Organizations (ISPSO) 1983–2008. London: Karnac, 23–49.

Kruse, Joachim (1976): Einführung in die Ausstellung 'Illustrationen zu Melvilles Moby-Dick'. In: Schleswig-Holsteinisches Landesmuseum (ed.), Illustrationen zu Mellvilles 'Moby-Dick'. Schleswig: Schleswig-Holsteinsches Landesmuseum, 13–32.

LaBier, Douglas (1986): Modern Madness. The Emotional Fallout of Success. Reading, MA: Addison-Wesley.

Lawrence, W. Gordon (1995): Social Dreaming as a Tool of Action Research. Paper presented at the 1995 Symposium, International Society for the Psychoanalytic Study of Organizations, London, 7–9 July.

Lawrence, W. Gordon (1998a): Unconscious Social Pressures on Leaders. In: Edward B. Klein, Faith Gabelnick & Peter Herr (eds), The Psychodynamics of Leadership. Madison CT: Psychosocial Press, 53–75.

Lawrence, W. Gordon (1998b): Social Dreaming as a Tool of Consultancy and Action Research. In: W. Gordon Lawrence (ed.), Social Dreaming @ Work. London: Karnac, 123–40.

Lawrence, W. Gordon (2000): Thinking Refracted. In: W. G. Lawrence (ed.), Tongued with Fire: Groups in Experience. London: Karnac, 1–30.

Linebaugh, Peter & Marcus Rediker (1990): The Many-Headed Hydra: Sailors, Slaves, and the Atlantic Working Class in the Eighteenth Century. Journal of Historical Sociology 3, 3, 225–52.

Linebaugh, Peter & Marcus Rediker (2000): The Many-Headed Hydra: Sailors, Slaves, Commoners, and the Hidden History of the Revolutionary Atlantic. London & New York: Verso.

Long, Susan (2008): The Perverse Organisation and Its Deadly Sins. London: Karnac.

Mann, Thomas (1901/1993): Buddenbrooks: The Decline of a Family. New York: Knopf, 1993.

Marx, Karl (1867): Das Kapital. Kritik der politischen Ökonomie. Hamburg: Otto Meissner; reprint (1980), Hildesheim: Gerstenberg Verlag.

Marx, Leo (1956): The Machine in the Garden. The New England Quarterly 29, 27–42.

Marx, Leo (1964): The Machine in the Garden. Technology and the Pastoral Ideal in America. London: Oxford University Press.

Mathiessen, Francis Otto (1941): American Renaissance: Art and Expression in the Age of Emerson and Whitman. London: Oxford University Press.

McDougall, J. (1974): The Psychosoma and the Psychoanalytic Process. International Review of Psychoanalysis, 1, 437–59.

Melville, Herman (1849/1969): Redburn, His First Voyage; Being the Sailor-boy Confessions and Reminiscences of the Son-of-a-gentleman, in the Merchant Service. Evanston, IL: Northwestern University Press.

Melville, Herman (1850/1990), White-Jacket or The World in a Man-of-War. Oxford: Oxford University Press.

Melville, Herman (1851/1967): Moby-Dick. Edited by Harrison Hayford & Hershel Parker. New York: Norton.

Melville, Herman (1856/1993): Benito Cereno. In: Billy Budd, Sailor and Other Stories. London: J.M. Dent, 209–84.

Melville, Herman (1924/1962): Billy Budd, Sailor. Harrison Hayford & Merton M. Sealts, Jr. (eds). Chicago: University of Chicago Press.

Misik, Robert (1997): Zur unpolitischen Ökonomie des Rentners. Pensionsfonds—ein Phänomen des neuesten Kapitalismus. Merkur 51, 955–958.

Mumford, Lewis (1926): The Golden Day. A Study in American Experience and Culture. New York: Boni and Liveright.

Mumford, Lewis (1929): Herman Melville. New York: The Literary Guild of America.

Mumford, Lewis (1966): The Myth of the Machine: Technics and Human Development. New York: Harcourt.

Murray, Henry A. (1929): Review of Lewis Mumford (1929). The New England Quarterly 2, 523–6.

Murray, Henry A. (1949): Introduction. In: Herman Melville (ed.), Pierre or the Ambiguities. New York: Hendriks House, XIII–CIII.

Myers, Henry A. (1956): The Tragic Meaning of Moby Dick. In: H. A. Myers (ed.), Tragedy: A View of Life. Ithaca, NY: Cornell Paperbacks, 57–77.

Ohlmeier, Dieter (2008): Herman Mellvilles 'Billy Budd, Sailor'. Über Urschuld und Urkonflikt einer Organisation. In: Arndt Ahlers-Niemann, Ullrich Beumer, Rose Redding Mersky & Burkard Sievers (eds), Organisationslandschaften. Sozioanalytische Gedanken und Interventionen zur normalen Verrücktheit in Organisationen/The Normal Madness in Organizations: Socioanalytic Thoughts and Interventions. Bergisch-Gladbach: Verlag Andreas Kohlhage, 97–104.

Pelzer, Peter (2005): Contempt and Organization: Present in Practice—Ignored by Research? Organization Studies 26, 8, 1217–27.

Rogin, Michael Paul (1985): Subversive Genealogy. The Politics and Art of Herman Melville. Berkeley: University of California Press.

Ruggiero, Vincenzo (2002): Moby Dick and the Crimes of the Economy. The British Journal of Criminology 42, 96–108.

Rycroft, Charles (1968/1995): A Critical Dictionary of Psychoanalysis. Harmondsworth: Penguin.

Sellers, Charles (1991/1994): The Market Revolution. Jacksonian America 1815–1846. Oxford: Oxford University Press.

Sexton, Timothy (2005): Leadership Compares to Captain Ahab's in Moby-Dick. Associated Content November 16, http://www.associatedcontent.com/

article/13807/how_president_bushs_monomaniacal_leadership.html?cat=37 (01/04/2010).

Shaw, Peter (1993): Cutting a Classic Down to Size. The Virginia Quarterly Review 69, 1, 61–84. http://www.vqronline.org/articles/1993/winter/shaw-cutting-classic/ (8/23/2009).

Sievers, Burkard (1986): Beyond the Surrogate of Motivation. Organization Studies, 7, 335–51.

Sievers, Burkard (1994a): Work, Death, and Life Itself. Essays on Management and Organization. Berlin: de Gruyter.

Sievers, Burkard (1994b): In Search of Vengeance: Lessons on Management and Organization from Herman Melville's Moby-Dick. Paper presented at the 12th International Conference of the Standing Conference on Organizational Symbolism (SCOS), Calgary, Alberta, Canada, July 10–13, 'Organizing the Past', Manuscript.

Sievers, Burkard (1995): Characters in Search of a Theatre. Organization as Theatre for the Drama of Childhood and the Drama at Work. Free Associations, 5, 2 (No. 34), 196–220.

Sievers, Burkard (1999a): Psychotic Organization as a Metaphoric Frame for the Socio-Analysis of Organizational and Interorganizational Dynamics. Administration & Society 31, 5, November, 588–615.

Sievers, Burkard (1999b): Accounting for the Caprices of Madness: Narrative Fiction as a Means of Organizational Transcendence. In: Richard A. Goodman (ed.), Modern Organizations and Emerging Conundrums. Exploring the Postindustrial Subculture of the Third Millennium. Lanham: Lexington Books, 126–142.

Sievers, Burkard (2003a): Competition as War: Towards a Socio-Analysis of War in and Among Corporations. Socio-Analysis 2, 1, 1–27.

Sievers, Burkard (2003b): Your Money or Your Life? Psychotic Implications of the Pension Fund System: Towards a Socio-Analysis of the Financial Services Revolution. Human Relations 56, 2, 187–210.

Sievers, Burkard (2006): Psychotic Organization—A Socio-Analytic Perspective. ephemera 6, 2, 104–20. http://www.ephemeraweb.org/journal/6-2/6-2sievers.pdf (7/18/2010).

Sievers, Burkard (2008): The Psychotic University. Ephemera 8, 3, 238–57. http://www.ephemeraweb.org/journal/8-3/8-3sievers.pdf (7/18/2010).

Sievers, Burkard (2009a): Before the Surrogate of Motivation: Motivation and the Meaning of Work in the Golden Age of the American Whaling Industry Part 1. Critique: Journal of Socialist Theory 37, 3, 391–413.

Sievers, Burkard (2009b): On My Way to Herman Melville's *Moby Dick*, I Found … *Some Preliminary Remarks from an Unwritten Book*. Society and Business Review 4, 2, 97–109.

Sievers, Burkard (2010): Before the Surrogate of Motivation: Motivation and the Meaning of Work in the Golden Age of the American Whaling Industry Part 2. Critique: Journal of Socialist Theory 38, 1, 1–17.

Sievers, Burkard & Rose Redding Mersky (2004): Some Socio-Analytical Reflections on Vengeance and Revenge. Journal of Psycho-Social Studies 3, 1, 4. http://www.btinternet.com/~psycho_social/Vol4/JPSS4_BSRRM1.htm (7/18/2010).

Sievers, Burkard & Rose Redding Mersky (2006): The Economy of Vengeance; Some Considerations on the Aetiology and Meaning of the Business of Revenge. Human Relations 59, 1, 241–59.

Smith, Henry Nash (1976): The Madness of Ahab. Yale Review 66, 14–32.

Stein, Howard F. (2007): Organizational Totalitarianism and the Voices of Dissent. Journal of Organizational Psychodynamics 1, 1, 1–25; again in: Stephen P. Banks (ed.) (2008): Dissent and the Failure of Leadership. Northampton MA: Edward Elgar Publishing Ltd, 75ff.

Stein, Howard F. (2008): Traumaitic Change and the Inconsolable Organization. In: Arndt Ahlers-Niemann, Ullrich Beumer, Rose Redding Mersky & Burkard Sievers (eds), Organisationslandschaften. Sozioanalytische Gedanken und Interventionen zur normalen Verrücktheit in Organisationen/The Normal Madness in Organizations: Socioanalytic Thoughts and Interventions. Bergisch-Gladbach: Verlag Andreas Kohlhage, 74–95.

Stein, Howard F. (2009): Personal e-mail communication 08/24.

Turquet, Pierre (1974): Leadership: The Individual and the Group. In: G. S. Gibbard (ed.), Analysis of Groups. San Francisco: Jossey-Bass, 349–72.

Van Doren, Carl (1921): The American Novel. New York: Macmillan.

Vickers, Daniel with Vince Walsh (2005): Young Men and the Sea: Yankee Seafarers in the Age of Sail. New Haven: Yale University Press.

Warner, Nicholas O. (2008): Of 'Gods and Commodores': Leadership in Melville's *Moby-Dick*. In: Joanne B. Ciulla (ed.), Leadership at the Crossraods. Vol. 3: Leadership and the Humanities. Westport, CT: Prager, 3–19.

Winnicott, D. W. (1935/1975): The Manic Defence. In: D. W. Winnicott (ed.), Through Paediatrics to Psychoanalysis. London: Hogarth.

Zola, Émile (1891/1994): L'Argent. Paris: Biibliothèque-Charpentier. Money. London: Chatto & Windus.

5
Nevil Shute: *Pastoral*

David Weir

In this chapter we offer an account of the career and contribution of Nevil Shute Norway, best-selling novelist, pioneering aircraft designer, an airship engineer who took over as Chief Design Engineer from the great Barnes Wallis on the successful R100 Airship that flew safely from the UK to Canada and back, youngest fellow of the Royal Aeronautical Society, and entrepreneur and founder of his own highly successful aircraft manufacturing company. He wrote of managers and leaders in his novels and he outlined a theory of industrial leadership in his memoirs in which he carefully distinguished two types of manager, the 'starter' and the 'runner', identifying himself as a 'starter' who could initiate new ventures but would tire of the chores of diurnal management. As engineer, CEO and novelist, Nevil Shute breaks the mould of the banal stereotypes of leadership that inhabit our textbooks.

Nevil Shute Norway was born in 1899 in West London to a middle-class family whose head was Arthur Hamilton Norway, a civil servant and writer of successful travel books who became head of the Irish Post Office. His second son was educated at Shrewsbury School, just missed serving in the Great War and went up to Oxford to read engineering, where he obtained a third. As a youth he caught the aviation bug, and never recovered. The aviation industry was in its infancy and offered ample opportunity for both adventure and application. Shute knew that there were old pilots and there were bold pilots but there were no old bold pilots. Shute recognised that the aviator who understood the nature of the engineering principles and practice, on which this precision craft was based, owed a duty of care not only to himself but also to his machine.

Shute rehearses this scenario many times in his life and writings, and the theme of several of his novels concerns the young man who has learnt how to take risks and survive. He understood the necessity of mastering one's craft before one forays into unknown territory. He was modest about his engineering, noting that 'an engineer is a man who can do for five bob, what any damn fool can do for a pound'.

Shute, still known, as he was throughout his career as an engineer and entrepreneur, as Nevil Norway, obtained a very junior position in the developing aviation industry through sheer persistence; throughout the 1920s he worked as a stress calculator in airship design. He lived the life of a single man and in many of the evenings, as a relaxation from his laborious daily grind of calculation, he wrote novels.

The R100 and the R101

His career in the airship industry reached its zenith in 1929 with his appointment as second in command to Barnes Wallis, the great engineer of the period who was subsequently to become famous as the inventor of the bouncing bomb, with which the Royal Air Force (RAF) destroyed the Mohne Dam. Together they worked on the development of the airship R100 for a subsidiary company of Vickers, the Airship Guarantee Company. Individual initiative was encouraged within the company—which was more than could be said for its state-owned rival.

Nevil Shute Norway shared a general belief in the future of airships, but the industry's hopes foundered in the crash of its government-supported competitor, the R101, subsequently wrecked with the loss of Lord Thompson, the Minister of Aviation who had invested his personal backing in the venture, and most of those on board. Norway had been privately critical of the procedures and systems with which the R101 was being constructed at Cardington in Bedfordshire. His experience bred in him a lifelong distrust of politicians and civil servants. He was to write about the disaster of the R101 in his memoir, *Slide Rule*.

Slide Rule is far from objective history: many of those who died in the R101 fireball were personal friends and colleagues and he wanted to memorialise them as well as this significant phase in his career. Subsequently, Shute raised funds for and became managing director of a company that produced a highly successful aeroplane, the Airspeed Oxford, of which several thousand were constructed and in which were trained the RAF bomber crews who won the air war against Nazi Germany. Airspeed built its aircraft initially in a converted bus garage in York that can still be seen, and subsequently at Portsmouth. This company was bought out at the end of the 1930s and the new owners made it clear that the awkward, irascible Nevil Shute Norway's services would no longer be required in the company that he had founded and built up. With the proceeds of an advance from Hollywood for his latest book, *Ruined City*, he became a full-time writer.

During the Second World War he was ordered to become a member of a top-secret team in the Ministry of Defence devising new and unusual weapons of war. During this period he continued to write in his evenings. He produced several successful novels, of which one, *Pied Piper*, became a best seller and the basis of an award-winning Hollywood film. Another, *Pastoral*, deals with the life of a bomber crew flying nightly over Germany. The 'hero' of the book is a young flying officer, Peter Marshall. In the remainder of this chapter we concentrate on the insights into leadership that are found explicitly and implicitly in this book, assess the impact of the book and comment on other aspects of Shute's life and work.

If we had to summarise Shute's views on leadership in a phrase, it would be about ordinary people being able to do extraordinary things; in his views on leadership, as in his success in the aircraft industry, he was able to rely on his own informed judgement, to anticipate developments and more often than not to be proved right. Nevil Shute Norway, who succeeded in more than one career and became a best-selling novelist, some of whose works were also filmed, is not easily categorised, and is the more interesting because of it.

Pastoral

The core of the plot concerns the tensions between the heavy responsibilities that this young leader carries for his crew, and the trauma of his love affair and rejection by his girlfriend, a Women's Auxiliary Air Force (WAAF) section officer at his aerodrome. These are eventually resolved as the bomber crew support their leader, understanding his personal crisis but determined that it must not affect their collective endeavours. After a near-disaster they come together as a team.

Leadership in a bomber crew

Nevil Shute's *Pastoral* at first appears a fairly straightforward wartime romance, almost written to a Mills and Boon formula: boy in the RAF meets WAAF girl; girl dithers about commitment; boy loses girl; boy and girl come together. But there is much more to the novel than that, and it is firmly rooted in the complex practicalities of leadership in wartime.

Indeed, some of the leading themes in the post-war literature on social psychology, group dynamics and leadership are foreshadowed in Shute's apparently artless tale of a man, a woman and a bomber crew. Let us examine the artful ways in which Shute weaves his leadership themes into the narrative text.

Plotting as a structural exercise

Shute plotted his books carefully. Implicit in his depiction of character, details of incidents and the evolution of plot are solid lines of construction. The airships he had designed supported a large mass and larger areas of lighter than air material crafted on a rigid framework of girders, with the load-bearing members each precisely calculated, so that the structure remained stable no matter what the stresses imposed upon it. As a novelist, Shute imposed a similar structure, and worked out his themes in terms of polarities of meaning around which the action occurred. Strong, spare lines of construction and hard skeletal struts supported extended, softer nets and carried the narrative tissue.

In *Pastoral* the life on the ground—safe, relaxing, enjoyable and free— is contrasted with the constrained, stressed, risky and threatened life in the air. Marshall is a man. His girlfriend, Gervase, is clearly a woman. These polarities are clear and ineluctable. They frame the action, but each of them also represents other polarities. Marshall has come to service life from a job as an insurance salesman based in London's Holborn. In the England of the 1930s such a position had little potential. Gervase is the daughter of a country doctor in Yorkshire, and perhaps has greater prospects.

Each of them brings certain elements to the relationship, which are intrinsic to the view of leadership which Shute implies. The critical incident which brings them together is the catching of a giant fish in a millpond. Fishing, for Marshall, represents a unique form of solace from the rigours and tensions of life in the air. His regular fishing companion is his Danish colleague and dependable co-pilot and navigator, Gunnar Franck. Marshall wants to go fishing, and cannot find Franck in the officers' mess. Instead, he finds Gervase Robertson—or rather, she finds him:

> Section Officer Robertson looked up from *Punch* as he passed her. He looked like a little boy she thought, disappointed because nobody would play with him. It was too bad. She got up from her chair. 'I'll come and see your fish,' she said.

Shute has introduced the dynamic tension created by the balance of the forces of man–woman, town–country, ground–air, day–night and life–death to initiate the framework of his narrative journey. He has started to describe a landscape of the mind through which his characters will travel. But the development of the action creates the need to transcend these easy polarities and to delve into the complex interpersonal dynamics of a performative team, the bomber crew, and in particular, to highlight the nature of leadership in these exposed and vulnerable conditions. Another polarity, that of the special role of the bomber pilot as the young leader and his team created to wage war in the air, increasingly becomes the central pivot of the action.

Later, Marshall, who is the captain of his crew and the pilot of his machine, makes a nearly disastrous error and almost loses his plane and crew through failing to accept feedback from Gunnar Franck in a desperate situation over the target. There is tension and lack of trust between the crew and the pilot as they start to lose faith in his ability, on which they have all previously been able to count, to get it right on the night. Marshall is going through a dark night of his own soul because Gervase has turned down his offer of marriage, but the lives of others depend on his retaining control of his emotions.

The bomber loses its way, they run out of fuel and crash in Yorkshire, miles off course, but close to Gervase's home territory. But she is not there in the flesh and he has to bypass this unfriendly territory to get back to his base. A long train journey, which the captain shares with his crew, brings them back to the reality of the aerodrome and a critical enquiry into the nearly catastrophic events of the night. His superior recognises that this has been a failure which very nearly turned into a disaster and considers splitting the crew. Something has clearly gone wrong and even worse could happen if they stay together. His crew are nonetheless willing to trust Marshall again. They realise, however, that he needs to resolve the conflicts in his emotional life, or they may all perish.

Now, the woman in the case has to move her ground. In an engineering sense, she has become the fulcrum of the stresses that have built up. In order to prevent catastrophic failure she has to readjust and reposition this fulcrum. Gervase recognises that she can restore the leader to his rightful position in the eyes of the crew, and the resolution of all of the themes occur as Gervase creates an opportunity of team-building by obtaining access to a private lake, well stocked with fish, to which the whole crew are invited. Her offer of reconciliation is a present of time and space—an outer landscape with an inner symbolisation.

Group dynamics

It is now clear to the reader that 'leadership' even in time of war is not just a question of inner personality, traits or good breeding, but is multi-faceted and group-based. Gervase has to reconcile her personal feelings with the needs of the group for the collective task of the bomber crew to be performed. Gunnar Franck, who had understood what is needed before Peter Marshall, has used his own leadership abilities to reinforce those of the formal leader of the crew. But Gunnar, a subtly played character in Shute's exposition, has to lead from the middle, to respect the hierarchy of the crew and his leader's increasing entanglement in matters of the heart.

Shute's capacity for anticipation

One of the important and fascinating aspects of Shute's writing is his capacity to anticipate both technical and psychological events and developments before they have actually occurred. In *No Highway*, he anticipates the Comet airliner crashes due to metal fatigue by half a decade. In *Pastoral* the theme which links the action in the bomber itself and on which the incidents bear is that of *leadership and team work in combat*. These factors combine to produce what was subsequently identified as 'morale'.

Morale and its study

The seminal report *Morale Among Bomber Crews* (1946), drafted by T T Paterson (later to become Head of the Business School at the University of Strathclyde), was not commissioned until two years after the publication of Shute's book, and not published officially until some years after that. Shute knew the significance of the phenomenon we now understand as 'morale' without having to read the social psychologist's report because he understood how men in aeroplanes need to work together and the factors which sustain and, in their absence, corrode human trust.

The use of poetry

The finer texture of Shute's novel is not simply a matter of description and analysis. Shute wishes his work to be construed as true art, and much as composers quote phrases and themes from other and earlier composers in order to demonstrate their different handling of them, so each sector of *Pastoral* is headed by quotations from English poetry. Shute quotes from A E Housman, Robert Herrick, John Keats, Rupert Brooke and Sir Henry Newbolt, whom he would have read at school. He also knew what the popular music of the era had to say, and his final quotations are from the wartime hit song 'A Nightingale Sang in Berkeley Square'.

Shute counterpoints dialogue with staccato bursts of exact specification. A country mill is the locus of the fishing that first introduces Marshall's relationship with Gunnar Frank.

> Coldstone Mill was a tall, factory-like building set in the countryside along the river Fittel. A lane crossed the river on a stone bridge of two arches: a hundred yards below the bridge the mill stood by the weir, and below that again was the mill pool. It was a broad, gravelly pool, scoured wide by the mill stream and the weir, overhung by trees at the lower end. It stood in pasture fields, very sunny and bright.
>
> (Shute, 1944, Page 16)

Shute uses words economically, sparingly and with no exaggerated emphasis. The style is plain, aiming, like the typical engineer 'to do for five bob, what any damn fool can do for a pound'. But it does not lack detail. It is exact in its specification. The pool is 'broad and gravelly'. The bridge is stone with two arches. We could draw that mill by that pond beyond that bridge and could recognise it if we came upon it. This is precision engineering with the written word.

Later Marshall talks to a 'civilian from the district' in the pub about the pike he has caught. He finds that the man has been, like himself in civvy street, a salesman in London. He reflects on his own situation and his likely future prospects, of 'the life he had known in his insurance office before the war. Everything had to end sometimes, it was undesirable to be killed, but it was also undesirable to go creeping back into the office when the war was over' (Shute, 1944, Page 41–3).

Marshall is beginning to understand who he is, and not merely for personal interest but because self-knowledge is the key to team leadership. In the confined space of the bomber and in the terror of aerial combat, insincerity and overconfidence can be found out and the leader's credibility can be shot away—as well as his life.

The influence of A E Housman

Shute was stunned by the death of his older brother in 1916. He died

> ... with my mother by his side ... He was only 19 when he died, and after nearly 40 years it still seems strange to me that I should be older than Fred ... For the remainder of my time at Shrewsbury I don't think I had the slightest interest in a career or any other life. I was born to one end, which was to go into the army and do the best I could before being killed. The time at school was a time for contemplation of the realities that were coming as a spiritual preparation for death.
>
> (Shute, 1958, Page 24)

This is the atmosphere of Housman. In penning these reflective phrases in *Slide Rule,* Shute catches exactly the mood of early death and frustrated promise that infuses Housman when he writes, of an athlete dying young,

> Smart lad to slip betimes away,
> from fields where glory does not stay,
> and early though the laurel grows,
> it withers quicker than the rose.
>
> (Housman, 1896, stanza xii)

Throughout his writings, Shute was conscious of the debt owed by the living to the dead and his landscape is infused with the call to activity symbolised by Housman in *Reveille:*

> Up lad up, 'tis late for lying,
> Hear the drums of morning play,
> hark the empty highways crying,
> who will be on the hills away,
> play lies still but blood's a rover,
> breath's a ware that will not keep
> up lad when the journey's over,
> there'll be time enough to sleep.
>
> (Housman, 1896, stanza iv)

Shute's appeal

In his engineering and in his writing alike, Shute pursues the steadfast and the enduring. His plotting is exact, his characterisation limited, but all is pinned on a steadfast and enduring framework. The great polarities in Shute's writing are those that have engaged writers down the ages: youth and age, life and death, north and south, boy and girl, and of the leader and his men, in a case of England against the world. He writes for his generation of a sceptred isle set in a silver sea openly, straightforwardly and without fuss. Shute's landscape is painted on a sturdy canvas with bold colour. His tapestry is woven on a robust texture with strong thread.

Shute's ability to empathise with ordinary people doing extraordinary things perhaps explains his wide appeal to readers in the New Worlds of America and Australia. It was said of Andrew Jackson that he 'had the Western faith that the common man is capable of uncommon achievement' (Nevins and Commager, 1942), and Shute understood this principle. It imbues all his writing and his perceptions of physical and social reality. But his heroes and heroines have to respect both natural and technical constraints.

New forms of leadership

Pied Piper

In other works, especially those written during the war and afterwards, Shute develops these insights into the new leadership of the ordinary people. In *Pied Piper*, he describes how leadership of a party of children is thrust on a lonely old man, whose son has been killed in action, as he treks through the Jura and on through Occupied France, to lead them to safety in England and then the USA. John Sidney Howard first has to attract the attention of the children, and he makes a little wooden whistle to do so.

> He sat down again, and began to fashion a whistle with the penknife that he kept for scraping out his pipe...The Cavanagh children stood by him watching his slow, wrinkled fingers as they worked; in their faces incredulity melted into interest. He stripped the bark from the twig, cut deftly with the little knife, and bound the bark into place. He put it to his lips, and it gave out a shrill note.
>
> (Shute, 1942)

A Town Like Alice

In *A Town Like Alice* his leader is a woman, who has leadership of a party of women uprooted by the Japanese invasion of Malaya thrust upon her, and who subsequently uses an unexpected legacy to create a new town in a new continent. Jean Paget, a London typist, understands the need for leaders to craft objectives that are achievable and can be owned by others. As she settles into her new role as a transformational leader in a one-horse Australian town, she discusses her precisely formulated ambition with her friend.

> He glanced around the ice-cream parlour. 'If everything you want to do works out like this,' he said slowly, 'you'll have a town as good as Alice Springs in no time.'
>
> 'That's what I want to have,' she said. 'A town like Alice.'
>
> (Shute, 1950, Page 332)

Ruined City

In *Ruined City* Shute reviews the ethical basis of leadership in a capitalist society. The values of finance capital associated with the City of London are subtly dealt with and contrasted against the apparently solid provincial values of industrial leadership in a northern ship-building town. In many of his writings he argues the need for capitalists to be close to the locations and regions and ways of life in which their investments are used. In *Ruined City* he is scathing of the selfishness of the original owners of the shipyard, a well-to-do family of local capitalists, who had taken excessive profits out of the company in times of plenty and left it to rot when the depression set in.

At the heart of the book is a love story. Shute's hero forms a liaison with someone of another class, recognising the decency and stability of the young woman almoner as a contrast to the feckless and selfish antics of his unfaithful wife. But the hero, Henry Warren, is not a plaster saint. He commits the ultimate sin in a finance capital environment, that of issuing a knowingly false prospectus to attract capital into the shipyard by deliberately over-egging expectations of financial gain for prospective investors. He does wrong and knows it. He does it in order that the greater good of the greater number may follow. He is prepared to take his punishment and serve his time in prison, though he finds even this experience brings its own rewards. He is 'accountable' and this accountability is central to Shute's conception of the moral life. Leaders are accountable. They cannot plead special status; they are subject to the common standards of behaviour.

Shute's heroes and heroines do not feel the need to justify their actions in terms that others outside the situation will find generally acceptable. But the leader has to be able to be understood by the immediately led. Leaders are reflective creatures positioned within, but not imprisoned by, their own culture. And that, for Shute, is enough.

A global appeal

To my generation, which grew up during the Second World War and the years immediately following it, Shute's account of leadership speaks to the social landscape of our childhood, for it is this England which made us. These are our blue remembered hills. But Shute's fictional leaders are not only to be found in England. Shute's 'leaders' are ordinary people who, through strength of character and the support of their teams, are empowered to achieve extraordinary outcomes.

The writings of Nevil Shute were best-sellers, wherever in the world English was the language of communication. But he never became a member of any literary establishment and remained to the end a provincial, colonial, marginal and critical figure, in relation to the contemporary prejudices of the rich, famous and powerful. His life took him from Cornwall, a peninsular attachment of England, to the Mornington peninsula, a peripheral location of Australia, an antipodean continent on the margins of empire. His heroes are ordinary, middle of the road people, who have heroism thrust upon them. But, like Joseph Conrad's flawed heroes, they have to survive moral hazard.

So although his narrative of leadership is resolutely an 'English' one, it is that of a universal Englishness, capable of global stretch. He created a language and a set of justifications for an emergent style of leadership that is more scientifically expounded in the post-war oeuvres of the Tavistock school of Bion, Jacques and Wilson and the North American social psychologists following Kurt Lewin. Kelly (1965) summarises these traditions in a succinct article, but two decades earlier *Pastoral* and *Pied Piper* had been little classics of group dynamics and team leadership written in accessible prose.

Transaction and transformation

Leadership in real life is not easy. *The transformational opportunity arrives only after mastery of the transactional duty.* Nevil Shute understood this and was able through his craft to transmit these values to an England at war, up against the world, and needing leadership from a new, technically literate and ethnically diverse generation of individuals from disparate backgrounds, with, at best, a grammar-school education, and with class-less aspirations. His work has much to teach us about leadership in our challenging times.

Bibliography

Housman, A. E. (1896) *A Shropshire Lad*, Kegan Paul, Trench, Trubner and Co: London.

Kelly, J. (1965) The group dynamics approach to leadership: *Education and Training*: vol. 7, no. 2, pp. 62–5.

Nevins, A. and Commager, H. S. (1942) *America: The Story of a Free People*, Oxford University Press: Oxford.

Paterson, T. T. (1946) *Morale Among Bomber Crews*, Report to the Air Ministry: London.

Potter, D. (1979) *Blue Remembered Hills*, Play for Today: BBC: 30/01/79.

Priestley, J. B. (1960) *Literature and Western Man*, Harper and Row: New York.

Shute, N. (1933) *Lonely Road*, Heinemann: London.

Shute, N. (1938) *Ruined City*, Cassell: London.

Shute, N. (1940) *An Old Captivity*, Heinemann: London.

Shute, N. (1942) *Pied Piper*, Heinemann: London.

Shute, N. (1944) *Pastoral*, Heinemann: London.

Shute, N. (1945) *Most Secret*, Heinemann: London.

Shute, N. (1948) *No Highway*, Heinemann: London.

Shute, N. (1950) *A Town Like Alice*, Heinemann: London.

Shute, N. (1951) *Round the Bend*, Heinemann: London.

Shute, N. (1952) *The Far Country*, Heinemann: London.

Shute, N. (1954) *Slide Rule*, Heinemann: London.

Shute, N. (1955) *Round the Bend*, Heinemann: London.

Shute, N. (1957) *On the Beach*, Heinemann: London.

Shute, N. (1958) *The Rainbow and the Rose*, Heinemann: London.

Shute, N. (1962) *Trustee from the Toolroom*, Heinemann: London.

Stafford-Clark, D. (1956) *Psychiatry Today*, Pelican: London.

Films

Many of Nevil Shute's novels were filmed, whether for cinema or later television, and at least two achieved a global success. They were:

A Town Like Alice 1951.
Directed by Jack lee. Starring Virginia McKenna and Peter Finch.
On the Beach 1959.
Directed by Stanley Kramer. Starring Gregory Peck, Ava Gardner, Fred Astaire and Anthony Perkins.
Pastoral does not seem to have been filmed.

Song

Sherwin, M. and Mashwitz, E. (1940) *A Nightingale Sang in Berkeley Square*.

6
Things Fall Apart: Chinua Achebe

Jonathan Gosling

> Turning and turning in the widening gyre
> The falcon cannot hear the falconer;
> Things fall apart; the centre cannot hold;
> Mere anarchy is loosed upon the world
>
> W B Yeats, 'The Second Coming'

Considering ours as a time of crisis, this chapter asks: what if this were not simply an *episode*, but really the end of an era?; for example, if we face fundamental changes of the scale and order that affected African societies when impacted by colonialism.

Pursuing this analogy, the chapter will focus particularly on *Things Fall Apart*, the first of the African Trilogy by Nigerian author and critic Chinua Achebe, taking its name from a poem by W B Yeats and opening with the quotation reproduced above. The novel was published in 1958, and has sold over 8 million copies in many languages: it is the most translated of any African novel. It is the story of Okonkwo, a young man growing up in an Ibo village; the psychological and social forces by which he crafts his ascension to greatness; and the unforeseeable transformation of this world brought about by the arrival of Christian missionaries and white colonial rule.

The scale of this transformation is almost unimaginable. Indeed, it is probably one of the few eras of change that really merit the term 'transformation': everything by which value was assessed, thrown into doubt; facts known with absolute certainty, revealed as illusory almost from one moment to the next; everything that marked out a good person—a life lived well, honoured, cultured, wealthy—became empty and meaningless within one generation. *Things Fall Apart* paints a fascinating picture of life in the village Umuofia lived much as it had for hundreds of years—not monotonously, but full of the real and most meaningful dramas of people figuring out how to live and get on with each other in their own community, how to grow up and make their own way under the eyes of older generations, how to cope with growing old, with crimes and injustices. And one day some white missionaries arrive, much as people from other foreign tribes had passed through Umuofia from time to time. There were some unpleasantries, reinforced by news that the whites had killed many people, unprovoked, in another village on the edge of the territory: it was a crisis, as war always is; and the people of Umuofia knew how to prepare for war.

But they were tragically mistaken. This was not an episode of war like countless others before: it was the end of things, and the last part of the book charts an appalling, unremitting collapse of every aspect of cohesion and social order. The people of Umuofia had no way of foreseeing such a catastrophe, and absolutely no sense of what might emerge from it: it was unprecedented. In reviewing this novel now, in 2011, I am explicitly asking if the world order is on the edge of such a collapse, if the crises in environment, government and business are not mere episodes like others we have faced; what if they are harbingers of things falling apart, a centre that cannot hold.

What if mere anarchy is to be loosed upon the world? And most pertinently for this volume, what can we learn about the predicament of leaders in such circumstances: when all that is praiseworthy, virtuous, glorious and heroic is no longer seen as such, but becomes ridiculous and out of place; and when everything that marks out a man or woman as an authority has been turned upside down?

Father to son

These opening words of the novel introduce the hero thus:

> Okonkwo was well known throughout the nine villages and even beyond. His fame rested on solid personal achievements. (Page 3)

We learn what is meant by his fame, and the measure of his achievements, and also about his poise and character.

> When he walked his heels hardly touched the ground and he seemed to walk on springs as if he was going to pounce on somebody. And

he did pounce on people quite often. He had a slight stammer and whenever he was angry and could not get his words out quickly enough he would use his fists. He had no patience with unsuccessful men. He had no patience with his father. (Pages 3–4)

Okonkwo's drama begins with longing to repair the shame he feels about his father Unoka, described as 'lazy...improvident...a debtor....a slight sloop. He wore a haggard and mournful look except when he was drinking or playing on his flute' (Page 4). Okonkwo found little charm in his father's fecklessness: 'Unoka, the grown-up, was a failure. He was poor and his wife and children had barely enough to eat. People laughed at him because he was a loafer, and they swore never to lend him any money because he never paid it back' (Page 5).

'Unoka was never happy when it came to wars. He was in fact a coward and could not bear the sight of blood. And so he changed the subject and talked about music, and his face beamed' (Page 6). Thus he remained outside the circle of great men who exemplified the virtues and accomplishments of leadership.

When Unoka died he had taken no title at all and he was heavily in debt. Any wonder then that his son Okonkwo was ashamed of him? Fortunately, among these people a man was judged according to his worth and not according to the worth of his father. Okonkwo was clearly cut out for great things. (Pages 7–8)

Okonkwo had no need to figure out what counts as greatness: everyone in the village knew how to assess his prowess and his hard work; and from these early passages we see that his ambition to achieve was driven by a relentless desire to exorcise his shame about his father. He goes on to amass great wealth; but it is reputation that matters to him, especially because it brings inclusion in the cadre of leading citizens. The thing he most wants is to belong; and one of the personal tragedies of the novel is that he never learns to recognise the humanity in his father, or to feel sympathy for the weak. His rise to leadership is accomplished by unremitting attention to being strong, physically and morally, and we have a narrator's voice to give us an account of the complex motives that lie beneath his observable behaviour.

The ambition and drive that is so often admired in leaders may often be fuelled by inner demons akin to Okonkwo's, as revealed in psychoanalytically informed accounts of, for example, Enron (Stein, 2007), Alexander the Great (Kets de Vries, 2004) and the CEOs of finance firms in the years preceding the 2008 financial collapse (Sievers, 2010; Stein, 2011). Part of the appeal of *Things Fall Apart* is that it gives us insight into such inner complexes, and how these help to explain self-destructive and emotionally painful behaviour. We see in Okonkwo a man for whom suffering and cruelty are an acceptable defence against shame: 'Okonkwo never showed any emotion openly unless it be the emotion of anger. To show affection was a sign of weakness; the only thing worth demonstrating was strength' (Page 27).

His predicament is recognisable across the cultural divide between his way of life and our own. One strand to the narrative, concerning a boy called Ikemefuma, gives a particularly poignant example of this; although the details seem to emphasise the cultural differences between Okonkwo and we readers, the dénouement is painfully resonant.

In Chapter 2 we hear how the village of Umuofia found cause for war with a neighbouring village but in accord with tradition, accepted instead two young people, a boy and a girl, as hostage. The boy, Ikemefuma, was placed in Okonkwo's charge and brought up in his family, becoming a close friend with the oldest son, Nwoye. Okonkwo comes to love the boy, who excels his own son in skill and aspiration. Perhaps Ikemefuma's need to please his adoptive father, having been torn from his own family, is resonant with Okonkwo's felt need to create his own role models; maybe it is the shame that their fathers were not able to protect and fend for them. In any case, Ikemefuma becomes the recipient for Okonkwo's paternal hopes, in contrast to which Nwoye appears to him as increasingly inadequate.

Thus shame about his father is reflected in shame about his own son, and emerges as the inescapable accompaniment of his greatness. Its potency becomes terrifyingly apparent when the village elders determine that Ikemefuma should be killed in sacrifice; they advise Okonkwo to stay home, to excuse himself from participating in this communal duty: 'That boy calls you father, bear no hand in his death' (Page 54). But he accompanies the men to the forest, and when the blow is struck 'he heard Ikemefuma cry "my father, they have killed me!" as he ran towards him. Dazed with fear, Okonkwo drew his matchet and cut him down. He was afraid of being thought weak' (Page 57). How often do we witness displays of ruthlessness in our leaders—fuelled perhaps by their fear of being seen as weak, or more disturbingly, their fear of experiencing weakness and vulnerability as integral to who they are?

The self-made man

Okonkwo was not paralysed by this fear, nor was he driven only to such destructive violence. For the most part, he was able to channel his energies into extraordinary achievements. ' "Looking at a king's mouth," said an old man, "one would think he never sucked at his mother's breast." He was talking about Okonkwo, who has risen so suddenly from great poverty and misfortune to be one of the lords of the clan' (Page 25).

High achievers are by definition those who excel in activities that have iconic status in a society. Okonkwo's accomplishments were at the heart of Umuofia's cultural life, so he became a natural representative of the community in its dealings with others.

> If ever a man deserved his success, that man was Okonkwo. At an early age he had achieved fame as the greatest wrestler in the land. That was not luck. At the most one could say that his *chi* or personal god was good. But the Ibo people have a saying that when a man says 'yes', his *chi* says 'yes' also. Okonkwo said yes very strongly; so his *chi* agreed. And not only his *chi* but his clan too, because it judged a man by the work of his hands. That was why Okonkwo had been chosen by the nine villages to carry a message of war to their enemies unless they agreed to give up a young man and a virgin to atone for the murder of Udo's wife. And such was the deep fear that their enemies had for Umuofia that they treated Okonkwo like a king ... (Pages 25–6)

There is much in this paragraph, and it repays closer attention. 'If ever a man deserved his success, that man was Okonkwo.' Here we are presented with a theory of poetic justice, that what happens to someone is a proportionate effect of causes for which he or she is responsible. Rewards go to those who deserve them, and punishments likewise. This implies a rather predictable moral order, although admittedly the phrasing here allows for some ambiguity: 'If ever a man...' suggests that some men might not so obviously deserve their success. If so, naïve poetic justice might not be such a comforting certainty after all: a place must be allowed for luck, the unpredictable will of God, or sheer muddle. It is a curiously double-edged phrase, hinting that a man's fate is not all in his own hands, however great his present success.

'At an early age he had achieved fame as the greatest wrestler in the land.' This at least was surely his own achievement, 'That was not luck'. So we are reassured that there is something special about him. 'At the most one could say that his *chi* or personal god was good. But the Ibo people have a saying that when a man says "yes", his *chi* says "yes" also. Okonkwo said yes very strongly; so his *chi* agreed'. The way to face the uncertainties of fate, all gaps in poetic justice, is to be strongly affirmative, and things will go with you; by positive thinking, you can affect your fate. 'And not only his *chi* but his clan too, because it judged a man by the work of his hands'. Okonkwo's qualities were recognised, affirmed and lauded socially.

'That was why Okonkwo had been chosen by the nine villages to carry a message of war to their enemies...And such was the deep fear that their enemies had for Umuofia that they treated Okonkwo like a king.' His own greatness was enhanced by the power of his community; what made him a powerful leader was more than his own greatness: it was the greatness of the community he led, which he did in ways that exemplified what was most valued in Umuofia.

A profound interdependence between individuals and the collective is a defining feature of strong organisational cultures and coherent communities. In the abstract, this can appear tautological: leaders are valued because they value what is valued. But in specific situations the tensions and dilemmas are real enough: for example, someone expected to represent a whole community may subsume personal intimacies beneath a supra-personal façade tailored to public expectations; familiar domestic relationships can suffer if they threaten to undermine the psychological effort required to maintain such a persona.

Domestic violence is often linked to such dynamics, where person-to-person intimacy is experienced as a threat to a precarious social persona—a precariousness that is not unusual for those in leadership positions. We see this in Okonkwo's life, when he lashes out at one of his wives at precisely the time that the village is observing a week of peace, and his actions cannot possibly be considered as a purely domestic affair.

> You know as well as I do that our forefathers ordained that before we plant any crops in the earth we should observe a week in which a man does not say a harsh word to his neighbours.... The evil you have done can ruin the whole clan. The earth goddess whom you have insulted may refuse to give us her increase, and we shall all perish. (Page 29)

This illustrates the complex identity-related pressures on leaders. They are in danger of losing themselves in the morass of social expectations;

and the social milieu itself is endangered by a leader's uncontrolled emotional outbursts.

In Umuofia's traditional culture the danger represented by a strong-willed person has cosmological significance because personal and social behaviour is in interaction with a wider world of natural and divine forces. In governing himself, or in this case, losing the struggle to do so, Okonkwo, might act out of turn and bring harm to the community. So what might be called 'care of the self' (Foucault, 1983; Case and Gosling, 2008) is a crucial component of leadership, comprising rather more than management of one's own emotions or 'emotional intelligence'; it is a defining activity of leadership, important because it is a struggle with the inner forces that, as we have seen, make for greatness. 'Okonkwo was not the man to stop beating somebody half way through, not even for fear of a goddess' (Page 29).

Okonkwo was punished and repentant for his breach of the Week of Peace, but this episode illustrates a feature he shares with many leaders: an inner conviction, probably only semi-conscious, that he is able to transgress common moral boundaries because the moral order is, in his imagination, no more than an extension of his own will. This is dangerous territory for narcissistic leaders and the collectives of which they are members. Recent corporate scandals provide many examples of leaders whose narcissism has fuelled a sense of confidence and direction, impelling them to the most senior positions, where they have confused their own driven self-interest with the moral responsibilities of their socially sanctioned authority. For any organisation—community or business—there are times when the vision and enthusiasm of the narcissist provides a welcome sense of focus and conviction: when people call for a strong leader, this is generally what they want.

But the social and political world is inherently plural, and even the most entrenched narcissist cannot brook the multiplicity of concerns of community life—one reason why they so often take themselves and their followers off into cults and sects, which modern pluralistic societies can generally tolerate unless the cults become violent. But in Okonkwo's world there was really nowhere else to go: he must either remain included, or be outcast. On this occasion he was punished and forgiven. Nevertheless, it was a major event:

> This year they talked of nothing else but the *nso-ani* which Okonkwo had committed. It was the first time for many years that a man had

broken the sacred peace. Even the oldest men could only remember one or two other occasions somewhere in the dim past. (Page 30)

Manliness and masculinity

Okonkwo's greatness is ultimately as a member of Umuofia society, but it is an uneasy membership in several ways. He finds it hard to join in the more relaxed and sociable aspects of village life, where the marks of achievement and success are less relevant.

> But somehow Okonkwo could never become as enthusiastic over feasts as most people. He was a good eater and he could drink one or two fairly big gourds of palm wine. But he was always uncomfortable sitting around for days waiting for a feast or getting over it. He would be very much happier working on his farm. (Page 36)

These days we might call him a workaholic, and we see here perhaps the limits of his ability as a rounded leader of his community, which is, after all, about more than production and wealth. But for him, wealth was intimately connected to his sense of identity, and especially the manliness that he so missed in his father.

> Yam stood for manliness, and he who could feed his family on yams from one harvest to another was a very great man indeed. (Page 31)

Manliness in this sense is inherently fragile, requiring constant attention and effort, all too easily subverted by bad luck, doubtfulness or too much thinking. Potency, literal and figurative, is a crucial component of such masculinity; any doubt about it is experienced as an attack on the self that incites the swiftest response:

> And so when he called Ikemefuna to fetch his gun, the wife who had just been beaten murmured something about guns that never shot. Unfortunately for her . . . . (Page 37)

Conversely, practices that bolster and inflame physical potency are powerfully affirmative. The drumming at a wrestling match, for example:

> Okonkwo cleared his throat and moved his feet to the beat of the drums. It filled him with fire as it had always done from his youth. He trembled with the desire to conquer and subdue. It was like the desire for a woman. (Page 41)

Habitual domestic violence is linked to masculine anxiety. That is perhaps easily said but in this book the relentless violence is quite shocking, and has been criticised by some who accuse Achebe of painting too bleak a picture of pre-colonial society. In any case, I think it is still a plausible analogy with the psychosomatic effects of power on men in political and corporate leadership roles, given the high levels of incipient bullying in some organisations. *Things Fall Apart* contributes an astute insight into the frequent, if not ubiquitous links between leadership, power and domination.

The fragility of greatness

In the first part of the book we are presented with the story of a man whose life seems by no means secure; whose accomplishments are hard-won and strenuously maintained, fragile and constantly at risk. Okonkwo would not have said that his life, or that of his village, is devoid of change and danger: indeed, a man's greatness is measured by his ability to stand up to and respond to such threats. But from the outside, in hindsight, we can see this as a way of life critically dependent on constants that are taken for granted, and the second half of the book charts what happens when underpinning assumptions are torn away.

The first hints are unremarkable: some casual mentions of a different kind of person in the margins of Umuofia's world.

'It is like the story of white men who, they say, are white like this piece of chalk', ... 'And these white men, they say, have no toes.' (Page 69)

These are passing references, and not recognised as having special significance, or requiring a leadership response. A far more prominent cataclysm occurs in the personal life of Okonkwo, and his place in Umuofia, an accident that brings chaos to much that he has accomplished:

The drums and the dancing began again and reached a fever–heat. Darkness was around the corner, and the burial was near. Guns fired the last salute and the cannon rent the sky. And then from the centre of the delirious fury came a cry of agony and shouts of horror. It was as if a spell had been cast. All was silent. In the centre of the crowd a boy lay in a pool of blood. It was the dead man's sixteen year-old son, who with his brothers and half-brothers had been dancing the traditional farewell to their father. Okonkwo's gun had exploded and a piece of iron had pierced the boy's heart. (Pages 116–17)

This event tips Okonkwo's world into instant collapse. He has killed a clansman and in accord with the law, he immediately packs up his entire family and leaves the village an outcast for seven years. His home is destroyed, the walls of his compound broken down, his wealth confiscated.

The next morning Okonkwo's friend Obierika asks himself: 'Why should a man suffer so grievously for an offence he had committed inadvertently? But though he thought for a long time he found no answer' (Page 118). The law in this case expressed a fundamental tenet of the moral order of Umuofia's cosmos. There could be no conceivable rationale for clansmen killing each other: it can only be an utter abomination. Society is precisely and fundamentally composed of clan loyalty, so transgression is not fixable by personal goodness or ability. For similar reasons, in many Western countries today, crimes against property are punished more severely than crimes against the person.

The institution of private ownership—of land or goods—is fundamental to our sense of order. If I were to look at your book and ask, 'why can't I take this?' you might reply, 'because it is mine', and that would be a good enough answer. For us, who owns a thing or a place is crucial to defining it. In the same way the clan to whom a person belonged was crucial to personhood. Okonkwo's fall is a personal tragedy, for here is a man brought down by an unlucky accident. 'His life had been ruled by a great passion—to become one of the lords of the clan. Then everything had been broken. He had been cast out of his clan like a fish on to a dry, sandy beach, panting' (Page 123). He may not have personally deserved this, according to his own deeds, but this is not a matter for poetic justice; yet the outcome is nonetheless just, because it affirms the foundations of social order: clansmen cannot conceivably be at war with each other; if such were to occur, things would really have fallen apart, the centre could not hold. Okonkwo the leader, the personification of common values, enacts his leadership by abandoning it, a destroyed but honourable man. Anarchy is not let loose upon the world.

Outcast

Part 2 of the novel comprises the years of Okonkwo's exile. It is largely an essay on suffering. As one elder says in commiseration:

For whom is it well, for whom is it well?
There is no-one for whom it is well. (Page 127)

This instantly evokes the famous Christian mystic Julian of Norwich, whose famous mediation on suffering concludes 'All shall be well, all shall be well; and all manner of things shall be well' (Chilson, 2008, Page 229). The irony is hardly bearable as one reads of the coming of missionaries. The clans recognise them as dangerous, and respond positively at first, but have no concept of the scale of the problem. After two years of exile Okonkwo receives a visit from his friend Obierika, who brings almost incredible news:

> [The clan of] Abame is no more.... During the last planting season a white man had appeared in their clan ... the elders consulted their Oracle and it told them that the strange man would break their clan and spread destruction among them ... and so they killed him. (Pages 129–30)

White men returned on market day and massacred everyone: the clan and village were destroyed.

' "They were fools," said Okonkwo after a pause. "They had been warned that danger was ahead. They should have armed themselves with their guns and their matchets even when they went to market" ' (Page 132). His response is understandable: it is not so different to the 'war on terror' of recent years, and the determination to stand against those who threaten our way of life. But these are strange times: when Obierika gives Okonkwo the proceeds from the sale of his confiscated yams, he says 'Who knows what may happen tomorrow? Perhaps green men will come to our clan and shoot us' (Page 133).

Two years later Obierika brings more news from Umuofia. Missionaries had arrived and won some converts, and

> That was a source of great sorrow to the leaders of the clan; but many of them believed that the strange faith and the white man's god would not last. None of his converts was a man whose word was heeded in the assembly of the people. None of them was a man of title. They were mostly the kind of people that were called *elulefu*, worthless, empty men.... Chielo, the priestess of Agbala, called the converts the excrement of the clan, and the new faith was a mad dog that had come to eat it up. (Page 135)

Among these converts was Nwoye, Okonkwo's son. Okonkwo disowned him, but now he, like everyone else was faced with the appalling dilemma: to fight this new religion would bring him into war with his clansmen. The unthinkable had come to pass in a few short years, and Umuofia, like all the clans, was in an irresolvable dilemma. Their coherent identity was split apart by the new religion, and to fight its adherents would be self-destructive, and unwinnable. At a personal level these events are a total abnegation of Okonkwo's personal project, his self-made greatness. Now the weak, 'worthless, empty men' have the power of the new regime and its arms. Every criterion of his success, universally acknowledged and self-evident, suddenly becomes provisional and relative.

> Suppose when he died all his male children decided to follow Nwoye's steps and abandon their ancestors? Okonkwo felt a cold shudder run through him at the terrible prospect, like the prospect of annihilation.... And immediately Okonkwo's eyes were opened and he saw the whole matter clearly. Living fire begets cold, impotent ash. (Pages 144–5)

What can he do? Popularly known as the 'Roaring Fire' (Page 145), he rages on. Returning after his seven-year exile to Umuofia he urges his clansmen to resist the degrading onslaught.

> If we fight the stranger we shall hit our brothers and perhaps shed the blood of a clansman. But we must do it. Our fathers never dreamt of such a thing, they never killed their brothers. But a white man never came to them. So we must do what our fathers would never have done. (Page 193)

As a leader, he rekindles some success: he organises to oppose the most severe attacks on traditional rites. But already they are in a world of alternatives, where it is a matter of choice whether one takes a traditional or a 'new' worldview, and Okonkwo's assumptions about honourable behaviour are not reciprocated by his counterparts in the religious and civil authorities he confronts. In fact they see no need to pay him any respect whatsoever, and his end is inexpressibly pathetic. As Obierika says in the closing passage of the book, 'That man was one of the greatest men in Umuofia... and now he will be buried like a dog' (Page 197). But the final words go to those of the colonial district commissioner, who considers the little he knows of Okonkwo's story:

One could almost write a whole chapter on him. Perhaps not a whole chapter but a reasonable paragraph, at any rate. There was so much else to include, and one had to be firm in cutting out details. He had already chosen the title of the book, after much thought: *The Pacification of the Primitive Tribes of the Lower Niger.* (Page 197)

Conclusions and continuities

So ends this novel. It has much to tell us about men and women who would be great, of the internal drives and social expectations that sustain leaders and the likely predicaments of those in leadership roles when established cultures face cataclysmic change. The lessons are rather bleak: Okonkwo remains true to the values that made him great, is unable to adapt to the new circumstances and is destroyed. Some of his contemporaries survive, but they do so by abandoning greatness in the old sense because nothing remained that might count as an act of greatness.

Wars and festivals, farming, drumming and wrestling—all are reduced to matters of personal competence. They no longer hold vital existential meaning for the community. Rather than aspiring to greatness, the next generation will struggle with doing well and being good as matters of personal conduct. This is the theme of the second in the trilogy, *No Longer at Ease* (1960), about Okonkwo's grandson Obi; it is a book about adaptability, but not about leadership.

I think Achebe's novel teaches us to be sceptical about the possibility of leading through such catastrophic destruction of a culture, at least in any way that we might recognise as leadership, in the terms of the losing side. But there is a counter argument to be made, that a leader (less flawed than Okonkwo) might be able to remind constituents of the continuing presence in their lives of ideals, even when an ideal life seems no longer possible. The philosopher Jonathan Lear (2006) suggests that this is precisely how Chief Plenty Coups of the Crow nation of American Indians led his people through the near total destruction of their way of life on the plains of North America in the latter half of the nineteenth century. Plenty Coups told his reporter, Frank B Lindeman 'I can think back and tell you much more of war and horse-stealing. But when the buffalo went away the hearts of my people fell to the ground, and they could no longer lift them up again. After this nothing happened. There was little singing anywhere' (Lear, 2006, Page 2).

Unlike Okonkwo, his fictional counterpart, Plenty Coups nonetheless found a way to lead his people to a new way of life on a reservation and to discover a reservoir of hope (Case and Gosling, 2010). This is a theme of *The Arrow of God* (1964), the third in Achebe's wonderful trilogy that commenced with *Things Fall Apart*.

References

Achebe, C. (1958/2006) *Things Fall Apart*. London: Penguin.

Achebe, C. (1960/1987) *No longer at ease*. Oxford: Heinemann.

Case, P. and Gosling, J. (2008) 'Wisdom of the Moment: Pre-modern Perspectives on Organizational Action', *Social Epistemology*, 21(2), 87–111.

Case, P. and Gosling, J. (2010) *'Through the Veil: Leading to the other side of catastrophe'*, paper presented to the Standing Conference on Organizational Symbolism, Lille, France, 7–10 July.

Chilson, R. (ed.) (2008) *All Will Be Well: Julian of Norwich*. Notre Dame, Indiana: Ave Maria Press.

Foucault, M. (1986) *The Care of the Self: The History of Sexuality*, Volume 3. Harmondsworth: Penguin.

Kets de Vries, M. (2004) *Are Leaders Born or Are They Made? The Case of Alexander the Great*. London: Karnac.

Lear, J. (2006) *Radical Hope: Ethics in the Face of Cultural Devastation*. Cambridge, MA: Harvard.

Sievers, B. (2010) 'Scene 6: Beneath the Financial Crisis' in: Brunning, Halina & Perini, Mario (eds) *The Psychoanalytic Perspective on the Turbulent World*. London: Karnac.

Stein, M. (2007) 'Oedipus Rex at Enron: Leadership, Oedipal Struggles, and Organizational Collapse', *Human Relations*, 60(9), 1387–410.

Stein, M. (2011) 'A Culture of Mania: A Psychoanalytic View of the Incubation of the 2008 Credit Crisis', *Organization*, 18(2), 173–86.

7
Leadership and Improvisation:
A Bell for Adano, by John Hersey

Norman W Provizer

The ghost

In search of new rules for 'managing the world' in the twenty-first century, writer Robert Kaplan visited Fort Bragg—the North Carolina home of the United States Army's Special Operations Command. At Fort Bragg, Kaplan asks Major Paul Warren about the model for civil affairs officers in Special Operations. 'Read John Hersey's *A Bell for Adano*,' the major replies, 'it's all there.' It's all there, of course, in the person of Major Victor Joppolo, the novel's senior civil affairs officer assigned to the newly 'liberated' Italian town of Adano during the ending phase of the Second World War. And it is from this character that Kaplan draws his first rule for America concerning the management of an untidy world: 'Produce More Joppolos' (2003, Page 69).

Kaplan's first rule, which appears in an *Atlantic Monthly* article, would not surprise the man responsible for *A Bell for Adano*. After all, in the 1946 Modern Library edition of the novel that was originally published in 1944, Hersey added an introductory comment on the character. 'Therefore', he writes,

> I beg you to get to know this man Joppolo well. He is our future in the world. Neither the eloquence of Churchill nor the humaneness of Roosevelt, no Charter, no four freedoms or fourteen points, no dreamer's diagram so symmetrical and so faultless on paper, no plan, no hope, no treaty—none of these things can guarantee anything. Only men can guarantee, only the behavior of men under pressure, only our Joppolos.
>
> (1988, Page vii)

'You see', Hersey continues, 'the theories about administering occupied territories all turned out to be just theories, and in fact the thing which determined whether we Americans would be successful in that toughest of all jobs was nothing more or less than the quality of the men who did the administering' (1988, Page v–vi). It is in that quality, ultimately, that leadership is lodged; and, from that perspective, to use Kaplan's words, 'One good man is worth a thousand wonks' (2003, Page 69).

Despite Hersey's admonition, Joppolo has not played any significant role in contemporary leadership studies. Neither he nor the writer who created him receives mention in leading texts on the subject, nor does Joppolo make much of an appearance in leadership courses. He should. For Joppolo's ghost speaks volumes on the role of individuals in the structured, reciprocal and multi-dimensional relationship we call leadership.

Creating Joppolo

Born to American missionary parents in Tientsin, China, in 1914, John Hersey spent the Second World War as a correspondent for *Life* and *Time* magazines. In 1942, he published his first book, the non-fiction *Men on Bataan*. And in August of the following year, Hersey produced a two-page article for *Life* titled 'AMGOT at Work'. The piece on AMGOT (Allied Military Government Occupied Territories) was based on a day the writer spent observing a real-life civil affairs officer, Major Frank Toscani, at work in the Sicilian town of Licata. After just three months of writing, Hersey turned that Sicilian episode into *A Bell for Adano*, a book filled with characters drawn from the writer's experience in Licata, in addition to reflecting his strong distaste for General George Patton— a distaste expressed through the character of General Marvin. In fact, Hersey would say, according to David Sanders's study of the author, the entire book began as a platform for him to write what he truly felt about the famed but seriously flawed Army general though the final result moved in a quite different direction (1991, Page 9).

While it took Hersey only a few months to write *A Bell for Adano*, the book captured a Pulitzer Prize in 1945. It was also turned into a play, a movie (which, according to Bosley Crowther's review in the *New York Times* of 6 July 1945, is 'the sort of picture that should do more for "understanding" than ten million moralizing words') and a television drama, emerging, with the exception of *Hiroshima*, as Hersey's most widely read work. In that work, the reader discovers that Joppolo, who was born in the Bronx to Italian-American immigrants, is about 35 years old and of medium height, with dark skin and moustache. Along with such facts, the reader learns that while Joppolo has known poverty, he has not known elite educational prep schools and universities such as Kent or Yale (though Hersey, himself, went to Hotchkiss and that university in New Haven).

At one point, the sentimental Major, who speaks Italian, explains that he became a clerk in New York City's Department of Taxation and Revenue, making $20 a week after placing 177th out of 1,100 people taking a government exam. After a change in the city's government with the election of progressive Republican Fiorella La Guardia as mayor, Joppolo lost his city job and turned to his mother-in-law for a loan to open a grocery in the Bronx. He owned the grocery for two years before hard times forced him to sell. Then it was back to the city and a job with the Sanitation Department, rising from a third-grade clerk to a second-grade clerk, making $42 a week before going into the Army.

Such fundamentals, of course, do not provide the material for an intimate, in-depth character study. Instead, Hersey presents Joppolo as he is, describing him as 'a good man, though weak in certain attractive, human ways' (1988, Page vi). One of those weaknesses is his attraction, while in Adano, to Tina, a daughter of the fisherman Tomasino. That attraction interestingly enough produced a lawsuit against the book by the real-life model for Joppolo, who claimed, as an earlier book on Hersey by Sanders notes, that his wife was emotionally upset over the episode in the novel and that it damaged his reputation as a husband, as well as a civil affairs officer (1967, Page 145).

Along with the lawsuit, *A Bell for Adano* faced criticism for its contrived simplicity, including the cardboard description of Joppolo as a good man, and a Foreword that reads like a script for a radio show. Still, despite such criticism and the dust of decades, there is something very compelling about the fictional Army major. 'A man of patience and integrity with a concern for honesty and justice', John Diggins writes, 'Joppolo feels that only simple good works reaching those at the bottom will reconstruct ravaged Italy' (1966, Page 607). Such a person-centred message continues to haunt the study of leadership, though in a manner quite different from what Barbara Kellerman, in her exploration of the role played by bad leadership in leadership studies, calls 'Hitler's ghost'.

Improvisation and the expression of leadership

Victor Joppolo would have been almost 70 years old when James MacGregor Burns published his path-breaking book *Leadership* in 1978. But back in Adano some three-and-a-half decades earlier, the Major understands much of what would later unfold in the volume produced by Burns. In both words and deeds, Joppolo expresses leadership by addressing, on the ground, the needs and aspirations of those over whom he had authority, while striving to elevate those needs and aspirations to a higher plane.

Think, first, of the bell from which the novel draws its title. Before the arrival of the American troops in Adano, the Italian government removed the town's historic bell so that it could be melted down for gun barrels. As soon as Joppolo arrives, he is regaled with tales about the 700-year-old bell, its loss and the people's need for its return. Although he understands that immediate needs (such as food for the town's residents) are a top priority, the civil affairs officer also recognises the bell's symbolic significance to the people and launches efforts to recover it. Those efforts provide a thread that runs throughout the novel.

When he discovers that the bell no longer exists, Joppolo arranges, with the Navy, for a substitute, a bell from the *USS Corelli*—a destroyer named for an Italian-American naval officer in the First World War that displays the words *America ed Italia*. But on the night after the bell's arrival—and before it is in place—Joppolo discovers that his conflict with General Marvin (the Army's divisional commander and the novel's anti-type of leadership) has led to the Major's immediate removal as the town's civil affairs officer. That clash between Joppolo and his superior, of course, represents another thread that runs through the novel.

It begins when Marvin is travelling on a road into Adano. Frustrated by a mule-drawn cart that delays his progress, the General orders the mule shot and the cart removed. Following that, Marvin meets with an out-of-uniform Joppolo and issues an order to ban carts from the roads to prevent them from hampering military transportation. Upon reflection, Joppolo realises that such a ban will cause the people of the town enormous difficulties and so he countermands it. Throughout the book, a report documenting Joppolo's action hits several detours, created by soldiers along the chain who agree with what the civil affairs officer is doing. But eventually, the information on Joppolo finds its way to Marvin and the General orders the Major out of Adano just as the bell arrives.

Beyond carts and bells, Joppolo's words and deeds make it easy to understand why Kaplan was told that the novel contains everything a civil affairs officer needs to know. First, there are his words. Among Joppolo's attributes, the novel tells us, is the fact that 'he could speak pompous sentences with a sincerity and passion so real that his Italian listeners were always moved by what he said' (1988, Page 156). When he talks to the town leaders, he informs them 'democracy is that the men of the government are no longer the masters of the people. They are the servants of the people.... And watch: this thing will make you happier than you have ever been in your lives' (1988, Page 45).

Additionally, the civil affairs officer attempts to convince the extremely anti-authority character Tomasino to lead his fellow fishermen back to work by telling him:

> You said I was different. You could be different too. It is possible to make your authority seem to spring from the very people over whom you have authority. And after a while, it actually does spring from them, and you are only an instrument of their will. This is the thing that the Americans want to teach you who have lived under men who imagined that they themselves were authority.
>
> (1988, Page 78)

Taken as a whole, such statements and their individual components clearly illustrate that Joppolo was way ahead of the curve followed by leadership studies in the decades to come. Not only did he pursue the right thing, to borrow from Warren Bennis, he also managed to do things right as well (1994, Page 45).

We are told that the trials conducted by Joppolo are impressive 'because he managed by trickery, by moral pressure and by persuasion to make the truth seem something really beautiful and necessary' (Kaplan, 1988, Page 75). Not a bad combination. And when it comes to the question of truth, the civil affairs officer tells the town's residents, 'As my friends, I will consider it my duty to tell you everything I think, for we do not want Adano to be a town of mysteries and a place of suspicion' (1988, Page 45).

In terms of simple actions, Joppolo hits the mark by showing respect for those over whom he has authority and earning, in turn, their respect. For example, when Tomasino refuses to come to Joppolo's office in the Palazzo, because all those who have authority are the same, the Major goes to see him causing a stir. After all, 'Never in the memory of anyone in the town had an official gone calling on a citizen on business. Either the citizen had come willingly to the Palazzo, or else the citizen had been arrested, and had come against his will' (1988, Page 69). But then, neither had previous officials expressed, as does Joppolo, a willingness to stand in line to buy bread just like everyone else.

Halfway through the novel, a high official from the allied occupation government, Lord Runcin, visits Joppolo and asks him to explain what he has done in Adano. The Major runs through a substantial list of accomplishments, including the establishment of a public assistance programme, arranging transportation for refugees in Adano to return to their hometown, obtaining rolls of muslin from a Liberty Ship to deal with the shortage of cloth in Adano, organising garbage collection in the town, convincing the fishermen to go out to sea and discovering railroad cars filled with wheat at a siding and turning it into flour for those in need. All that was still needed was a bell.

In response, the high-level occupation official imperiously tells the civil affairs officer, 'We can't afford to be too sentimental, you know, Joppolo. Can't afford to let these people be *too* happy, you know. Can't afford to let discipline get too loose.' Joppolo then explains that the he 'can't see that happiness and discipline don't go together . . . . Every time I've done something for these people, I've found they did two things for me just out of thanks' (1988, Page 134). In the end, Runcin agrees to help with the bell and tells Joppolo whom to contact with his request.

As the novel continues to unfold, the Major adds to his list of substantive achievements by developing plans to address inflation and the safety problem produced by the children chasing trucks to get candy from American troops. When there are rumours of a gas attack on the town, Joppolo goes to the harbour and takes deep breaths at various locations to show there is no basis for the rumour. And when, the Major discovers that beneath the water in the harbour there is a small ship, with cargo that can benefit the town, he convinces the Navy to raise the ship. Despite the obvious inter-service rivalry, the Major succeeds in working with the Navy because he is, in the words of Lieutenant Commander Robertson, 'the first Army man I ever saw that was willing to give the Navy credit' (1988, Page 207).

Within his own branch of the military, Joppolo is widely considered to be 'the best goddam guy I ever seen in *this* Army', while the population of Adano loves him because the people there can always count on him to deliver justice (1988, Pages 38–9). Combine those sentiments with that expressed by those in the Navy and you know the potential of an individual exercising leadership.

In his book *Leadership without Easy Answers*, Ronald Heifetz tells us:

> Leadership operates within particular worlds and requires an experimental mindset—the willingness to work by trial and error—where the community's reactions at each stage provide the basis for planning future actions. Research about each particular context is

critically important, but no analysis or catalogue can substitute for a leader's improvisational skills.

(1994, Pages 242–3)

That is an idea well recognised before it was articulated by Heifetz in 1994, and one that was definitely understood by Joppolo 50 years earlier. Right after his arrival in Adano, the major begins to read the official *Instructions to Civil Affairs Officers*. After looking at a few pages of that catalogue, he places the detailed list of activities in the trash. He then turns to his own notebook labelled *Notes to Joppolo from Joppolo*. 'Don't make yourself cheap. Always be accessible to the public. Don't play favorites. Speak Italian whenever possible. Don't lose your temper. When plans fall down, improvise...' (1988, Pages 14–15). Immediately, Joppolo recognises that the best advice he has for himself is found in that last point, 'When plans fall down, improvise'. In this sense, he clearly knows that in an adaptive situation, improvisation, as Heifetz puts it, 'is the norm' (1994, Page 272).

From this perspective, leadership, like jazz, can be viewed as the art of the improviser in which all members of the group can have their moment to solo. That art requires an ability to imagine where you want to go, to arrange a method of getting there within a given set of circumstances and to adapt your playing by listening to others and recognising changing contexts. In incident after incident in the novel, Joppolo displays all of those talents. Following the view expressed by Gary Wills concerning Franklin Roosevelt, Waller Newell argues in his book *The Soul of a Leader*, 'that tactical flexibility in the service of a core moral aim is a hallmark of great leadership' (2009, Page 199). That's exactly the path Joppolo follows.

Remembering Joppolo

The military's civil affairs officer in the town of Adano clearly believes, as John Diggins writes, that 'America's only chance for permanent recovery of Europe depended not on abstract slogans but on simple deeds, not on governments but on those who govern' (1966, Page 608). True, the argument can certainly be made that the novel presents that view in a rather monochromatic manner and thus fails to capture the complex animosities that marked the occupation of Italy. Still, in the words of Rowland Egger, 'The sheer virtuosity of *A Bell for Adano* carries John Hersey's monochromatic portrayal of the relations between Major Joppolo and the people of Adano to heights of artistry seldom reached in novels of any sort, and almost never in administrative novels' (1959, Page 450).

Continuing in that vein, Egger notes, in an article that appeared in the *American Political Science Review*, 'Much of our knowledge of society is of this essentially humanistic kind, whatever claims we may make on impersonality or timelessness for our learning about man in his relationships to other men' (1959, Page 453). Remembering Joppolo serves as a reminder of that very thing. The scope of his sphere of activity was limited and its nature influenced by both his connection to the military and the factor of occupation. Yet, even within those special contexts, he conveys a message of broad applicability to leadership—a message that indicates how, to borrow the title of a 1999 study by Richard Haass, a 'bureaucratic entrepreneur' blurs the lines between transactions and transformations, between administrating and leading.

It was F Scott Fitzgerald who observed, in a 1936 essay, that 'the test of a first-rate intelligence is the ability to hold two opposed ideas in the mind at the same time, and still retain the ability to function' (Fitzgerald, 1990, Page 69). In similar fashion, the test of first-rate leadership, like that exercised by Joppolo, is found not in the singular commitment to either carrying out transactions or stimulating transformations. It comes, instead, from knowing how and when to transact and how and when to try to transform things as a significant actor within a complex, structured context filled with multiple participants, many of whom have their own motives, means and opportunities to act. Like a hybrid vehicle, hybrid leadership at any level underscores the value of having two distinct yet interrelated sources of motivational power rather than relying on only a single source.

In his foreword to a book of Nelson Mandela's words, former United Nations Secretary General Kofi Annan writes, 'People often ask me what difference one person can make in the face of injustice, conflict, human rights violations, mass poverty and disease. I answer by citing the courage, tenacity, dignity and magnanimity of Nelson Mandela' (Mandela, 2003, Page xiii). While not many figures, real or fictional, can measure up to Mandela and his ability to practise hybrid leadership, Major Joppolo, in his own way, also reminds us of the difference one person can make, especially one who is willing to recognise and reflect on his own weaknesses, as Joppolo does regarding Tina and the question of whether he was playing favourites in violation of one his own cardinal rules.

In this sense, Joppolo combines a passionate, though never naïve commitment to the fundamental principles of democracy and decency with the flexible art of improvising. And by so doing, he highlights how important it is along the path of leadership to have the right individual who can bridge what Fareed Zakaria refers to, in a *New York Times* review of *The Assassin's Gate*, 'as the staggering gap between abstract ideas and concrete reality' (2005, Page 10). Perhaps that helps explain why Lt Col Patrick Donahoe ends his *Military Review* article on preparing leaders for the process of nation building with the simple line, 'The Army needs more leaders like Major Victor Joppolo' (2004, Page 26).

Truth and fiction

'The fundamental issues of leadership—the complications involved in becoming, being, confronting, and evaluating leaders—are not' James March and Thierry Weil write in their book *On Leadership* 'unique to leadership. They are echoes of critical issues of life more generally' (2005, Page 1). And serious works of fiction frequently provide the greatest insight when it comes to understanding those critical issues.

Two days before the 2008 presidential election in America, David Margolick highlighted this point in the *New York Times* by emphasising how Ernest Hemingway's character Robert Jordan in *For Whom the Bell Tolls* resonated with both of the major-party candidates then vying to move into the White House. According to Margolick, few figures, real or fictional, exerted as much influence on Senator John McCain as Jordan, the fictional American volunteering for the republican side in the Spanish civil war. McCain, in fact, borrowed the title for his 2002 autobiography *Worth the Fighting For* from words delivered by Jordan in the novel published in 1940.

At the same time, Margolick also notes that 'Senator Barack Obama told *Rolling Stone* that Hemingway's novel is one of the three books that most inspired him.' As someone willing 'to give his life for a cause greater than himself', Jordan connects with the military man McCain. As someone driven by a sense of mission and a vision, the literary figure connects to the transformational side of Obama's character (2008, WK 3).

Interestingly, on the same day that Margolick's article appeared, the newspaper's book review section contained an essay by Jon Meacham that also discussed Jordan's impact on McCain and Obama. 'Like Robert Jordan', Meacham writes,

> they want to make things better and are willing to put themselves in the arena, but they know that nothing is perfectible and that progress

is provisional. Things fall apart; plans fail; planes are shot out of the sky. Their attraction to Hemingway suggests a willingness to acknowledge unpleasant facts not always found in those who enter elective politics.

(2008, Page 27)

An attraction, you might say, that makes Jordan 'Hemingway's Bipartisan Hero' (Stamberg, 2008, Page 1).

Additionally, McCain, who first discovered the Hemingway novel when he was 12 years old, tells Meacham, 'Robert Jordan is what I always thought a man ought to be' (2008, Page 27). In Jordan, McCain writes, he discovered someone who was 'brave, dedicated, capable, selfless', a man who 'possessed in abundance that essence of courage that Hemingway described as grace under pressure, a man who would risk his life but never his honour'. Expressing what McCain calls 'beautiful fatalism', Jordan is 'an individual committed to a cause he believes in' (McCain, 2002a, Pages xxi–xxiii).

In life, to use McCain's words from a 2002 interview, 'There may be events you can't control but as long as you remain true to your ideals, your beliefs and your causes, then it is ok and you're willing to accept your fate.' In this sense, Jordan not only inspired McCain but, as the Senator says, was 'as real to me as any human being in my imagination' (2002b). So real, in fact, that as a prisoner of war in Hanoi, McCain thought if Jordan were in the cell next to his, Hemingway's hero 'would be stoic, he would be strong, he would be tough, he wouldn't give up. And Robert would expect me to do the same thing' (Margolick, 2008, WK 3).

Great fiction informs us about people at the profoundest level; it tells stories that explain much about leadership. 'One death', to use a quote attributed to Stalin, 'is a tragedy, one million is a statistic.' That's because one death has a story, one million deaths has only a large number of zeroes. In telling such stories, as Murray Edelman notes in his study *From Art to Politics*, art serves as 'the fountainhead from which political discourse, beliefs about politics, and consequent actions ultimately spring'. In other words, according to Edelman, 'Works of art generate the ideas about leadership, bravery, cowardice, altruism, dangers, authority, and fantasies about the future that people typically assume to be reflections of their own observations and reasoning' (1995, Page 2–3).

The ideas generated by the two novels that share the imagery of a bell are quite different. For Hemingway, the bell tolls for the novel's hero and those who would emulate him, while in Hersey's tale, it rings for the people of Adano. Although less the grand heroic figure, the former shopkeeper Joppolo is, in reality, a considerably more effective exemplary leader than Jordan, the American professor who sacrifices all in the Spanish civil war. Yet both individuals mirror the human condition, reminding us, in the process, why it is that literature counts when it comes to studying leadership.

References

Bennis, W. (1994) *On Becoming a Leader*. Addison-Wesley, Reading, MA.

Burns, J.M. (1978) *Leadership*. Harper and Row, New York.

Crowther, B. (1945) 'The Screen: In Military Role', *The New York Times*, 6 July, at http://movies.nytimes.com/movie/review?res=9B02EEDB133 BEE3BBC4E53DFB16683838E659DE.

Diggins, J. (1966) 'The American Writer, Fascism, and the Liberation of Italy', *American Quarterly* 54: 599–614.

Donahoe, P. (2004) 'Preparing Leaders for Nationbuilding', *Military Review* May/June: 24–26002E.

Edelman, M. (1995) *From Art to Politics*. University of Chicago Press, Chicago.

Egger, R. (1959) 'The Administrative Novel', *American Political Science Review* 53: 448–55.

Fitzgerald, F.S. (1990) 'The Crack-Up' in Edmund Wilson (ed.) *F. Scott Fitzgerald*. New Directions, New York.

Haass, R. (1999) *The Bureaucratic Entrepreneur*. Brookings Institution Press, Washington, DC.

Heifetz, R. (1994) *Leadership without Easy Answers*. Harvard University Press, Cambridge, MA.

Hemingway, E. (2003) *For Whom the Bell Tolls*. Scribner, New York.

Hersey, J. (1988) *A Bell for Adano*. Vintage Books, New York.

Kaplan, R. (1988) *The Atlantic* 292(1).

Kaplan, R. (2003) 'Supremacy by Stealth: Ten Rules for Managing the World', *The Atlantic Monthly* 1(292): 65–83.

Kellerman, B. (1999) 'Hitler's Ghost: A Manifesto' in Barbara Kellerman and Larraine Matusak (eds) *Cutting Edge Leadership 2000*. Burns Academy of Leadership, College Park, MD, 65–8.

Mandela, N. (2003) *In His Own Words*. Little, Brown and Company, New York.

March J.G. and Thierry Weil. (2005) *On Leadership*. Blackwell Publishing, Oxford, UK.

Margolick, D. (2008) 'Papa's Gift to the Fire-in-the-Belly Crowd', *The New York Times* 2 November: WK 3.

McCain, J. with Mark Salter (2002a) *Worth the Fighting For: A Memoir*. Random House, New York.

McCain, J. (2002b) 'Interview with the Author for the Radio Show', *Colorado Close Up*, 31 October 2002.

Meacham, J. (2008) 'How to Read Like a President', *The New York Times Book Review*, 2 November: 27.

Newell, W. (2009) *The Soul of a Leader*. HarperCollins, New York.

Sanders, D. (1967) *John Hersey*. Twayne Publishers, New York.

Sanders, D. (1991) *John Hersey Revisited*. Twayne Publishers, New York.

Stamberg, S. (2008) 'Robert Jordan, Hemingway's Bipartisan Hero', National Public Radio (NPR), Washington, DC, 14 December, at www.npr.org/templates/story/story.php?storyId= 95604448.

Zakaria, F. (2005) 'Review of *The Assassin's Gate* by George Packer', *The New York Times Book Review*, 30 October: 10.

8
The Silhouette of Leadership: James Bond and Miss Moneypenny

Beverley Hawkins

Introduction

This chapter reflects on the way images of heroic leaders from popular culture can be used within organisations. I link my ethnographic data to some extracts from Ian Fleming's '007' novels to suggest why Bond's heroic style of action-focused leadership acts as a template for organisational heroics. I also highlight the implications of Miss Moneypenny's role as the heroic leader's 'trusty sidekick' (Maccoby, 2000). I suggest that figures from popular culture, like Bond and Moneypenny, can act as 'leadership silhouettes', resurrecting heroic models of leadership within post-heroic workplace structures.

I begin the chapter by outlining some of the literature on leadership, heroes and corporate culture narratives. After a brief explanation of my ethnographic research method, I recount my experience as a member of a self-managed team of recruitment consultants in a branch of 'Strongstaff' (a pseudonym), an international recruitment agency.

The return of the leader–hero in the post-heroic age

Over the past two decades the field of leadership studies has witnessed a trend towards more relational, constructivist approaches to leadership in organisations. Theorists have rejected the notion of leadership as rooted within the attributes and actions of just one 'great man', or hero, in favour of a conceptualisation of leadership which emerges through the collaborative, sense-making activities of individuals (Gronn, 2002; Pye, 2005). Leadership is thought of as a collective, distributed, shared and creative *process,* through which members of a group negotiate with and influence each other.

This trend parallels a move within organisations towards more collab-orative, participative forms of workplace organisation. Organisations are streamlining their bureaucratic structures and changing work arrange-ments in a bid to achieve flexibility and quality, two buzzwords of the post-Fordist society. Often, these structural changes have involved a move towards self-managed team-working set-ups.

Under the principles of self-managed teamwork (Katzenbach and Smith, 1993), members of a team share equal responsibility for allo-cating and carrying out work tasks. They are facilitated, rather than directed, by a team leader who occupies a more participative supervisory role. Day et al. (2006) argue that distributed, collaborative leadership models are more appropriate for understanding leadership within self-managed teamwork because they allow for the plurality of influencing processes that occur as team members negotiate their work through social interaction.

Nonetheless, the mythical leader–hero figure remains heavily rooted in our everyday understanding of leadership (Pfeffer, 1981). In sales organisations like 'Strongstaff', individual sales workers are ranked and categorised, with the highest achieving employees reaching heroic status: recognised during prize ceremonies and in the pages of corpo-rate magazines as the embodiment of the organisation's purpose and success.

The emphasis on heroes in sales organisations is, however, embedded in a wider cultural narrative. The value we place on heroes is reinforced by the stories of 'modern-day heroes' in the tabloid sports pages, and similarly perpetuated by the actions of the fictional heroes we see in countless television series and comic strips. In the NBC television series 'Heroes' (Kring, 2006–08), for example, the main characters are each born with a 'superhuman' power which sets them out as 'different' from the friends and family surrounding them. Embedded in an overarching quest to conquer evil, the ensuing story describes each of the heroes' battles with adversity and with his or her own sense of identity. Our fictional superheroes often find it hard to maintain intimate personal relationships as they fight to save the world. Take, for example, the comic book hero Batman, who has few family and friends, and finds that his relationships with romantic interests Vicki Vale and Catwoman hamper his efforts to save society from crime. Being a hero, we learn, requires sacrifice and hard work, and is often related to a sense of moral duty to assist those who are not similarly endowed with heroic qualities. This heroic status occurs at the expense of having to live in a 'bat-cave' and renounce our social relationships.

Heroes and corporate culture narratives

Fictional hero–leader narratives, with their emphasis on commitment to a moral cause and the sacrifice of personal relationships in favour of a public-sphere, heroic role, appear to have much to offer as a corporate culture theme. Pettigrew (1979) argues that organisations can construct a corporate culture using narratives, symbols and material objects which generate a shared cultural identity. This identification with the culture of the corporation is thought to inspire in workers a sense of moral commitment towards the pursuit of organisational goals. In other words, enacting organisational values becomes part of a higher purpose, embedded in morality and a sense of self. This approach became popularised by managerialist texts in the 1980s, which argued that a 'strong culture' was central to corporate success (Pettigrew, 1979).

Critics of so-called 'corporate culturism' have argued that this management technique amounts to 'nascent totalitarianism' (Strangleman and Roberts, 1992; Willmott, 1993). They argue that corporate cultures aim to provide a framework for thinking, being and doing that precludes workers from being aware of possible alternatives. Yet others (Smircich, 1983; Hawkins, 2008) have questioned the extent to which culture can be imposed on members of an organisation. Culture, from an anthropological viewpoint, emerges from the collective social interactions of its members: it cannot be designed by managers, although they may have more access to the material resources which act as cultural artefacts, to be interpreted by employees (Meek, 1988; Smircich, 1983).

Parry and Hansen (2007) argue that while leaders often employ stories as part of a corporate culture aimed at inspiring followers, the stories themselves also act like leaders by linking goals and values to specific actions. Stories can be inscribed with normative discourses which delimit the expected ways of behaving in an organisation. By interpreting stories about, for example, exemplary leadership, followers actively construct a narrative for themselves about how to enact organisational values (ibid.). This is the process which I observed during my fieldwork as an employee at a branch of 'Strongstaff'.

Methodology

My arguments in this chapter are drawn from a longitudinal ethnographic research project involving a branch of an international recruitment consultancy I have called 'Strongstaff'. For two months, I was a full-time, temporary member of 'DriveTeam', a self-managed team of recruitment consultants, who recruited haulage drivers for the transport industry. Having secured the consent of my colleagues, I recorded field-notes at my desk and during the subsequent three years I made return trips to the field to conduct formal (tape-recorded) and informal interviews. The interviews enabled me to engage more deeply with the themes which had emerged from the fieldwork, focusing on teamwork processes, gender and identity work, and the negotiation of and resistance to corporate culture.

I make no claims about the reliability or validity of ethnographic research, preferring instead to argue that the integrity of ethnographic writing lies in its *plausibility*, through the relaying of contextual specificities which enable the text to convince the reader (Geertz, 1999), and in its *criticality*: the degree to which the resulting analysis can call existing assumptions and theories into question (Golden-Biddle and Locke, 1993). The events that took place on the 'Sales Day' are presented here in the form of an account, interspersed with links to theory and literature, and, as Van Maanen (1979) points out, the subjective recounting of ethnographic data means that there is a fictional element in any 'tale from the field'.

What would James Bond do? Becoming Bond and Moneypenny for the Strongstaff 'Sales Day'

Rosen's ethnographic work (1985, 1988) portrays organisational ceremonies as social dramas, used to reassert social norms and hierarchies. In this chapter I describe what happened at one such event, a sales competition, which took place at a branch of an international recruitment consultancy I have called 'Strongstaff'. The events in this chapter are therefore drawn from the events which took place on one day.

For the Sales Day occurring during my third week at Strongstaff, a fancy-dress theme was chosen by senior management, which, Sarah suggests, is intended to reflect the purpose of the Sales Day:

> Sarah: [the theme is intended] to make people think a little bit more about what they have to achieve ... the costumes, what they're wearing, how they act, the day itself, just to give it a bit more of an edge ....
>
> (Team leader, AdminTeam, in interview)

Sarah describes how Strongstaff's senior management are deliberately harnessing a narrative which they believe will demonstrate to consultants the kinds of appearances and actions ('their costumes, what they're wearing, how they act') are appropriate for this important day. She believes that the theme was chosen on purpose with the aim of motivating the consultants because it links with Strongstaff's hard-hitting sales focus. She suggests that enacting this fancy-dress theme will help the consultants prioritise their goals in line with the Strongstaff's expectations ('...make people think a little bit more about what they have to achieve').

Senior managers chose the theme of 'James Bond and Miss Moneypenny'. These characters are taken from Ian Fleming's series of novels about fictional spy James Bond, and became iconic figures through the 22 internationally screened films in the James Bond film franchise. Bond's solo endeavours represent one man's heroic struggle to uphold Western (capitalist) values and the British Empire, traditionally against communism and, in more recent films, against alternative regimes and terrorists threatening Western domination.

Iconic figures change over time (see the various versions of Dr Who) and there are differences of style and approach in the James Bond novels, written by Ian Fleming, and the films that followed. Just as leadership may now be seen as a collective enterprise, so the image of James Bond is no longer in his creator's hands, but in those of many others. It would appear consistent, though, that Bond's work, and the priority he gives it, has a destructive influence on his ability to form personal relationships and connect emotionally; it is significant that he is unmarried. (Bond marries in *On Her Majesty's Secret Service* (1963) but his new wife is murdered by his enemies.)

The Bond/Moneypenny theme was the subject of even more discussion than our plans for how we should conduct our work on the Sales Day. We were inspired to translate the theme into objectified dress and behaviour codes and the fortnight preceding the Sales Day was taken up with lengthy discussions about what each employee should wear. The hunt for appropriate costume time took over our personal time, as well as working hours. 'Costume talk' ate into the boredom of many slow afternoons, and presented us with opportunities for bonding and collaboration. Many of us trawled the town centre enthusiastically together during our lunch hours, hunting for accessories, which were paid for out of our own pockets or given to teammates as presents.

As the day progressed, we got into our stride, comparing our results with those of other teams over the Intranet, placing valueless bets on which team would win. We found plenty of inspiration in the Bond theme. Geoff had written 'WWJBD?' in large letters at the top of the whiteboard—a variation on the 'WWJD?' (What would Jesus do?) car bumper sticker we had seen on television. This reminder indicates how the James Bond narrative caught the imagination of the consultants, and was deemed suitable for use as a control mechanism through which we regulated our own and each others' behaviour. Certainly, nobody was under any doubt what James Bond would do if he was a *recruitment*, rather than a *secret* agent: we ticked call after call off our lists, were chucked out of the office by the caretaker at 8 pm, and scattered, exhausted, towards our buses, trains and cars.

'The man who is only a silhouette': The significance of James Bond for Strongstaff's core team values

The role of James Bond is written in contrast to his enemies' characters. In Fleming's books, and in the films, Bond battles powerful men whose wickedness is represented in their various physical deformities (a cleft palate, claws for hands, inability to feel pain, metal teeth, eyes that bleed) and supposed sexual perversions (homosexuality, lesbianism). By comparison, Bond is portrayed as the ultimate emblem of masculine physicality and heterosexuality, to the point that the various actors playing Bond's character in the films are subjected to endless scrutiny, ranking and comparison by critics and laypersons. Almost everyone has an opinion on their favourite Bond! When Daniel Craig was chosen to play Bond in the 2006 film version of *Casino Royale,* he was variously described in advance by critics as 'too blond', 'too short' and, after wearing a lifejacket on a publicity stunt involving a speedboat, 'too effeminate' to make an effective Bond (Woods, 2006).

The first appearance of 007 in every film is in silhouette form, pictured in cartoon-like shadow through an enemy sniper's rifle scope. The viewer gazes through the scope at a shadowy figure, armed with a revolver. Hovey (2005) argues that the unmistakeably masculine suit and hat signify that the figure is a man, and that his revolver and stance indicate the *type* of man he is: 'violent ... graceful and fascinating' (ibid., Page 44). In this iconic opening sequence, Bond has no features. He could be any man, and yet, as Amis (1966) and other critics have suggested, the Bond stereotype represents a hyper-heterosexuality and masculinity, an heroic leadership identity which it is impossible for any one man to embody. Woods writes in the *Daily Telegraph* (13 November 2006, Page 19) that Bond is a reflection of the national zeitgeist. He has become

... more than a mere fictional character. He is a totem of the nation's identity, a testosterone-charged barometer of our sexual mores ... 007 has to inspire our menfolk to raise their game.

The choice of a James Bond template by senior managers is particularly interesting because it represents firstly a silhouette, or template of (masculine) leadership which is apparently unachievable in reality, and secondly, a keen nostalgia for a lost time when British industry was at the height of its power. Despite these apparent drawbacks, all the male consultants at Strongstaff were expected to adopt the role of secret agent James Bond: active, autonomous, the ruthlessly masculine and irresistible hero, always present at the centre of the action, and 'representative of the virtues of Western Capitalism triumphing over ... Eastern Communism'. (Bennett and Woollacott, 2003, Page 16). By living out this template during the Sales Day, male team-workers could try to demonstrate leadership values of autonomy, proactive behaviour and heroism. Yet it seems that Bond is an unliveable character, representative of a kind of leadership that cannot be fully realised or embodied because its very purpose is to be aspirational, not achievable.

Correspondingly, the legend of James Bond, as an emblem of active, heroic surveillance, entrepreneurial endeavour and the suppression of emotional intimacy in favour of physical conquests, has caused Symons (1972, Page 232) to claim him as the 'perfect pipe-dream figure for organization man'—and certainly, Bond's fictional enemies have agreed. In *From Russia with Love,* the Russian spy agency SMERSH seeks out a British hero, in order to destroy the resolve of the British people and the Secret Service:

> This myth, of Scotland Yard, of Sherlock Holmes, of the Secret Service ... is a hindrance which it would be good to set aside .... Have they [the Secret Service] no one who is a hero to the organization? ... Myths are built on heroic deeds and heroic people. Have they no such men?
>
> (Fleming, 2002, Pages 55–6, 58)

Bond is selected as 'such a man' (ibid., 59) because of his reputation within the British Secret Service and its overseas equivalents as 'someone who is admired and whose ignominious destruction would cause dismay'. His elimination would 'destroy the myth and thus strike at the very motive force of the organization' (ibid., 58). To his enemies, and perhaps to his creator Ian Fleming, Bond is the life force of 'the organization', the Secret Service.

The relationships between Bond, his sexual conquests and Moneypenny, whose relationship with Bond remains unconsummated throughout the Bond novels, are particularly interesting because they represent early examples in popular culture of what Denning (2003, Page 73) calls the 'libidinization of the workplace and daily life', a process which he links to the shift towards consumer capitalism. This argument is especially significant within the context of Strongstaff, whose consultants are expected to construct their gender identities and expressions of sexuality according to the cultural demands of the industry within which they recruit (see Hawkins, 2008). Unsurprisingly then, all the male consultants at the branch I worked for chose to dress as Bond, and all the women, including Sarah and Anna, the team leaders, decided to dress and act in the character of Miss Moneypenny. When I asked during a coffee break why this might be, Kate laughed at me and said 'Bev, that's just wrong! The boys have got to be Bond and the girls have got to be Moneypenny! And anyway, it wouldn't look right on the Intranet photos....' Where then, does this leave the women consultants as they attempt to embody Strongstaff's leadership values? The following section explores the implications of the Miss Moneypenny silhouette for enacting leadership.

Miss Moneypenny and the Bond/Moneypenny dyad

Miss Moneypenny has an ambiguous, marginal role in the Bond narrative (Brabazon, 2003), but has appeared in more Bond novels and films than any other character except for Bond himself. As assistant to M, head of the British Secret Service, Moneypenny does not seem to represent any form of heroic leadership. She performs low status back-office and secretarial work to facilitate Bond's heroic actions. Kingsley Amis, in his analysis of the Bond phenomenon, describes Moneypenny as a 'sister—or possibly domestic servant type' (Amis, 1966, Page 58). This occupation hardly reflects the leadership values prioritised by Strongstaff in their 'sales culture'. Yet the fleshing out of a 'Moneypenny silhouette' serves as a foil which both strengthens and challenges Bond's image as heroic leader.

These Bond/Moneypenny silhouettes have many implications for the Strongstaff consultants. Firstly, even within self-managed teams, the templates separate the consultants along gender lines, re-establishing a gendered hierarchy. Miss Moneypenny's static, desk-bound character emphasises the masculine-ness of Bond: her supportive capacity reinforces his role as 'agent'; her marginal presence highlights his centrality. The contrast between Moneypenny and Bond is significant because it accentuates the supposed ability of men—and inability of women—to uphold the actions and values of heroic leadership.

Following this, the team becomes separated so that despite the distributed leadership rhetoric which is espoused by proponents of self-managed teamwork, the ability to enact 'heroic leadership' is no longer the premise of all members of a team. The Sales Day was intended to promote inter-team competition and therefore to strengthen team bonds, but the Bond/Moneypenny theme legitimised and rationalised a hierarchical gendered division of labour between (male) 'leaders' and (female) 'followers'. The social norm of male-dominated organisation was reasserted in that the female team leaders also had to enact the subordinate Moneypenny silhouette.

Nevertheless, the women consultants seemed happy to adopt the Moneypenny silhouette as their own. I argue here that this is because Moneypenny allows them to challenge the heroic leadership assumptions embedded in Strongstaff's culture. As Maccoby argues, every heroic leader requires a 'trusty sidekick', who is able to point out the narcissism and self-centredness within the leader's actions. Certainly, a similar sense of irony and knowing is manifest in Miss Moneypenny's later guises (Brabazon, 2003). As Brabazon (2003) points out, the later Bond films portray Moneypenny as a wry, knowing observer of Bond's haphazard actions as secret agent, and ultimately unrewarding and destructive relationships with Bond girls. Miss Moneypenny is the possessor of 'secret knowledge' (Fleming, 2002, Page 134) about 007's missions, and about the man himself. There is undoubtedly more ambiguity to Moneypenny's character than Amis's (1966) sister/servant label implies.

Although the earlier films sometimes show Moneypenny as being infatuated with 007, she does not constantly simper after Bond, and in the novel *You Only Live Twice,* she regards him 'with ill-concealed dislike' (Fleming, 2006b, Page 27). Bond, on the other hand, has a certain amount of respect for Moneypenny: in the film *On her Majesty's Secret Service* (Hunt, 1969), he refers to her as 'Britain's last line of defence'. Brabazon (2003) argues that Moneypenny's character, as portrayed in cinema, is an example of filmic feminism, in that it reveals the fractures in dominant masculine discourses. By remaining *Miss* Moneypenny, she exists outside the standard discourses involving marriage and domesticity. While the Moneypenny in the Roger Moore Bond films was represented as a powerless old maid, invisible to Bond yet enthralled by him, the Pierce Brosnan era signalled a shift in the way her character was defined. Brabazon explores the following conversation from the film *GoldenEye* (Campbell, 1995, in Brabazon, 2003, Page 210) to show Moneypenny begins to give as good as she gets:

> *Bond*: Out on some professional assignment – dressed to kill!
>
> *Moneypenny*: I know you find this crushing 007, but I don't wait home every night waiting for some international incident, so I can rush down here to impress James Bond. I was on a date, if you must know, with a gentleman.
>
> *Bond*: Moneypenny, I'm devastated. What would I do without you?
>
> *Moneypenny*: As far as I can remember, James, you've never had me.
>
> *Bond*: Hope springs eternal.
>
> *Moneypenny*: You know, this sort of behaviour could qualify as sexual harassment.
>
> *Bond*: Really? What's the penalty for that?
>
> *Moneypenny*: Some day you will have to make good on your innuendo.

Brabazon suggests that this interaction is significant because by highlighting her unavailability, Moneypenny is reminding Bond of his limitations: he is conforming to the stereotype of masculine heroism, which is without essence.

While Miss Moneypenny contradicts the values espoused in Strongstaff's corporate culture messages, her maternality in earlier films, and her role in later films as unattainable female other and wry commentator on Bond's sexual shenanigans with interchangeable Bond 'girls' (Brabazon, 2003), might characterise the opportunities which the Strongstaff consultants take up to distance themselves from the leader/follower (subject/object) dyad. These possibilities for distance (Collinson, 1988) offered by the Bond/Moneypenny templates offer a further reason why the women consultants took up the Moneypenny narrative so enthusiastically and repeatedly. She represents the shifting ways (mother figure, sexual object and so on) that women consultants play with gender and leadership during their interactions with teammates and other work contacts.

A quantum of solace—Resisting heroic leadership as a 'Double Agent'

While Bond at first appears to offer the male consultants a leadership silhouette more closely aligned with the entrepreneurial, action-oriented values in Strongstaff's sales culture, he also highlights some of the more confusing tensions in this culture which consultants must reconcile during the course of their work. Although our work was a *collaborative* process, Strongstaff's values prioritise *individual* acts of heroic leadership.

Yet by representing these tensions, Bond makes clear the fractures within the Strongstaff ethos. He offers the male consultants an opportunity to infuse their days at the office with notions of heroic derring-do, but in doing so, highlights the monotony of the consultants' working day and symbolises an ambivalent attitude towards teamwork and organisation. In the novel *From Russia with Love* (Fleming, 2002, Page 131), for example, Bond is stifled with boredom during the wait for a new mission. He considers his motives for opposing a new Secret Service directive:

> Bond wondered, as at nine o'clock he walked out of his flat and down the steps to his car... was he so bored that he could find nothing to do with himself except make a nuisance of himself within his own organization?

Rather than the company man that Symons suggests (1972), Fleming portrays Bond as a maverick, reluctant to become embroiled in organisational bureaucracy, dismissive of the organisation he works for and willing to upset the status quo in the office in his search for a more exciting life. This was perhaps not the characterisation of Bond that the senior management at Strongstaff had anticipated, but was certainly one that we consultants could all relate to—the constant hunt for ways to make our work more bearable, to make the day seem different from yesterday, to pass the time until our working days ended at six or seven. 'The thing about the Bond [event]', Phil suggested to me as we carried boxes of files into a back room for sorting,

> 'is that it helps you get through the day quicker, don't it. Everyone looks different; you could be in a different office. It's stressful work, this, but that don't mean it's not boring when you do it day in, day out. Dressing up, having a laugh... gives you something to

laugh about...' 'Yeah', agreed Kate. 'And you know what they say – a change is as good as a holiday!'

Authors such as Amis (1966) have suggested that part of Bond's appeal lies in the escapism contained in 007 as a fantasy figure. Amis suggests that the secret agent aspect of Bond's character is central to his attractiveness as an alter ego because this role requires an outward appearance of normality. This allows the male recruitment consultant to 'say to himself and without any special preparation, "Under this fiendishly clever bank clerk [recruitment consultant] etc disguise, lurks intrepid, ruthless 00999" ' (Amis, 1966, Page 12).

Concluding discussion

Enacting Bond and Moneypenny silhouettes therefore offers the consultants a maze of different, gendered routes which distance them from team values. Nonetheless, this tactic is not without jeopardy. Engaging in 'Bond-ing' draws the team together, tightening the bonds between individuals and giving a strengthened moral responsibility to teammates.

'Becoming Bond' requires a visible compliance with the masculinity and performance orientation encouraged by Strongstaff's organisational culture. The men who continue to enact the Bond role risk becoming further entrapped in the unending struggle to 'do' heroic leadership. Bond can therefore only offer a partial way out of the normative values established within the team and through the Strongstaff corporate culture, leaving the male consultants still vulnerable to the gaze of their teammates, who assess their performances with relish, ranking them and comparing them to the unachievable norm (Foucault, 1979) provided by 007. Yet this way out might go some way to exposing the *performance* of heroic leadership discourses: the consultants' over-the-top, parodied renditions of Bond could indeed be an attempt to 'destroy the myth and thus strike at the very motive force of the organization' (Fleming, 2002, Page 58) which links sales to masculine heroics.

Enacting Miss Moneypenny, however, offers women consultants an array of ambiguous, alternative ways to respond to the gaze of their teammates. Unlike the aeroplane-flying, weapon-toting Pussy Galore, Moneypenny is not defined through a sexual relationship to Bond. However, the 'Moneypennys' have occasional, momentary opportunities to roll their eyes at the hyper-heroic aspects of their work which are so evidently entrenched in the James Bond silhouette. Miss Moneypenny, as a knowing observer and trusty sidekick (Maccoby, 2000), therefore provides a risky alternative to the sex symbol logic of the Bond girl and to Bond's narcissism. By allowing women consultants to express their awareness of the irony of enacting a passive secretarial role in comparison to Bond's unflinching heroics, the character Miss Moneypenny 'undoes' the heroism in 007 (Butler, 1999), and in Strongstaff's leadership culture: she draws attention to its groundlessness.

Bibliography

Amis, K. (1966) *The James Bond Dossier*. New York: Signet Books.

Bennett, T., and Woollacott, J. (2003) 'The moments of Bond' in C. Lindner (Ed.) *The James Bond Phenomenon: A Critical Reader*: 13–33. Manchester: Manchester University Press.

Brabazon, T. (2003) 'Britain's last line of defence: Miss Moneypenny and the desperations of filmic feminism' in C. Lindner (Ed.) *The James Bond Phenomenon: A Critical Reader*: 202–14. Manchester: Manchester University Press.

Butler, J. (1999) *Gender Trouble: Feminism and the Subversion of Identity*. New York: Routledge.

Collinson, D. (1988) 'Engineering humour: Masculinity, joking and conflict in shop-floor relations', *Organization Studies* 9: 181–99.

Day, D. V., Gronn, P., and Selas, E. (2006) 'Leadership in team-based organizations: On the threshold of a new era', *The Leadership Quarterly* 17(3): 211–16.

Denning, M. (2003) 'Licensed to look: James Bond and the heroism of consumption' in C. Lindner (Ed.) *The James Bond Phenomenon: A Critical Reader*: 56–75. Manchester: Manchester University Press.

Fleming, I. (2004) *On Her Majesty's Secret Service*. London: Penguin Modern Classics.

Fleming, I. (2002) *From Russia with Love*. London: Penguin Books Ltd.

Fleming, I. (2006a) *Casino Royale*. London: Penguin Viking.

Fleming, I. (2006b) *You only live twice*. London: Penguin Books Ltd.

Foucault, M. (1979) *Discipline and Punish: the Birth of the Prison* (trans. Alan Sheridan). New York: Vintage Books.

Geertz, C. (1999) 'Thick description: Toward an interpretive theory of culture' in A. Bryman and R. Burgess (Eds) *Qualitative Research Volume III*: 346–68. London: Sage.

Golden-Biddle, K. and Locke, K. (1993) 'Appealing work: An investigation of how ethnographic texts convince', *Organization Science* 4(4): 595–616.

Gronn, P. (2002) 'Distributed leadership as a unit of analysis', *The Leadership Quarterly* 13(4): 423–51.

Hawkins, B. (2008) 'Double agents: Organizational culture, gender and resistance', *Sociology* 42(3): 418–35.

Hovey, J. (2005) 'Lesbian Bondage, or why Dykes like 007' in E. P. Comentale, S. Watt, and S. Willman (Eds) *Ian Fleming and James Bond: The Cultural Politics of 007*: 42–54. Bloomington, IN: Indiana University Press.

Katzenbach, J. R. and Smith, D. K. (1993) *The Wisdom of Teams: Creating the High Performance Organization.* Boston, MA: Harvard Business School Press.

Lynn Meek, V. (1988) 'Organizational culture: Origins and weaknesses', *Organization Studies* 9(4): 453–73.

Maccoby, M. (2000) 'Narcissistic leaders: The incredible pros, the inevitable cons', *Harvard Business Review* 78(1): 69–77.

Parry, K. W., and Hansen, H. (2007) 'The organizational story as leadership', *Leadership* 3(3): 281–300.

Pettigrew, A. (1979) 'On Studying Organizational Culture', *Administrative Science Quarterly* 24: 570–81.

Pfeffer, L. (1981) 'Management as symbolic action: The creation and maintenance of organizational paradigms', *Research in Organizational Behavior* 31: 1–52.

Pye, A. (2005) 'Leadership and oarganizing: Sensemaking in action', *Leadership* 1(1): 31–49.

Rosen, M. (1985) 'Breakfast at Spiro's: Dramaturgy and dominance', *Journal of Management* 11(2): 31–48.

Rosen, M. (1988) 'You asked for it: Christmas at the Bosses' Expense', *Journal of Management Studies* 25(5): 463–580.

Smircich, L. (1983) 'Concepts of culture and organizational analysis', *Administrative Science Quarterly* 28: 339–58.

Strangleman, T. and Roberts, I. (1999) 'Looking through the window of opportunity: The cultural cleansing of workplace identity', *Sociology* 33(1): 47–67.

Symons, J. (1972) *Bloody Murder: From the Detective Story to the Crime Novel: A History.* London: Faber and Faber Ltd.

Van Maanen, J. (1979) 'The fact of fiction in organizational ethnography', *Administrative Science Quarterly* 24(4): 539–50.

Willmott, H. (1993) 'Strength is ignorance, slavery is freedom: Managing culture in modern organizations', *Journal of Management Studies* 30(4): 515–52.

Woods, J. (2006) 'Best ever Bond?', *The Daily Telegraph,* Monday, 13 November 2006: 19.

Film/Television references

Campbell, M. (dir) (1995) *GoldenEye.* Eon Productions.

Hunt, P. R. (dir) (1969) *On Her Majesty's Secret Service.* Danjaq.

Kring, T. (creator) (2006–08). *Heroes* [Television Series]. NBC.

9

A Wild Sheep Chase: Haruki Murakami

Chris Land, Martyna Śliwa and Sverre Spoelstra

Introduction

In Book III of the Laws, Plato (1997) lays out a series of qualifications that make a leader fit to rule. The first four of these relate to traditional forms of authority through birth and social status: the right of the noble to rule the serf, the parent the child, the master the slave and the old the young. The fifth relates to the authority of those with a superior nature, over the weak. This indeterminate, 'superior nature' parallels the trajectory of trait theories of leadership as well as Great Man theories of leadership, both of which posit a nature (sometimes of divine origin)—'leadership'—then set out in pursuit of this nature. Plato's sixth qualification is knowledge or expertise and the power of those who know over those who do not. Here we find the precursors for the second major tradition in leadership studies: the idea that the right to lead derives from mastery of a set of skills that can be taught and learned. As the French political philosopher Jacques Rancière (2001) notes, however, there is a seventh qualification: the paradoxical qualification of having no qualification but, by chance or lottery, being thrown into a position of leadership.

In this chapter we explore these 'qualifications' to lead through a reading of Haruki Murakami's *A Wild Sheep Chase*. We first introduce the novel and then explore four distinct, but not exclusive, perspectives on leadership: Great Man theories, knowledge-based theories, attribution theories and, finally, what we shall refer to as the 'Weak Man' theory of leadership. While these different perspectives appear sequentially in the novel, giving a suggestion of theoretical development and progress towards our final perspective—the Weak Man theory of leadership—this linear narrative is undercut throughout the novel by its lack of adherence to the genre conventions of the realist novel. In the same way, the structure of our chapter in one sense follows that of a sequential line of inquiry in which a series of perspectives on leadership is explored through the novel, then rejected, building to a final resolution in the Weak Man theory of leadership. However, it is our contention that the real contribution that a novel like *A Wild Sheep Chase* can make to our understanding of leadership is through its refusal to offer an unambiguous resolution to what leadership is and how it works. The power of the novel as a vehicle for organisational studies is not so much in its ability to represent the 'reality' of organisation, however messy, subjective and contradictory that reality may be, but in its opening up of the entire matrix of intelligibility, within which 'organisation', or leadership in this case, takes place (Land and Sliwa, 2009). In seeking inspiration for our thinking of leadership, we use the imagery and events from the novel—in both metaphorical and representational senses—to challenge and restructure dominant understandings of the leadership phenomenon (cf. Sliwa and Cairns, 2007).

Chasing wild sheep

In his text, Murakami does not follow the conventions of a realist novel. Some of the characters are equipped with supernatural features while the narrative itself is full of absurd, surreal and improbable events. The protagonist and narrator, a disillusioned and recently divorced advertising worker, is called into a meeting with a representative of 'the Boss', a shadowy, right-wing political leader and entrepreneur who has effectively monopolised the Japanese media, as 'he keeps a grip on certain centres of political authority and on the core sectors of the public relations industry, there's nothing he can't do' (Murakami, 2003, Page 58). In this meeting, the representative informs our hero that the Boss ascended to his position of leadership from a mundane and even humble life before the Second World War. During the war, while he was sheltering one night in a cave, it appears that the spirit of a mystical sheep entered into him, giving him remarkable powers of leadership and organisation:

> Starting from the spring of 1936, the Boss was proverbially born again, a new man. Up to that point the Boss had been, in a word, a mediocre right-wing activist ... Yet by the summer of 1936, when

he was released from prison, he had risen to the top, in every sense of the word, of the right wing. He had charisma, a solid ideology, powers of speech making to command a passionate response, political savvy, decisiveness, and above all the ability to steer society by using the weaknesses of the masses for leverage.

(Murakami, 2003, Page 117)

Over the years the Boss has used these powers to build a media empire that controls communication and politics in Japan. However, we are told that the sheep has now departed from him, and left him not only bereft of his powers but with a terminal cyst—'a blood bomb' (Murakami, 2003, Page 114)—in his brain.

The novel's protagonist has come to the attention of the Boss's representative because he has recently received a photograph that, on closer inspection, contains this mysterious sheep, and has published it in a small-circulation pamphlet that his company produces. The photograph is considered as evidence that the sheep exists and that there is something exceptional about it that distinguishes it from other sheep on the photograph and from all other sheep in the world:

Aside from that particular sheep, all the others are ordinary Suffolks. Only that one sheep differs. It is far more stocky than the Suffolk, and the fleece is of another colour. Nor is the face black. Something about it strikes one as howsoever more powerful. I showed this photograph to a sheep specialist, and he concluded that this sheep did not exist in Japan. Nor probably anywhere else in the world. So what you are looking at now is a sheep that by all rights should not exist.

(Murakami, 2003, Page 112)

Unwilling to reveal the source of this photograph—an old school friend called 'the Rat' whom he has not seen for years—the protagonist and narrator is charged by the Boss's representative with finding the sheep himself. As the Boss's representative puts it, finding the sheep—and hopefully thereby a new leader—is important in order to make sure that the organisation does not 'plunge into a sea of mediocrity' (Murakami, 2003, Page 119). Deprived of his Boss's vision and direction, the immaculately dressed and conspicuously competent representative is lost as to what to do with himself and can only think to cast about for a replacement leader 'not for reasons of my personal loss, but for the greater good of all' (Murakami, 2003, Page 121).

The Great Man theory of leadership

At a first reading, the premise of the novel suggests a twist upon the classical tradition of the 'Great Man' theory of leadership (Carlyle, 1841; Adair, 1989; Huczynski, 1993, Page 88, cf. Gemmill and Oakley, 1992), which holds that leaders have inherent qualities, either by nature or gifted from above, that make them fit to lead. While some men[1] may be born great, in this tale the Boss is made great by a life-changing encounter and is gifted with leadership: an indeterminate, superior nature, which people naturally follow. The Boss's representative—the 'strange man' as he is called in the book, in which none of the characters has a proper name—here stands as complement and foil to the Boss's leadership; he is a manager, an administrator of things, while the Boss is a leader who can motivate and inspire people to truly exceptional acts (cf. Kotter, 2000). Without the guidance and vision of his leader, the manager is lost and adrift. As such, his sole act of creativity is to commission another to head out in search of leadership and once again bring meaning and direction to his administrative actions. The point here is not only that the manager's own life would lose meaning with the passing of the Boss but that without real leadership to endow action with significance, all that is left is pointless, technocratic calculation:

> The Boss will die. That one Will shall die. Then everything around that Will shall perish. All that shall remain will be what can be counted in numbers. Nothing else will be left. That is why I want to find that sheep.
>
> (Murakami, 2003, Page 122)

Here, then, leadership is juxtaposed with accountancy. While the latter is devoid of meaning and significance, leadership is the creation of a Will that can unite and mobilise, giving significance and meaning to numbers and functions, giving an enterprise direction and purpose. Without this leadership there is no 'enterprise' at all, just meaningless, directionless activity.

But how does one start in a search for leadership? With only four weeks to find the sheep, our hero falls back upon his girlfriend, who spends her life pursuing a portfolio of professional activities:

> She was a part-time proof-reader for a small publishing house, a commercial model specializing in ear shots and a call girl in a discreet

intimate-friends-only club. Which of the three she considered her main occupation, I had no idea. Neither did she.

(Murakami, 2003, Page 27)

The girlfriend's ears are so beautiful that she must keep them covered, or at least, close them so that others are not awed by their beauty. With her ears covered, she is a very plain woman but with them open she is not only exceptionally beautiful but also more sexually potent:

> She'd become so beautiful, it defied understanding. Never had I feasted my eyes on such beauty. Beauty of a variety I'd never imagined existed...
> 'You're extraordinary', I said, after catching my breath.
> 'I know', she said. 'These are my ears in their unblocked state.'
> (Murakami, 2003, Page 38)

The girlfriend is the only significant female character in the novel and both her appearance and behaviour stand in contrast with the rest of the characters. For example, while the Boss's representative is consistently portrayed as rational, calculating, impeccably dressed, clean and tidy, she can be both logical and irrational, plain-looking and extraordinarily beautiful, empathetic, in an understated way, and extremely sexual. She is also generally comforting and engaged, whereas 'the strange man' is threatening and detached from the protagonist's problems. Set against 'the Boss', she figures as parody and counterpoint. While the Boss's exceptional ability to lead is a result of having been possessed by the mystical sheep—an incident about which he was not able to do anything—the girlfriend is in the position to control her supernatural powers through turning off, or closing, her ears:

> If I add up everything you've told me, it seems to come down to this: that up to age twenty you showed your ears. Then one day you hid your ears. And from that day on, not once have you shown your ears. But at such times that you must show your ears, you block off the passageway between your ears and your consciousness.
> (Murakami, 2003, Page 34)

This ability to exercise her agency by active refusal also puts her in contrast with the narrator who becomes completely absorbed in his quest, finding meaning and entering wholly into it. While the girlfriend is crucial to the success of the quest, she chooses to turn back before the chase has ended.

The narrator's girlfriend, of course, plays a pivotal role in the development of the novel's plot. But, in addition, paying attention to this particular character, especially in juxtaposition with those of the Boss's representative, the Boss and the protagonist, allows us to observe with greater clarity how strongly the model of leadership articulated here corresponds with, and can be read as simultaneously an exemplar and critique of, the Great Man theory of leadership. While the representative's need for the Boss's will, and the 'chase' itself, suggest that the Great Man is needed for leadership, and that such a man cannot easily be replaced, the lack of agency of the other characters, compared to the girlfriend, undercuts this interpretation by which the Great Man is the source of all direction and meaning. Unlike the representative and the narrator, the girlfriend is able to manage not only her unusual portfolio of employment, but also the search for leadership itself, all without the direct, external direction of a sheep or leader.

In contrast to this self-direction, the Boss is endowed with leadership only because of his strange possession, the sheep, and the hallucinations and visions that this gives him. With the great leader about to die, it is impossible that his second in command should succeed him because he is not gifted in the same way. 'The strange man' is a manager and as such cannot learn to become a leader but must search around for another to replace his dying Boss. By identifying the one discernable feature that distinguishes his Boss from all the others around him—his possession by the sheep—the manager concocts a search for leadership that is based on finding the source of leadership, the sheep itself and finding another who it may enter and endow with great vision and leadership.

Although the process of reasoning by which the Boss's representative reaches the conclusion that it is the sheep that is the determinant of great leadership is entirely rational, this is not a form of leadership that anyone can learn. As the representative acknowledges when asked what he will do once he finds the sheep:

> Nothing at all. There is probably nothing I could do. The scale of things is far too vast for me to do much of anything. My only wish is to see it all out at last with my own eyes. And if that sheep should wish anything, I shall do all in my power to comply. Once the Boss dies, my life will have lost almost all meaning anyway.
>
> (Murakami, 2003, Page 122)

From this account, leadership can be experienced—the manager here wishes to 'see it... with my own eyes' and the girlfriend can hear the voice of leadership—but it cannot be properly understood or known. Its source is a mysterious gift from above. When the Boss became a leader he was 'proverbially born again, a new man' (2003, Page 117). But what turned him into a new man (the sheep) does not lend itself to rational comprehension. As the Boss's representative says of sheep in Japan generally:

> ... up until Meiji, few Japanese had ever seen a sheep or understood what one was. In spite of its relatively popular standing as one of the twelve zodiacal animals of the ancient Chinese calendar, nobody knew with any accuracy what kind of animal it was. That is to say, it might as well have been an imaginary creature of the order say of a dragon or phoenix.
>
> (Murakami, 2003, Page 110–11)

The key point here is that sheep are characterised in near mythical terms, as something that can signify without direct connection to concrete reality. As such, the leadership that the sheep symbolises partakes of the fantastic and inexplicable and is not subject to rational analysis and empirical understanding. It is, then, suggested to us that leadership is something of a fantasy that exists as much, if not more, in the dreaming and needs of a follower as it does in the tangible reality of a leader. This overturning of leadership is reinforced by the Boss's physical absence from the action of the novel. He only ever appears as an object of indirect discourse, through 'the strange man's strange tale', for example, or through conversations with his chauffeur. This framing of the Boss—the exemplary leader—as an absent presence in Murakami's novel, coupled with the intimations of sheep's mythical, fantastic status already focuses our attention on the role of followers in constructing the phenomenon of leadership, another of the perspectives that Murakami weaves throughout his complicated and—from the point of view of leadership theories—often contradictory, tale. We will return to this theme later in the chapter.

The sheep professor

Immediately following his observations on the mythical significance of sheep in Japan, 'the strange man' enters into a discussion of how sheep were first imported from America and the subsequent economic demise of Japanese sheep farming when faced with competition from New Zealand and Australia. This move locates the model and image of leadership represented in the novel within a geo-political system of cultural, economic and military domination. It also suggests a material tangibility to leadership and sheep that renders them susceptible to more conventional scientific analysis and knowledge. This move from mythical explanation to a more prosaic material analysis also reflects the shift in leadership theories away from an attempt to identify the Great Man of leadership to an understanding of leadership as a set of identifiable skills that can be categorised, dissected, analysed and reproduced through training and teaching in an educational context. Here the leader is not so much marked out for greatness by fate or the gods— or by a sheep—but is carefully selected, nurtured and trained in requisite skills and techniques.

In a crucial episode in the novel, the narrator's girlfriend chooses a hotel for the couple, who, having travelled from Tokyo to Hokkaido in search of the sheep, need to find a place to stay. Scanning the local telephone directory over a cup of coffee, the girlfriend decides that she likes the sound of the hotel 'The Dolphin'. Initially the hotel proves to be a less than salubrious place to stay, infested with cockroaches, filth and having no café or restaurant. After a few days of fruitless research in the library and around town, the couple are talking to the owner/receptionist when he mentions that before he turned it into a hotel the building was the Hokkaido Ovine Hall, a repository for papers and resources concerning sheep and the home of the Hokkaido Ovine Association (HOA). At this point, the owner's father is introduced to the story and becomes a significant figure in the search for the sheep:

> ... he was the former director of Ovine Hall, and anyway he knows all there is to know about sheep. Everyone calls him the Sheep Professor.
> (Murakami, 2003, Page 178)

It transpires that, following a period in which sheep farming fell upon hard times, the HOA decided to disband. The owner's father bought the property and continued his previous research into sheep from his base on the second floor of the building while his son turned the rest of the premises into a hotel.

Following this revelation our protagonist shows The Dolphin's owner the picture that started off this whole wild sheep chase. The hotel owner immediately recognises it and shows the couple that there is an identical photograph, now dusty with age, hanging high up on the reception wall. As we are told the life story of the Sheep Professor, we discover that he has also been possessed by the strange sheep of leadership, and may even have brought it to Japan from China. The sheep, however, did not stay long with the Professor and left him in 1936, around the time that it entered into the Boss. As well as sharing his story over a meal, the Sheep Professor is able to identify the location where the photograph of the sheep was taken. It is his old ranch, high up in the mountains. He also reveals that someone else has been around to ask him about this photograph and the ranch: the narrator's childhood friend, the person who first sent him the photograph that started off the whole chase, a young man only ever referred to in the novel by his nickname, 'the Rat'.

As well as providing a crucial link on the road to finding the sheep, the episode with the Sheep Professor also suggests a somewhat different understanding of leadership. While 'the strange man'—the Boss's representative—is quite prepared to accept that leadership is mysterious, and something that he will neither attain nor understand, the Sheep Professor is an academic by inclination. A child prodigy at school and university, and a former rising star in the elite of the Japanese administration, the Sheep Professor seeks to understand the leader–sheep phenomenon through academic study. He reads 'ethnological studies and folklore relating to sheep', interviews people and gathers statistics and data on sheep, all to increase his knowledge (Murakami, 2003, Page 188).

But his study of sheep is not untouched by his experience of being possessed by the sheep of leadership. In the end, just like the Boss's representative, the Sheep Professor does not manage to objectify leadership and also delivers a version of the Great Sheep Theory of Leadership:

> The sheep that enters a body is thought to be immortal. And so too the person who hosts the sheep is thought to become immortal. However, should the sheep escape, the immortality goes. It's all up to the sheep. If the sheep likes its host, it'll stay for decades. If not—zip!—it's gone. People abandoned by sheep are called the 'sheepless'. In other words, people like me.
>
> (Murakami, 2003, Page 188)

He also believes that the understanding of leadership as something that comes to life through possession by sheep has a long history and can be found in geographical contexts outside Japan:

> In parts of Northern China and Mongol territory, it's not uncommon to hear of sheep entering people's bodies. Among the locals, it's

believed that a sheep entering the body is a blessing from the gods. For instance, in one book published in Yuan dynasty it's written that a 'star-bearing white sheep' entered the body of Genghis Khan.

(Murakami, 2003, Page 188)

If we also take the story as an allegory of the search for leadership, then we can see that this expertise, lodged in a book-filled, musty, old room in a decaying institution, is crucial for the quest for 'leadership'. Without the knowledge and understanding of the old professor, obtained through his capacity to spiritually commune with sheep, the search would have hit a dead end. It is only this mystical knowledge that allows the chase to move forward. It is not hard to see a link with academic studies of leadership, which also claim to produce objective and scientific studies of leadership but oftentimes romanticise their object of study to such an extent that they too appear to spiritually commune with Great Men.

Follow the sheep

This suggestion that 'leadership' is an ultimately inexplicable gift bestowed upon an individual, places the agency responsible for the production of leadership outside mere human beings, even great leaders themselves. As we have already suggested, the only character with active agency in the novel (other than the Rat, as we shall see shortly) seems to be the girlfriend, who is, at least, able to take control of her own actions and responses to the voice of leadership or the demands of the quest. Of course, if we read the novel literally and remain at the level of the dominant narrative, then we might suggest that the sheep is really the prime mover in the story. However plausible, this account is at best one of many presented in the novel. Once we step back from the action, this idea that great leadership is the product of possession by a sheep is quite clearly so absurd as to offer no explanatory traction. Even more crucially, throughout the novel we are given several indications that the characters do not themselves really believe this version of the leadership story. For example, before embarking on his chase, the protagonist questions whether the leadership sheep exists at all. However, it turns out that whether it does or not is irrelevant to the quest itself:

'Do I have any choice?' I asked. 'And what if no such sheep with a star on its back ever existed in the first place?'

'It is still the same. For you and me, there is only whether you find the sheep or not. There are no in-betweens. I am sorry to have to put it this way, but as I have already said, we are taking you up on your proposition. You hold the ball, you had better run for the goal. Even if there turns out not to have been any goal.'

(Murakami, 2003, Page 123)

At the end of the quest, when the sheep has finally been found, it becomes clear that it is the action of the protagonist in searching for, or *following*, the sheep that is necessary for the realisation of leadership.

After arriving at the house up in the mountains, where the sheep has been tracked to and is now in possession of the Rat, the narrator discovers that the Rat is not there. The girlfriend also disappears. The narrator drinks alcohol and spends the evening reading Sherlock Holmes. Later on, in the house, he finds a book about Pan-Asianism. In the book, he comes across the name of the Boss and the place of his origin—the location at which he had finally arrived after the long search. He realises that the things he has made so much effort to find out about, other people already knew, including 'the strange man'. He becomes angry and frustrated, and feels cheated:

Here I was, smack in the centre of everything without a clue. At every turn, I'd been way off base, way off the mark. Of course, you could probably say the same thing about my whole life. In that sense, I suppose I had no one to blame. All the same, what gave them the right to treat me like this? I'd been used, I'd been beaten, I'd been wrung dry.

(Murakami, 2003, Page 266)

If there was a purpose at all to sending the narrator on the search, it was not to find the sheep, whose location was already known, but because the chase itself was necessary to realise the Rat's potential as a leader.

It is the action of the protagonist in searching for, or *following* the sheep, that is necessary for the production/emergence of leadership, and his relations with ears (through the girlfriend) and expertise (through the Professor) that constitute him, not as a leader but as an *effective* follower, that is, one who can *effectuate* leadership through the convincing performance of *followership*. We thus consider this as not a simple production of leadership by the follower, but of leader through follower, both produced by a sensory and discursive articulation of 'leadership' that co-constitutes both parties, and which is made possible only on condition that this co-constitution is denied. The philosopher Slavoj Žižek puts this very clearly:

> The subjects think they treat a certain person as a king because he is already in himself a king, while in reality this person is king only insofar as the subjects treat him as one.... But the crucial point is that it is a positive, necessary condition for the performative effect to take place that the king's charisma be experienced precisely as an immediate property of the person-king. The moment the subjects take cognizance of the fact that the king's charisma is a performative effect, the effect itself is aborted.
>
> (Žižek, 1991, Page 33)

What does this performative effect establish? For Gemmill and Oakley (1992), the myth of leadership represents 'a regressive wish to return to the symbiotic environment of the womb', that is, a place without anxiety and existential insecurity. Such conceptualisation of the relationship between the leader and his followers as fulfilling the role of providing the followers with ontological security is directly referred to in the novel in the context of the protagonist's encounter with the Boss's chauffeur:

> 'The Boss is an honorable man. After the Lord, the most godly person I've ever met.'
> 'You've met God?'
> 'Certainly. I telephone Him every night.' (...)
> 'The Boss gave me it a few years ago' said the chauffeur out of nowhere.
> 'Gave you what?'
> 'God's telephone number.' (...)
> 'He told just you, alone, in secret?'
> 'Yes. Just me, in secret. He's a fine gentleman.'
>
> (Murakami, 2003, Page 127)

The relationship between the chauffeur and the Boss can therefore be seen as one of a religious nature. The Boss gives the chauffeur access to God himself, and thanks to this, the chauffeur's life concerns become resolved:

All you have to do is to speak honestly about whatever concerns you or troubles you. No matter how trivial you might think it is. God never gets bored and never laughs at you.

(Murakami, 2003, Page 128)

Devoid of the traditional forms of meaning and security, such as the religious beliefs in which the chauffeur takes solace, the majority of the characters in the book drift without purpose, seeking it ultimately in a sheep/leader. We also recognise this idea in the comments from The Dolphin hotel owner that the Sheep Professor, his father, has been happy (in a sense) because the search for the sheep gave his life structure and meaning. For the hotel owner, the search for leadership is a worthwhile way of going about one's life as it provides purpose:

'I sometimes wish I could go off in search of something,' he declared, 'but before getting even that far, I myself wouldn't have the slightest idea what to search for. Now my father, he's someone who been searching for something all his life. He's still searching today. Ever since I was a little boy, my father's told me about the white sheep that came to him in his dreams. So I always thought that's what life is like. An ongoing search . . . . My father's seventy-three now and still no sheep. I don't know if the thing even exists. Still, I can't help think that it hasn't been such a bad life for him. I want to see my father happy now more than ever, but he just belittles me and won't listen to a word I say. That's because I have no purpose in life.'

(Murakami, 2003, Page 194)

But what happens when the search is completed? What does our protagonist find when the quest ends and he discovers the sheep?

The Weak Man theory of leadership

When he finally speaks with his friend the Rat—which takes place during a spell of feverish hallucination—he is told that the necessary pre-condition of leadership lies not within the extraordinary abilities of an individual, but in a weakness:

'The key point here is weakness,' said the Rat. 'Everything begins from there. Can you understand what I'm getting at? . . . Weakness is something that rots in the body. Like gangrene. I've felt it ever since I was a teenager. That's why I'm always on edge. There's this something inside you that's rotting away and you feel it all along...It's the same as a hereditary disease, weakness. No matter how much you understand it, there's nothing you can do to cure yourself. It's not going to go away with a clap of the hand. It just keeps getting worse and worse.'

'Weakness towards what?'
'Everything. Moral weakness, weakness of consciousness, then there's the weakness of existence itself.'

(Murakami, 2003, Page 282)

The Rat suggests that the sheep which possesses an individual feeds on weakness. It takes advantage of the weakness and enters the individual by luring him into what it offers:

And it was enough to draw me in. More than I'd care to confess. It's not something I can explain in words. It's like, well, like a blast furnace that smelts down everything it touches. A thing of such beauty, it drives you out of your mind. But it's hair-raising evil. Give your body over to it and everything goes. Consciousness, values, emotions, pain, everything. Gone. What it comes closest to is a dynamo manifesting that vital force at the root of all life in one solitary point of the universe.

(Murakami, 2003, Page 283)

We now witness a dramatic reversal of the great man theory of leadership, and a highly original one: the gift of leadership, that presents itself in the form of a mysterious sheep, does not befall great men but, on the contrary, sneaks into weak men because they alone cannot deal with the realities of everyday life. Leadership, then, provides a comfort zone, not only for the led, as Gemmill and Oakley (1992) argue, but even for 'leaders', who necessarily allow themselves to be subjectively (re)constructed as leader, with all of the behavioural and performative expectations that this position demands.

But the most surprising twist is yet to come. From the conversation between our protagonist and the Rat we learn that the leadership sheep tried to find a new home in the body of the Rat, turning the Rat into 'the Sheep Man'. This time, however, the leadership sheep made a fatal misjudgement: the Rat was not as weak as the sheep with a star on its back thought. Contrary to the Boss and others possessed by the Will of this sheep, 'the Sheep Man's behaviour seemed to reflect *the Rat's will*'

(Murakami, 2003, Page 260, emphasis added). With the Rat's will being stronger than the will of the starred sheep, they both go down in the Rat's suicide:

> 'What happened was this,' said the Rat. 'I died with the sheep in me. I waited until the sheep was fast asleep, then I tied a rope over the beam in the kitchen and hanged myself. There wasn't enough time for the sucker to escape.'
> 'Did you have to go that far?'
> 'Yes, I had to go that far. If I waited, the sheep would have controlled me absolutely. It was my last chance.'
>
> (Murakami, 2003, Page 281)

So in the end the truly heroic sacrifice is not carried out by the leader, which is how we normally like to portray him, but is carried out against him. Murakami reminds us that truly great men (and *women* we may add at this stage) rebel against the reassuring but false comfort zone that leadership all too often establishes. This resistance against leadership, however, is not realised by demystifying the leadership phenomenon (this is what critical scholars of leadership often call for: for example, Gemmill and Oakley, 1992; Jackson and Parry, 2008). One must be as unreal as leadership itself. The strength to be unreal when it mattered most was indeed what characterises the Rat, as we learn from a much earlier passage in the book where our protagonist recalls that

> '[The Rat] was so...more than unreal. Do you know what I mean?'
> 'I think so.'
> 'I guess it took someone as unreal as him to break through my own unreality.'
>
> (Murakami, 2003, Page 100)

Perhaps this is also why fiction can tell us more about leadership than many of the Sheep Professors that we normally consult on the topic.

Note

1. The use of the gendered term is quite intentional here, reflecting not only a gender bias in writing on leadership but also a significant gender dynamic in the novel.

References

Adair, John (1989) *Great Leaders*. Guildford: Talbot Adair Press.

Carlyle, Thomas (1841) *On Heroes, Hero-Worship and the Heroic in History*. Oxford: Oxford University Press, 1904 edition.

Gemmill, Gary and Judith Oakley (1992) 'Leadership: An alienating social myth?', *Human Relations*, 45(2): 113–29.

Huczynski, Andrzej (1993) *Management Gurus: What Makes Them and How to Become One*. London: Thomson Business Press.

Jackson, Brad and Ken Parry (2008) *A Very Short, Fairly Interesting and Reasonably Cheap Book about Studying Leadership*. London: Sage.

Kotter, John (2000) 'What leaders really do', *Harvard Business Review*, 68(3): 103–11.

Land, Chris and Martyna Sliwa (2009) 'The novel and organization', *Journal of Organizational Change Management*, 22(4): 349–56.

Murakami, Haruki (2003) *A Wild Sheep Chase*. London: Vintage.

Plato (1997) *Complete Works*. Indianapolis, IN: Jackett.

Rancière, Jacques (2001) 'Ten theses on politics', *Theory & Event*, 5(3).

Sliwa, Martyna and George Cairns (2007) 'The novel as a vehicle for organizational inquiry: Engaging with the complexity of social and organizational commitment', *Ephemera: Theory and Politics in Organization*, 7(2): 309–25.

Žižek, Slavoj (1991) *Looking Awry: An Introduction to Jacques Lacan through Popular Culture*. Cambridge, MA: The MIT Press.

10
Leadership and Expectation: Thomas Pynchon

Peter Pelzer and Peter Case

'What can I do? There is absolutely nothing I can change.' This kind of statement will be familiar to anyone who has worked in a complex organisation. It denotes a vague feeling of helplessness brought on by one's perceived inability to influence the organisation or pursue meaningful courses of action in the face of its anonymous 'hierarchy' and powerful bosses. However, the statement takes on a different order of salience and implication when uttered by a top manager. In a concrete case known to one of the authors, this *crie de cour* came from a director of what was, at the time, the second largest bank in Germany. The author was, himself, a member of the second tier of management and responsible to the executive board. Together with one colleague he was responsible for the complete back-office activities concerning transactions for securities, custody and payments. These departments had a combined workforce of about 3000 employees.

The director's utterance was, in this instance, not only remarkable considering his position in the hierarchy, it was also in direct contradiction to his physical demeanour. Almost two metres tall with broad shoulders and a loud voice, he had an imposing, not to say intimidating, appearance. His behaviour in the workplace was invariably intended to reinforce his dominance and, all in all, he considered himself to be a very successful manager in several parts of the bank and its overseas branches. So why did someone in such a powerful position feel the need to make such an exclamation of helplessness? Is this an expression of doubt about the centre of power by a person who, during his entire career, aimed at becoming part of the centre? A desperate insight, told in a tone of disbelief, that sovereignty is just an illusion, an attribution by those who are far from the centre?

In his novel, *Gravity's Rainbow*, Thomas Pynchon (2000) seems to attack the seemingly self-evident assumption of the organisational concentration of power at 'the top'. Hidden in a complicated plot and disguised within his reflexively rich and florid style of writing, he holds a basic insight for organisation theory, we suggest. Such a view would certainly be consistent with Styhre's conclusion that Pynchon 'employs a highly complex and heterogeneous language to make certain social practices and conditions problematic' (Styhre, 2004, Page 317–18).

The action of *Gravity's Rainbow* takes place in a Second World War setting replete with paranoia and conspiracy. The novel imparts a social phenomenology of complex organisations that, in its psychotropic disorientation, speaks of the essentially imaginary nature of leadership and organisational processes. By analysing carefully selected quotations we want to indicate that this novel can help us to understand why 'imagined leadership' is such an attractive or seductive notion and why, moreover, the myth persists even after its fictional character has been revealed. The taken-for-granted centre of an organisation, the CEO, may be absent, or may even not exist at all (as in the example taken from Pynchon's novel), but the organisation can still function perfectly well. That the fiction of the existence of a centre must be maintained is the almost paradoxical conclusion we arrive at from our analysis of Pynchon's book. In a perhaps surprising turn, we will also point to the collusion of organisational researchers in reinforcing this imaginary construction.

It could be said that Pynchon's writing is philosophy put into practice: fiction disclosing organisational phenomena. When reading his novels the names of such philosophers and social theorists as Michel Foucault, Jean-Francois Lyotard, Jean Baudrillard, Jacques Derrida come immediately to mind. Out of the numerous possible examples, and being mindful of the present collection's preoccupation, we have selected one particular scene from the novel to illustrate our argument. Despite the sometimes bewildering complexity of perspectives in Pynchon's text, the following passage contains in miniature an entire thesis on organisation. In it one of the novel's main characters, Slothrop, has finally tracked down the location of what he has deduced must be the 'centre' of an organisation concerned with the design of a top secret military rocket:

> Here Slothrop stages a brilliant Commando raid, along with faithful companion Blodgett Waxwing, on Shell Mex house itself—right into the heart of the Rocket's own branch office in London. Mowing down platoons of heavy security with his little Sten, kicking aside

nubile and screaming WRAY secretaries (how else is there to react, even in play?), savagely looting files, throwing Molotov cocktails, the Zootsuit Zanies at last crashing into the final sanctum with their trousers up around their armpits, smelling of singed hair, spilled blood, to find not Mr. Duncan Sandys [the Shell Mex boss] cowering before their righteousness, nor open window, gypsy flight, scattered fortune cards, nor even a test of wills with the great consortium itself—but only a rather dull room, business machines arrayed around the walls calmly blinking, files of cards pierced frail as *sugar faces*, frail as the last German walls standing without support after the bombs have been and now twisting high above, threatening to fold down out of the sky from the force of the wind that has blown the smoke away...The smell of firearms is in the air, and there's not an office dame in sight. The machines chatter and ring to each other.

(Pynchon, 2000, Page 298f)

Imagination—nothing else. This is obvious from the outset, but nevertheless it is much more than *mere* fancy. Fiction overtakes reality via reality's fictional character. The search for a centre of organisation, access to the central person who *decides*, who is *responsible*, the *one* (in this case Mr Duncan Sandys), whom one has always already wanted to call to account, leads to *nobody*. In place of a flesh-and-blood human one finds merely a disembodied facsimile of organisation as could only be produced through the operation of a literary conceit. The disappointment, however, is real enough and offers insight into one's own self-deception:

But Duncan Sandys is only a name, a function in this. 'How high does it go?' is not even the right kind of question to be asking, because the organisation charts have all been set up by Them, the titles and names filled in by Them.

(Pynchon, 2000, Page 299)

The 'wrong question' about the subject which controls everything turns immediately and defensively into an inclination to answer this question positively. It was *Them* who wrote the organisational charts; it was *their* imagination set in the scene. Hence Pynchon deduces:

Proverbs for Paranoids, 3: If they can get you asking the wrong questions, they don't have to worry about answers.

(Pynchon, 2000, Page 299)

This proverb, however, sounds wrong. Who could be the one asking the wrong questions? This generalised 'other'—the 'you' of the proverb—is also just an act of imagination and, as such, the result of an incapacity to imagine a human order alternative to the one created and controlled by an almighty central controller. Trying to imagine it differently, one would start to consider a world without a centre. The absence of a truth or divine principle—a central rule—provided by a centre makes plurality of ethics, decision and action possible. This is a plurality which goes beyond a decentralisation to a de-centring; it becomes 'ex-centric' (Hutcheon, 1988, Page 65). Not simply eccentric in the sense of having moved out of the middle but in the double meaning of being out of norm and therefore not belonging to the centre. It is the creation of differences beyond hierarchies, of differences to the other that this text prompts us to contemplate. The centre which once judged the differences and brought alignment of thought and action becomes outmoded as a benchmark of organisational conduct. Difference no longer means erring from the straight and narrow, but, freed from normative constraint of a single truth defined by a central power, becomes the condition of the possibility of possibilities.

With Derrida's (1998) understanding of differences the supplementary character of a 'Slothropian' understanding of organisation and hierarchy comes into focus. The centre has no presence. It is just the trace left by supplementing the centre with the understandings of those who use the image of the centre in their daily actions. It is always changed by using it, supplementing slightly different meanings and changing the centre as such with each use of it. The centre is a *différance*, always already moved in time and space—differed and deferred. Revisiting the centre, therefore, always confronts one with its disappearance. One is disturbed to discover that the centre already vanished. Indeed, it is a disappearance that calls into question whether it ever existed at all. The centre is just an empty room and the suspicion arises that it would have made no difference even if Duncan Sandys—the person imagined to be at the top—would actually have been present when Slothrop penetrated the inner sanctum. 'What could I do?', we can almost hear Sandys saying; 'I'm not responsible. There is nothing I can change.'

Pynchon's organisation works without a heart. The important person—in the end the decisive one right in the centre of the organisation, without whom the organisation cannot exist—is nothing but an empty myth. As such, this 'leader' is a construction and reflection of a hierarchic worldview, within which notions of god, truth, science and rationality, as well as belief systems and eternal laws, are formed.

Everything follows from this worldview or is subsumed within it. Once the belief in ultimate explanations is lost, as for example Lyotard (1984) claimed with his proclaimed end of the grand narrative, the deductions from these narratives also become questionable. The men who invaded the heart of the London headquarters realise that 'the organisation charts have all been set up by Them, the titles and names filled in by Them' (Pynchon, 2000, Page 299). However, they, Slothrop and Waxwing, were not taken in by the myth. It is no trap, no wrong question that somebody got them to ask. *This is by no means less misleading from their point of view, however, if it results in denying the capillary effects of power, which, in the Foucauldian tradition, are no longer attributable to a single individual but, instead, are performed by interaction between innumerable points in a complex network.* Meaning? Power, in this sense, is the play of uneven and moving relations (Foucault, 1983, Page 115). Microphysics of power therefore is a more adequate term for interpreting this moment in the novel (and this moment only) in which the subject is profoundly perturbed by organisation.

The individual feels bewildered and lost in the face of ever more powerful and unfathomable structures, processes and obscure modes of organising. She does not determine her life any more; someone seems to be playing games with her yet she is unable to identify the facts and conditions which would prove, unequivocally, that she is the subject of this ludic conspiracy. She is left only with a persistent hunch that there is someone behind the whole affair. Accordingly, Pynchon formulates one more proverb for paranoids: 'You may never get to touch the Master, but you can tickle his creatures' (Pynchon, 2000, Page 282). The frivolous play with fantasies about conspiracies, unrecognised mechanisms and powers ruling the world is one way to compensate for the claustrophobic sense of there being no room for individual manoeuvre. Pynchon's novels are full of characters imputing the existence of dark forces and trying to discover the mechanisms behind complex conspiracies. That such paranoia is more a matter of subjective projection than objective fact is what Slothrop has to learn before realising that what led him to his goal was equally obscure. In his excitement the memory was lost: '... do you remember the way in, all the twists and turns? No. You weren't looking' (Pynchon, 2000, Page 299). In the daily routine many things are so self-evident that we do not think about them. The absence of the expected makes us hesitate and reflect on why a centre-less organisation is obviously functioning well in empowering and enabling the people working in it but can also have restricting, even destructive effects on the individual despite this central absence.

The organisation's centre is, to use a concept of Jean Baudrillard (1978), just a simulacrum; a simulacrum, however, that does productive or performative work. *When signs become simulacra they point to no reality at all.* It seems to me that this article requires a certain specialised knowledge before one can understand it. Will our readers have that knowledge? I do not. In Pynchon's description of the centre, the CEO Duncan Sandys is just such a simulacrum. Sandys is a sign for the centre from which all power and agency of the organisation seems to originate. But under closer scrutiny, the centre turns out not to exist at all. It is just an empty image which nevertheless serves the purpose of a justification for the actions of the organisation.

There is another level on which the Pynchon extract above can be read. Tyrone Slothrop and Blodgett Waxwing could be seen as organisational researchers facing the challenges involved in gaining access and making sense of what they subsequently encounter (Pelzer, 1995). Tyrone Slothrop realises after the event that he had 'asked the wrong questions'. He believed in the myth which positioned Duncan Sandys within the organisational sanctum; one in which Sandys seemed to be steering the fate of the organisation. Slothrop, as organisational researcher, *projected his subjectivity as co-creator of the object of research onto the sheerly imagined figure of Duncan Sandys?*—the 'real' creator of the organisation according to this paranoid mind. Through his encounter with a quotidian office void of human life, Slothrop confronts a complementary emptiness within himself—the self-induced myth that made him ask the wrong question in the first place. An equivalence of the categories of management and researcher, and workforce and researched, suddenly present themselves. This would not be in their role of taking revenge, machine guns in hand, but in their preparation of the org charts. This is not as arbitrary as it might appear. A surprisingly open description of the difference between workforce and top management can already be found in the work of the German economist Erich Gutenberg (1983). He understands work as comprising an 'elementary' and a 'dispositive' factor. The 'elementary' human resource is the factor which is at the *disposal* of the 'dispositive' factor, a framing which might lead one (mistakenly) to think that Gutenberg is proffering a managerialist theory of organisation. The dispositive factor decides how and what is done in the organisation; it is the creative element and as such more than human resource control. The dispositive factor gives orders and takes the basic decisions about the development of the organisation. It is the power concentrated at the top. The elementary factor is not creative; it has to be efficient. Top management is therefore assigned to the dispositive factor, which proves to be, ultimately, the main motor of organisation. While the elementary factors can be captured quantitatively by their productivity, the dispositive factor shows its independence not only by determining the performance of the other factor, but more importantly because it 'cannot be dissolved completely into rationality' (Gutenberg, 1983, Page 133). The border is drawn quite sharply. It is here, at the top of the company, in the bosses, where subjectivity manifests itself in each consequential decision of the leader. Scientific method is unable to reveal, inform or explain the secret of correct decisions: 'The dispositive factor cannot be dissolved into procedures. The big decisions have their roots in that irrationality which remains the secret of the individual kind of thinking and acting' (Gutenberg, 1983, Page 147).

Gutenberg's description of the dispositive factor corresponds well with the self-disclosures and accounts of prominent top managers (for example, as described in Iacocca and Novak, 1984; Trump and Schwarz, 1988; Hansen, 1992), whose apparent lack of empathy is quite astonishing, and contrasts markedly with attempts at rationally leading a company. The researcher, who sees herself as a subject, reproduces her image of herself in characterising those at the top of the company who are able to make 'big decisions'. These are projections of personalities who have an independent kind of thinking and acting. Organisation charts seduce: the shape of a pyramid leads the eye to the top where there are relatively few positions and occupants. One is led to conclude, of course, that only the important few can reside here at the top. Moreover, these kinds of charts are indifferent to the kind of organisation they represent, be it a private or public company with a CEO or research department with a professor at its apex. They look much the same and impart the same kind of message. With the safe feeling of congeniality one's feeling for a reality beyond this representation of order gets lost.

That the researcher wants to take part vicariously in the prestige of those who are capable of winning recognition for their subjectivity is one motive to consider. However, this is not the only point. What is demonstrated through this understanding of the human workforce as an elementary factor is just how easy and common it is for a subject (leader/researcher) to see and treat everyone else as an object.

This insight draws us to a moment when, or point at which, the role of theory in the production of practice could be analysed. We say 'could be', as long as the wrong question obscures one's line of sight.

Proverbs for Paranoids, 2: The innocence of the creatures is in inverse proportion to the immorality of the Master.

(Pynchon, 2000, Page 287)

The Master remains hidden while we tickle his [*sic*] creatures. His pleasure from successfully getting people to ask the wrong questions (and therefore not needing to worry about the answers) because of his so obvious absence is, at the same time, troubled by the feeling of his noticeable presence. The office is not empty after all. The narrator is present and everything we as readers/observers of the narrative know is down to his account. Yet we know still more: that it was *Them*, Slothrop and his partner, who drew up the plans and who are therefore confronted by the results of their own actions. *The trip around the mobius strip is completed: the insight into the self-referential nature of the situation points ineluctably to the enmeshment of social reality and imagination. The constraint of structures and the paranoid search for the Master, fiction and the fictional character of reality, are exposed.*

Unsuspecting, another subject—the commentator, Slothrop, who feels so bad about the Master's influence that he wants to take revenge—emerges in the guise of a creature who hatches plans to search for the Master in order to accuse him of his immorality. The Master's absence makes him wonder. Slothrop is thrown back on himself and realises the guilelessness as his own immorality, he himself being the Master of his own guilelessness. No conspiracy, just the normal ignorance of his own contribution to the construction of this puzzling reality. Entering the 'sanctum', Slothrop reveals his presupposition regarding the importance of the room and its potential inhabitant. Slothrop's reflections represent metaphysical thinking in an environment which has long since abandoned its belief in a god and trust in grand narratives. What remains is an understanding of the environment's local and temporal limitations. The belief in the centre, in an almighty figure standing for the organisation, defining its character, capable of being responsible for what the organisation does, is the fading ideal of lost times. This is the core message, we contend, of Pynchon's little scene. Believing in it denies the part we play in constructing the reality we feel restricted by, the strategies of self-defeat that we all pursue.

This is not to say that the iron cage (Weber, 1970), the panopticon (Foucault, 1977) or the castle (Kafka, 1986), to list a few iconic tropes of organisation theory, disappear. They persist and still have effects. The aporia that arises from acknowledging the absence of a centre while at the same time feeling the restricting effects of organisation must remain.

If we could acknowledge that we don't need a Duncan Sandys—that he is just a figure at the top representing the whole—we could achieve a less deluded view of the complexity of these social constructions. This is not, as may be inferred from the iconic tropes just mentioned, left unnoticed by academic research. German economic historian Werner Pumpe expresses a similar view in the context of the changing conditions faced by German export-oriented corporations who find themselves integrated into globalised markets (Pumpe, 2005). The demands on the board, he argues, have changed significantly. On the one hand, the companies are restructured with accelerating frequency, often following fashions (Kieser, 1996). Ideas like diversification are succeeded by completely opposing concepts like concentration on core competencies. The companies, however, follow the advice of international consulting companies (Kieser, 2002) in order to gain a better position in the view of the financial markets, which provide resources for the realisation of their strategies. This goes along with a different attitude of the markets[1] to the corporates themselves, or, to be precise, it is a logical consequence of this particular strategic nexus. The companies turn from actors into objects of investment where arguments like a strong local tradition, workforce, even good management do not have a significant value any more. The price of a company is set by the international financial markets and their actors on stock exchanges and in hedge funds and private equity funds. In fact, every company is exposed to market forces and potentially prey to a take-over by another company. Management in these fluid markets has to be able to handle both the complexity of global markets for commodities and services and the markets for companies. This leads Pumpe to a paradoxical conclusion: 'As this is practically impossible, the increasing acknowledgement of management and the comparably high salaries paid serve to hide exactly this incapability of management. Not least by extreme salaries, capacity and responsibility are fabricated exactly because they have become impossible' (Pumpe, 2005, Page 19, translation PP). The dilemma is that management has become impossible, but the belief in its possibility remains essential. This is a strong statement, denying facets of management dealing with sense-making, judgement and imagination, human aspects beyond the figures representing them. The changed circumstances as described by Pumpe, however, clearly describe the restricting factor: in the world of hedge funds, corporate finance and take-overs the rationality of figures prevails and leaves no space for the qualitative facets of leadership.

Pynchon confronts us with a world in which the organisation (dys-) functions perfectly well in the absence of a CEO, and Pumpe provides an explanation for this. The importance of the figure at the top is nothing but a consequence of the viewer's or subject's expectation—often paranoid in Pynchon's hands—that such a person *has* to be there. The general lesson for leadership is that *the power, influence and effectiveness of a leader rests not so much in the supposed objective qualities or capacities of the person at the top as in the often delusional assumptions and expectations of those having dependency on an organisation and its imagined leader.*

There is no way out, Slothrop realises:

> The smell of firearms is in the air, and there's not an office dame in sight. The machines chatter and ring to each other. It's time to snap down your brims, share a post violence cigarette and think about escape ... do you remember the way in, all the twists and turns? No. You weren't looking. Any of these doors might open you to safety, but there may not be time....
>
> (Pynchon, 2000, Page 299)

Indeed, you weren't looking on the way in, and missed the whole development of modernity leading to a completely organised world. The doors, however, do not lead to freedom—just to ever more rooms.

And we see the bank manager of our opening paragraph, looking with yearning into a room opulently furnished with a huge desk, exquisite carpets and art on the walls and representing everything he ever wanted to achieve. He has to stay outside, harbouring an awful suspicion that the world he longed for does not exist. Fiction can sometimes be very illuminating.

Note

1. Generalising the individual or corporate actors involved in the complex enactment of financial markets in faceless terms of 'the markets' engenders the same kind of feelings of helplessness in individuals as those confronted when facing the amorphous and overpowering organisation.

References

Baudrillard, Jean (1978): *Agonie des Realen*, Berlin: Merve.
Derrida, Jacques (1998): *Of Grammatology*, Baltimore, MA: Johns Hopkins University Press.
Foucault, Michel (1977): *Discipline and Punish*, Harmondsworth: Penguin.
Foucault, Michel (1983): *Der Wille zum Wissen. Sexualität und Wahrheit I*, Frankfurt/Main: Suhrkamp.

Gutenberg, E. (1983): *Grundlagen der BWL, Bd. I: Die Produktion*, 24th ed., Berlin.

Hansen, K. P. (1992): *Die Mentalität des Erwerbs, Erfolgsphilosophien amerikanischer Unternehmer*, New York and Frankfurt/Main Campus.

Hutcheon, Linda (1988): *A Poetics of Postmodernism*, London: Routledge.

Iacocca, Lee/ Novak, William (1984): *An Autobiography*, New York: Bantam.

Kafka, Franz (1986): *Das Schloss*, Frankfurt: S. Fischer.

Kieser, Alfred (1996): Moden & Mythen des Organisierens, *Die Betriebswirtschaft* 56(1), 21–39.

Kieser, Alfred (2002): *Wissenschaft und Beratung*, Heidelberg: Winter.

Lyotard, Jean-Francois (1984): *The Postmodern Condition*, Manchester: University of Manchester Press.

Lyotard, Jean-Francois (1987): *Der Widerstreit*, München: Wilhelm Fink.

Pelzer, Peter (1995): *Der Prozess der Organisation*, Chur: G+B Verlag Facultas.

Pumpe, Werner (2005): Das Ende des deutschen Kapitalismus, *WestEnd, Neue Zeitschrift für Sozialforschung* 2, 3–26.

Pynchon, Thomas (2000): *Gravity's Rainbow*, London: Vintage.

Trump, Donald and Schwarz, Tony (1988): *The Art of the Deal*, New York: Warner.

Styhre, Alexander (2004): Thomas Pynchon and the Scrambling of Literary Codes: Implications for Organization Theory, *Ephemera* 4(4), 315–27.

Weber, Max (1970): *From Max Weber: Essays in Sociology*, Trans. Hans Gerth and C. Wright Mills, London: Routledge & Kegan Paul.

11
Leadership: The Madness of the Day by Maurice Blanchot

Hugo Letiche and Jean-Luc Moriceau

Blanchot's *The Madness of the Day* shows that when we have to make sense of experience, we inevitably distance ourselves from the raw, naïve openness of the event. This is something we all know and it is a process that fiction (as well as a great deal of management literature) implicitly tries to deny by evoking a meaningfulness-in-itself that does not refer to lived processes of relatedness. Based on Blanchot, we go here a step further, claiming that leadership is an iconic exemplar of this process. Like narrative itself, leadership is inherently connected to the glorification of accountability, purposefulness and goal-directed orientations. In so far as this is so, *leadership is quite mad*.

Introduction

In this reading of Blanchot's *The Madness of the Day* (1981) we will examine three things:

(i) the genre of the text;
(ii) what the text has to say about accountability and leadership; and
(iii) how the difference between madness and sanity is understood.

Genre

The Madness of the Day is a very short novella. A single subject addresses a stream of consciousness to his questioners, which apparently include the readers. A descriptive monologue is offered approximating a thematic poem. The authorial persona examines writing, narrative and speaking from different angles and questions what text is, but never really resolves any of the issues or themes raised. Conventional essays respect a pattern of 'statement—exposition—conclusion'; this one does not. What is written seems to have no clear foundation, or to serve any prescribed cause, or to confirm any 'truth'. The beginning and end seem confused; memory floats and is displaced while remaining indefinite. Acute reflexivity seems to destroy clarity, purpose and intent. Significance is deconstructed; argument thwarted. The reader is carried along by a flow of images and the intensity of the prose.

Differences between types of text can be problematic. The distinction between fiction and non-fiction is anything but clear. As in any such definitional pair, the one exists in (negative) terms to the other, and the 'third term' upon which the polarity is based is, as is often the case, mute. Malinowski's Trobiand islanders (1922/2007; 1929/2005; 1935/2001) are a rather famous illustration: are they fictional or non-fictional? Saul Bellow's *Herzog* (2007) poses the question in reverse: people, places and situations in the so-called 'novel' are all (rather embarrassingly) recognisable. Social science seemingly makes its 'subjects' anonymous and depersonalises 'events', but is this any more real, objective or true than a text that shows individual emotions and personalities?

Blanchot's text is intimate and distanced, philosophical and descriptive. It raises all sorts of questions about the purity of genres. Ultimately, is text ever really trustworthy? Is there any real possibility of textual sanity, or is all text and identity untrustworthy, floating and possibly deranged? Can we be assured that the authorial persona is 'real', 'responsible' and/or 'rational'? Could it be that all text is mere linguistic artefact and as such it could just as well be a product of madness as of sanity?

Blanchot's novella repeatedly addresses the theme of accountability. What is it to make one's (non-)responsibility explicit? Who or what demands that explanations are given: the will that enforces accountability or the necessity that one gives an account of oneself, organises and orders? Language-ing is (en-)forced. Language and speech are not just vehicles for expression. Their 'grammars' organise the thinkable and determine what can be made operational.

In terms of our investigation here, organisation entails the formalisation and enforcement of goal directedness via texts of 'vision, energy, authority and strategic direction [...] [that] engage people and rouse their commitment to company goals' (Goffee and Jones, 2000, Page 63). 'Leaders' frame and declare such texts. 'Leadership' produces and communicates reality constructions that engender and/or support a state of relatedness (Hosking, 1988, 2001). In 'organisation' near continuous relationship is demanded and 'leaders' supposedly call the shots. Leadership is identified here with the power to provide and demand clarification. The leader is the person or force that requires explanation, defines liability and frames the boundaries to action. Leadership is the authority that instigates and commands explanation(s). Leadership entails that texts of identity are provided, demanded, controlled and revised.

The refusal to engage in accountability—that is, to tell and be told, to command and to follow, to speak and to respond—disorganises the speech and textual acts upon which organisation depends. An often-analysed illustration of speech/textual acts as described in a fictional text is Herman Melville's *Bartleby* (Miller, 1990; Deleuze, 1998; Agamben, 1999; Ranciere, 2004; Wood, 2005; Beverungen and Dunne, 2010). Bartlelby (Melville, 1853/1967) may be a model clerk—an anonymous, bored man without qualities—but this is not what makes him interesting. Bartlelby does not refuse to work, he mounts no opposition; he simply states a preference. The crucial point is that he ceases to exist *as a functionary, for 'the Other'*. He is a scrivener—not a writer, narrator or re-encounter, but someone who copies text. He does what is necessary for the accounts—legal and financial—to get done. But one day he discovers the 'I prefer not to', and he manifests his will. Instead of remaining a faceless extension of the organisation, he becomes a force of disorganisation—the ordering principle becomes the disordering one. But both before and afterwards, Bartleby is 'accountable'. Throughout, he is an agent of text without agency. In the story, the authorial 'I' is supposedly the lawyer who employs Bartleby. Principles of identity formation are not problematised. Bartleby changes his identity construction without changing his basic structural relationship to the Other. All the way through Bartleby is, in *phenomenal terms, relationally inscrutable*. He is unknowable and has next to no voice of his own, both as the perfect 'organisation man' and later as the 'misfit'. He cannot easily be interpreted, defined or acknowledged.

Blanchot's text is much more radical than Melville's. It has attracted commentary from Derrida (1986, 2000), Levinas (1975, 2000) and literary critics (Large, 2005; Hill, 2009), but with the exception of Robert Cooper (2006), organisation theory has not engaged with it. Blanchot's authorial 'I' speaks directly to its inquisitors. All demands made on the 'I' to speak are interpreted to be violent and (potentially) destructive. Melville's Bartleby dies; the problem is past. Blanchot's 'I' continues to threaten the spectator with speechless madness and fierce refusal. The reader is free to interpret Bartleby's stock phrase and attitude as he or she will. Blanchot's 'I' screams negation, conflict and doubt. Melville's story can be taken on several levels: political, psychological, ontological or in terms of organisational studies. Blanchot's text is insistent in its deconstruction of textuality, sense-making and the social interact(s) needed for communication. It refuses to accept the role of willingly bringing a message to a reader.

The Madness of the Day is very short, less than 15 pages. The genre is unclear: is it a short story, a narrative, a philosophical essay, a prose poem or a combination of any of these? The question of the genre is important because the text is extremely self-questioning and doubting. What is the text really all about? Blanchot questions whether and/or what text can be. He demands what it means for a text to be, and/or not to be, about something. He problematises the relationship of foreground to background: a text can only be about something because it accepts to not be about anything else. The *BEING* exists at the cost of, and/or as the complementary of, the *NOT-BEING*. The text is visible because there is an invisible that is covered, shrouded, denied and bullied. For Blanchot, the *NOT-BEING* of the text includes the existence, emergence and processes of life itself. Text denies raw experience and unmediated sensation. Text is sense-making that replaces events, feelings and perception.

Let's enter for a moment into the structure(-lessness) of Blanchot's text.[1] It has no beginning. We encounter near the end, the same sentences with which the text started. The beginning was not really a beginning at all, and there is no ending. The text ends with the beginning and refuses to be the narrative (that the text is). The very last sentences: 'A story? No. No stories, never again' (1981, Page 18) may or may not belong to the story. They may form some kind of meta-discourse. The text has no plot: we learn nothing about the outcomes of the described situations. The text is (at least) about the possibility of narrative and the madness of accountability, as well as the insanity of the demands of reason. But these themes do not really belong to the narrative. The text has no credible narrator. The one who says 'I' does not manage to constitute himself as an identity and is unable to sustain the narrative. And this 'I' paradoxically refuses to narrate. Is the text a narrative? At the first publication the title on the cover page was: *a narrative?*, and in the table of contents: *a narrative*. The manuscript was later reprinted as: *The Madness of the Day*. The text performs the impossibility of doing narrative. Is this fiction? At some moments the text relates events that actually did happen to Blanchot. The text could metaphorically be understood as referring to the author's experience(s); but very little of what gets talked about probably ever happened.

Blanchot's text turns constantly back on itself and questions its own possibility of existence. The text is about text. The narrative questions the possibility of narration. The authorial 'I' doubts its ability to exist and ponders its ability to ever get to the point: that ism for him- or herself to become self-accounted-for in text. Blanchot's novella is not a story and his account is not accountable. The novella contains bits of identity and moments of recall, but none of this conforms to the norms of a (traditional) narrative. The story is not clearly about anything. It has no succinct beginning, middle and end; there's really no plot or development. It is self-referential text, which is not traditionally novelesque. But it is not simply a philosophical manuscript. For Blanchot, forcing the narrative into an ordered or reasonable form creates an inescapability that is violent, repressive and leads to madness.

Conventionally the novella requires ordered, disciplined and purposeful rendering of a story. A demand that falsifies existence: life/death is not so structured. Life and death, as *The Madness of the Day* suggests, are mostly thought of as a sad story with a tragic ending. As early as the first paragraph, the narrator declares: 'I experience boundless pleasure in living, and I will take boundless satisfaction in dying'. He claims that he has hardly ever met people who welcome life and death as he does. The (happy) few that do not entrap life and death in a (sad) story are 'Other'. Submitting one's existence to the ordering of text puts the purpose and meaning of life to death. The narrator does not want any one story to capture his existence. He tries to stay with the 'Other'. He does not want to have his existence imprisoned in *The Madness of the Day*. His wants his life to be made up of multiple moments and events.

Blanchot's novella provokes the boundaries of narrative and of fictional form(s). The text interrogates and plays with the frontiers of leadership, narrative and literature. Leadership entails identity: of the leader and follower. It assumes boundaries (in text) that define, separate and unite leader and follower. Leadership depends on narratives of identity and on storytelling that marshal action consistent with identity. Leadership is a form of testimony: of self and of other, and of the two as interrelated.

Contemporary literature is often self-reflexive and questions its own structure, authorial 'I' and authority. It is a literature that points to the 'disappearing point' of leadership. Blanchot explores the boundaries of self and other, consciousness and mindlessness, leadership and followership. He leads his readers and forces his accounts onto them, but if that is a rational, determinant or understandable goal, it is left profoundly in doubt. *The Madness of the Day* is a novella wherein form triumphs above everything else. It is a narrative wherein narration exists for itself and not to tell a story. The text demands to be understood in how it is text; it is text that is not dedicated to plot and does not offer a window to some external reality. The *reflexivity* of the text and of the writing triumphs over all other themes. Leadership is not so much constituted as an effect exercised on the other, but as a possibility of speech, text and languaging.

Identity may continually be demanded of us, but is testimony possible: and to whom, why, how and when? To whom would we testify and why? To what 'truth', 'possibility' or 'reality' could testimony be directed? If existence is 'business as usual', one could testify to that absolute. If organisation produces itself as particularist economic rationality, then the narrative could testify to financial self-interest. But if a living human subject testifies, then human existing, mortality and consciousness define the horizon of the text. Is there something more, contained in leadership, organisation and its text, than what a purely materialist for-profit horizon could define? Is text reducible or irreducible to business (organisational) success?

The text you are now reading attempts to demand your attention and awareness, and thereby to demand accountability of you. It attempts 'leadership'. Leadership affirms reason and order via account and text. Coherence and purposeful text is expected of us. Text is not imagination unleashed, or words given permission to go every which way. Text is no-one's consciousness; its objectivised order avoids me, you, us and life. Text leads; it has a leadership of its own; it is inhuman and alien. The story is permanent, lasting and 'true'—organisation as storied and lived consciousness is deadening.

Blanchot's writing questions the possibility of write-ability—that is, of the possibility of text. Text entails self-assertion in narrative, which assumes the necessity of sense-making. This is what organisational studies produces via its textuality. But does this rendition of the space of writing do justice to writing? What if writing denies and forbids totalisation—that is, rejects assertions of truth, identity, place, time and order? What if writing and organisational rationality are fundamentally opposed to one another? Perhaps narrative does not have to affirm order, control and accountability, but could deny it. What if living narrative inherently denies the textual regime of substance and logocentricism? Organisational studies pretends to order, rationality, intentionality and purposefulness. But speech may inherently entail polyphony, multiplicity and heteroglossia. What if organisation is speech all the way down—and the very possibility of speech denies what is assumed by 'organisation'? Where would that leave 'text'—as living speech, or as deadened/deadening artefact?

These questions about writing and identity, substance and doubt, self and other, speech and text are what Blanchot's *The Madness of the Day* addresses. This madness is not local and limited (that is, of one and only one day). The madness is produced by awareness of the 'now' or of the time (duration) of direct existence. It is the madness endured by an 'I' that has lost faith in the right to say 'I'. It is the madness of a lucidity free of delusion. It is Blanchot's quintessential speech situation—open and indefinite, not propositional or systematic.

Accountability as text and leadership

Following Robert Cooper's deconstruction of organisation, we emphasise organisation/disorganisation (Cooper, 1986). The episteme of organisational studies is mostly grounded in the study of relationships between systems or organisations and their environments or ground. Critical management studies, contrastingly, emphasises how organisational order(-ing) can threaten to 'get out of order' (Munro, 2001). Cooper insists that there is no a priori justification for privileging order above disorder, organisation over disorganisation, utopia more than dystopia, leaders beyond the disenfranchised. Since each term only makes sense or can be defined in terms of the counter term, one either leaves first principles unexamined or one has to study the 'dis-'. Organisational studies tend to leave managerial principles unquestioned, prioritising profit above disinterestedness and obedience more than disobedience. An external referent of leadership—that is, one outside of text and mutual social construction—is assumed:

> [...] 'leaders make things happen' is an obvious and rarely questioned way of thinking. Indeed, it is inherent in management studies to consider 'the leader as consistent essence, a centred subject with a particular orientation' (Alvesson & Sveningsson, 2003: 961). [...] It is the same with charismatic, effective, visionary and transformational leadership. These beliefs in leadership often attribute power to individual social actors and it is they [supposedly] who cause events (Gemmill & Oakley, 1992). [...] Moreover, those who are led often find the responsibility a leader assumes for visioning and strategic direction to be important and comforting (Bolman & Deal, 1994). People look to a leader to frame and concretize their reality (Smircich & Morgan, 1982). (Wood, 2005, Pages 1105–6)

But is this 'misplaced concreteness', which mistakes abstraction for concrete reality, just an illusion? Is a simulacrum of clear-cut things being used to cover-over necessary constitutive processes? While a mainstream scholar like Pfeffer (1977) asserts that leadership is an unmitigated phenomenal occurrence, making use of Blanchot we argue that leadership is a textual effect of hierarchical governance. But we do not stop there: our aim is to investigate what sort of textual effect 'leadership' really is.

Leaders demand accounts of others—that is, they impose accountability, demand justification, enforce actions and decisions, and reward as well as punish. Blanchot's authorial 'I' refuses to be answerable to any such principle of Other. He rejects the obligation of accountability and problematises the (dis-)order that imposes the governance of leadership. Leadership is constituted in social- or socio-texts—that is, leadership brings text to organisation, replacing the multiplicity, complexity and chaos of life with the (dis-)order and structure of purposive narration. Leadership achieves the primacy of text by destroying the unlimited pandemonium of unstructured circumstance. If there is leadership, there is text or an intentional story, including narratives of goals, structures and processes. Leadership entails the presence of a certain type of text— text that prioritises order, legitimacy, responsibility, answerability and linear causality. If there is no such text, there is no leadership; and there is then (potentially) chaos, disorder and unstructured process.

Blanchot's novella is about the relationship between text and non-text. Blanchot's work centres on the refusal to transform existence into text-for-the-Other. Blanchot's text disavows having to provide text to the Other. The social and organisational legitimacy of having to provide narrative is what is denied. Organisation, as the social construction of purpose, goals, planning and order, hides the imposition of power via the rationale of goal-directedness. Why should one person impose accountability on others? Why should the one be willing to be subordinated to the other? Answerability requires submission; the subaltern (infamously) has no voice. Refusal of the obligation to report denies the very ground of leadership. The rejection of accountability undermines the roots of leadership. As long as participants in organisation are willing to provide narrative, the possibility for control and dominance is intact. Narrating for the Other is the key prerequisite to account-ability and control.

Blanchot refuses to narrate—story, storytelling and the social construction of narrating are called into question. His story does not want to be a story and his writing attacks the existential justification(s) of text-for-the-other. At issue is if there should be text or just process, perception and emergence? As long as the One answers to the Other, in social science categories, via business budgets, with research descriptions and/or through strategic plans, the regime of accountability prevails. If a story is forthcoming, then the structure of answerability is intact.

Blanchot's authorial persona claims: 'A story? No. No stories, never again.' Order and organisation require that there be a story. The basic relationship is not defined in terms of the content. If 'A' accounts for her- or himself to 'B', narrative structuration of accountability occurs. Governance is realised in every performative relationship of accountability. When story is demanded, Blanchot answers:

> I had been asked: Tell us 'just exactly' what happened. A story? I began: I am not learned; I am not ignorant. I have known joys. That is saying too little. I told them the whole story and they listened, it seems to me, with interest, at least in the beginning. But the end was a surprise to all of us. 'That was the beginning,' they said. 'Now get down to the facts.' How so? The story was over! (1981, Page 18)

The Other who listens and observes defines the relationship of answerability, dependence and power. Blanchot's 'I' asserts, 'No [...] never again.' Two issues are being raised here:

(i) how narrative relates to sense-making by destroying the duration of raw existence; and
(ii) why there should be no more narrative.

Narrative or destruction by sense-making

Blanchot's deconstruction of narrative problematises the listener, who dominates the speaker and the accountability that enforces the pretence of order, and it reveals the disorder of narration. Accounts are not innocent; answerability is a form of domination. Blanchot's argument is epistemological and not ontological. The issue is not if 'leadership' or 'answerability' *exists*, but if the demand for sense-making, justification and self-narration defines a knowledge episteme of subjugation. The imposition of narrative order—'A' justifies her- or himself by being answerable to 'B'—produces the basic power relation of accountability. Sense-making assumes that text has to 'mean'—that is, text must be proactive, consequential, significant, intentional and liable. Narrative entails self-creation via answerability to an Other. Narrative is constitutive of a controlled and subjugated self-identity.

The senseless necessity of sense-making is all pervasive. In its episteme, text cannot just *be*—that is, text must 'mean'. Meaning creation entails subjugation to the Other, who accepts or refuses to acknowledge the meanings. Accountability defines 'self' in terms of the Other's power to acknowledge or reject the meaning or identity on offer. Self and Other, when in a relationship of accountability, assume the necessity of 'meaning'. The relationship of Self and Other—the order or organisation that they define—has to make sense. In accountability, one party tells and one judges. And the judgement enacts the sense of organisation. In accountability, sense is granted or withheld.

In management, the Other prioritises vision, mission and purpose. Order exists as assumed and already thought. Concrete human interaction is beside the point. In narrative, the world is already thought, made sense of, and is reduced to concept. Thought, defined, distilled and reified is all-powerful. Thought is defined as pure necessity—as profit, success, quality, bench-marking, evidence-based, et cetera. Response-ability comes before observation, event or circumstance. Order is always already thought—that is, organisation is reduced to mission, purpose, goal and accountability. This is a world with few or no processes— things do not happen; they already mean. Anything the subject says can be weighted on its merit—account-ability or the judging of the Self's text knows no lacunae, limits or imperfections. Governance is total—the response-ability to the Other is unlimited. The Other as a subjective 'Self' is nothing. We know almost nothing about the Other's personal history or subjective existence. The Other is not a person but a narrative device that produces a world that is thought and which has to make sense. Purpose, text and reason are crucial, not autobiography or individual unicity.

In sense-making, Self is sacrificed to the function of sense-making. Sense-making is an all-consuming principle, insuring that order and motivation are always present. Experience is sacrificed to sense-making. Circumstance is always (already) remade (or remake-able) as narrative. And this is what order does. Order destroys pure process, raw environment and uncontrollable duration, replacing all messiness and chaos with total narrative inclusion. Supposedly there is nothing outside of the narrative. For basic raw human existing, there is no place. Narrative replaces human will, substance and possibility with 'response-ability' and 'account-ability'. The episteme of goals, tasks and functions is all-powerful. Existence without goals, intentions and structures is outside of the episteme. It is unspeakable, unknowable, beyond the pale. Existence prior to purpose—that is, not put into some intentional form and shape—is inaccessible. The speakable exists without the unspeakable; order acknowledges no disorder; narrative accepts no anti-narrative. A fallacy of pure positivity reigns.

No more narrative

Sense-making eats up all *being*. *Being* is subsumed to narration and is never accessible on its own terms. The discourse of goal(s) and purpose(s) dominates, and what is dominated remains invisible. Accountability is a discourse of 'truth'—what 'is' must be, and what ought to be has to be told. But who should be doing all of this, and in what circumstance, is invisible in the narrative itself. The messiness, serendipity and surprises of events are repressed; objectives and purposes are made paramount. Planned existence counts; existence prior to what has been planned is abjected. The signifier and its significance are exalted. Words of purpose replace those of raw circumstance. Unconceptualised event is unthinkable, unknowable and made inexistent. Only after it has been analysed and made to 'mean' does existence fit into narrative. Anything that has not been thought, processed, analysed and made purposeful cannot fit into narrative. Meaning is all encompassing, and not-organised existence is not (no longer) experience-able.

At a certain moment in Blanchot's text, the narrator is faced by a series of actions to which he cannot ascribe any meaning. A woman with a baby enters a building, a man gets out of a doorway, et cetera. No narrative is offered to make sense of these 'events'. The narrator is close both to the end of the text and of the day: 'I had seized the moment when the day, having stumbled against a real event, would begin hurrying to its end. Here it comes, I said to myself, the end is coming; something is happening, the end is beginning. I was seized by joy' (1981, Page 10). Event leads to no-meaning.

Blanchot's text is about 'the madness of the day'. What is more entirely commonplace, self-evident and quotidian than the demand for organisation, purpose, goals, order and structure? The madness of the day—that is, what is very common and popular but silly and preposterous—centres on the defined, identified and purposeful. All of these require 'identity-work'. Accountability requires that at any and every moment a narrative of missions, visions, stakeholders and results can be produced. Narration requires identity-work wherein existence is defined as goal-driven and purposeful. At any instant, the demand can be made—right now in the present—to produce a narrative of existence. The masters of narration make these demands.

Supposedly, identity, goals and purposes are necessary for organisational success. Accountability is necessary—after all, that is what planning and control entail. Accountability entails: 'I address a question to you; I demand your attention and awareness; I require that you are answerable to me'. The assumption that narrative is necessary is not discussable. Total accountability is assumed. It is a product of unexamined and unexaminable assumptions about Self/Other: a Self that renders accountability and an Other that demands accountability form the systemic assumptions of the regime or episteme of Self/Other. This epistemic system cannot be justified either by Self or Other, because both identities assume the system and do not exist without it. The order of Self and Other is pre-reflective and pre-conscious in the system of accountability. Accountability assumes, that the Other demands that Self is accountable. This is a closed epistemic system, which cannot be questioned or doubted from within.

In the novella, the narrator tries but does not manage to make a narrative from his life and experiences. But what is an 'I' with no narrative telling of its 'Self', that is, that has no identity? Identity requires that one make a narrative out of the events of one's life. The past, the present and the future have to form an all-encompassing narrative of self-identity. Blanchot's authorial 'I' tells us all sorts of things, but there is no narrative that successfully narrates his 'I'.

Blanchot protests against the right of some to demand accounts of others, but also against the assumption that 'I' requires self-narration. Blanchot produces a narrative that is not a narrative and an account that accounts for nothing. And the testimony attests to no identity (in particular).

Madness

Throwing open my rooms, they would say, 'Everything here belongs to us'. They would fall upon my scraps of thought: 'This is ours'. They would challenge my story: 'Talk,' and my story would put itself at their service. In haste, I would rid myself of myself. I distributed my blood, my innermost being among them, lent them the universe, gave them the day. Right before their eyes, though they were not at all startled, I became a drop of water, a spot of ink. I reduced myself to them. The whole of me passed in full view before them, and when at last nothing was present but my perfect nothingness and there was nothing more to see, they ceased to see me too. Very irritated, they stood up and cried out, 'All right, where are you? Where are you hiding? Hiding is forbidden, it is an offence', etc.

(Blanchot, 1981, Page 14)

It is the madness of the day (that is, the self-evident quotidian social norm) to ask for reasons, to demand accounts and to insist that laws explain. The leader requires the correct account: 'Tell us "*just* exactly" what happened.' And that is exactly what is demanded of the narrator. The assumption is commonplace that such a narrative is possible, and that it has to be given, and that we are thereby accountable. But is this possibility itself open to being held accountable? Do leaders have the right to demand accounts of others and/or of their organisations—and if so, what gives them that right?

Blanchot's 'day' is more directed to 'light' than to 'visibility' (the 'day' and the 'light' are the same word in French). Light enables sight, but at least since the Enlightenment, light is connected to reason and to an ordered universe (of laws). Light is both the medium and the milieu in which the world is seen. The leader requires light to be enlightened and to be able to keep the Other visible. Behaviour is to be ordered, lawful and reasonable. A logical account of behaviour needs to be possible. The normalness of behaviour needs to be ensured and checked. But the norm of mandatory 'normalness', logically and inevitably leads to its opposite: that is, to pathology.

The two doctors that interrogate the narrator are an eye doctor and a specialist in mental illnesses. The narrator should see as he ought to see. He should see a world of laws and reasons, a world that can be narrated and accounted for. Facing his two interrogators, the narrator enlightens them. He enables them to see him. By giving the right accounts, he creates and confirms them as leaders. But almost immediately, by making them leaders, he comes entirely under their sights and he becomes very small, nearly unnoticeable, and irrelevant or subordinate. Nothing worth seeing is shown. The interrogators become suspicious that the narrator is hiding his identity.

By giving an account, we count for the leader. We state (or imply) that the leader can count on us. Accounting entails recognition. And there is a whole game around recognition. The leader can acknowledge us, or he/she may not see and listen to us. Blanchot's narrator does not look for recognition. He does not seek the joy and gratitude of mutual understanding. He does not claim any agency in what happens to him. And above all, he refuses to be identified as an identity. Being identified or (re-)cognised, or thematised, is for him utmostly violent and senseless.

Being encapsulated in a definition of an 'I' and in an 'I can' is to be determined by the other's leadership.

> I nearly lost my sight, because someone crushed glass in my eyes. That blow unnerved me, I must admit. I had the feeling I was going back into the wall, or straying into a thicket of flint. The worst thing was the sudden, shocking cruelty of the day; I could not look, but I could not help looking. To see was terrifying, and to stop seeing tore me apart from my forehead to my throat. What was more, I heard hyena cries that exposed me to the threat of a wild animal (I think those cries were my own) (. . .) Yes seven days at once, the seven deadly lights, become the spark of a single moment, were calling me to account.
>
> (Blanchot, 1981, Page 11)

An event happened to the narrator. Someone crushed glass into his eyes. The event is unsufferably violent and painful. It deregulated his sight. He could, then, see the cruelty of the day, which is the cruelty of the light. This triggers a paradoxical situation. Seeing means realising and witnessing the violent cruelty of the light. But not seeing means not being able to know and testify about the cruelty. Everything is threatened by the chaos and savagery of darkness and lawlessness.

What his accidented eyes were able to see was the triumph of the madness of the day. It is the view of what we do not normally see. He sees that the light and clarity of modernity—synonymous with reason, order, knowledge and control—have gone mad. The imperialism of reason, orderliness and sensibility, has led to the most violent absurdity. The crisis is that we cannot see without light. Light is what cannot be seen, but it is the medium that enables us to see. We need light to see the madness of the light. Not seeing—in darkness or in the wilderness—is not a preferable option.

Conclusion

Accountability assumes a system of answerability wherein the one answers to the other. The texts that separate and unite Self and the Other are narrated. Such a structure of 'accountability' can just as well be called leadership. Persons, institutions and organisations constitute and repeat themselves in the narratives. Leadership requires both a system of Self and Other and some possibility of change. The structure of Self and Other is repeated over and over; but there is (normally) some change in the content narrated. The constitutive relational structure is more or less static, but concrete plans and activities change. The Other has to make real demands on the Self for the accountability to remain credible. But the Other normally does not want to change the structure of the relationship. The pain of the real can overwhelm the narrative structure. It may be impossible to accept, see and acknowledge the 'real'—that is, the social situation, nature of oppression or effects of the power differential may be overwhelming. Seeing the 'real' may just be too painful and 'seeing' may end up being replaced with blindness. Then the preservation of the discourse structure—that is, of the regime or episteme of leadership—requires the non-presence of life. Accountability or the affirmation of text can be deadening. There is only madness between being crushed by the 'real', escaping into simulacra and loosing all identity in pure process.

Does Blanchot and/or do we write from within the madness of the day, or from its boundaries, or from the outside? If we enter into the madness of the day, do we join into the 'no narrative, never'—and what would that be like? If we stay at a distance, we create a simulacrum of Blanchot that looks a little bit like Blanchot, but is not Blanchot. We produce a 'not-narrative' that most clearly, really is one. And if we enter into Blanchot, we may loose our readers and our minds. Thus we have produced a text that skirts around the boundaries and perhaps is afraid of itself. This text implies that organisation is something to be afraid of and that accountability and leadership terrifies 'I', Self and life.

Note

1. This paragraph is based on Derrida's (1986, 1994) analyses of this novella, which qualifies the text's structure as a structure of narrative in deconstruction.

References

Agamben, G (1999) *The Coming Community*. Minneapolis: Minnesota University Press.

Alvesson M & S Sveningsson (2003) 'Good visions, bad micro-management and ugly ambiguity' *Organization Studies* 24:6 961–88.

Bellow, S (2007) *Herzog*. London: Penguin.

Beverungen, A & S Dunne (2010) " 'I'd Prefer Not To' Bartleby and the excesses of interpretation' *Culture & Organization* 13:2 171–83.

Blanchot, M (1981) *The Madness of the Day/La folie du jour*. Barrytown, NY: Station Hill Press (bilingual edition).

Bolman, G L & T E Deal (1994) 'The organization as theater' in H Tsoukas (ed.) *New Thinking in Organization Behavior*. Oxford: Butterworth-Heinimann, 93–107.

Cooper, R (1986) 'Organization/disorganization' *Social Science Information* 25:2 299–335.

Cooper, R (2006) 'Making present' *Organization* 13:1 59–81.

Deleuze, G (1998) 'Bartleby; or, the formula' in G Deleuze (ed.) *Essays: Critical & Clinical*. London: Verso.

Derrida, J (1986) *Parages*. Paris: Galilée.

Derrida, J (1994) *Demeure. Maurice Blanchot*. Paris: Galiléee.

Derrida, J (2000) *The Instant of My Death/Demeure*. Stanford: Stanford University Press.

Gemmill G & J Oakley (1992) 'Leadership an alienating social myth' *Human Relations* 45:2 113–29.

Hill, L (2009) *Radical Indecision: Barthes, Blanchot*. Derrida Notre Dame: University of Notre Dame Press.

Large, W (2005) *Emmanuel Levinas & Maurice Blanchot: Ethics and the Ambiguity of Writing*. London: Clinamen.

Levinas, E (1975) *Sur Maurice Blanchot*. Montpellier: Fata Morgana (trans. *The Levinas Reader* Sean Hand (ed.) New York: Wiley-Blackwell).

Levinas, E (2000) *Emmanuel Lévinas-Maurice Blanchot, penser la difference*. Paris: PUF.

Malinowski, B (1922/2007) *Argonauts of the Western Pacific*. London: Read Books.

Malinowski, B (1929/2005) *The Sexual Lives of Savages*. London: Kessinger Publishing.

Malinowski, B (1935/2001) *Coral Gardens and Their Magic*. London: Routledge.

Melville, Herman (1853/1967) 'Bartleby the Scrivener' in H Melville (ed.) *Billy Budd, Sailor and Other Stories*. London: Penguin.

Miller, H J (1990) 'Who is he? Melville's 'Bartleby the Scrivener' in H J Miller (ed.) *Versions of Pygmalion*. Cambridge, MA: Harvard University Press.

Munro, R (2001) 'Unmanaging/disorganization' *Ephemera* 1:4 395–403.

Pfeffer, J (1977) 'The ambiguity of leadership' *Academy of Management Review* 2:1 104–12.

Ranciere, J (2004) 'Bartleby and the literary formula' in J Ranciere (ed.) *The Flesh of Words: The Politics of Writing*. Stanford: Stanford University Press.

Smircich L & G Morgan (1982) 'Leadership: the management of meaning' *The Journal of Applied Behavior Studies* 18:3 257–73.

Wood, M (2005) 'The fallacy of misplaced leadership' *Journal of Management Studies* 42:6 1101–21.

12

Leadership and Dharma: The Indian Epics *Ramayana* and *Mahabharata* and Their Significance for Leadership Today

Harsh Verma

Introduction

As Shakespeare's Henry IV put it: 'Uneasy lies the head that wears a crown' (Henry IV, Part 2, Act 3, Scene I, Pages 26–31). This adage is so because a leader faces bewildering choices and an array of possibilities that make decision-making difficult. On the one hand, the leader is circumscribed by tradition. Yet to go forward he must embrace modernity. There might be a course of action that has enjoyed historical legitimacy, but it is either inapplicable in the present era or a newer and clearer vision reveals it to be prejudiced, discriminatory and unjust to various sections of people who were excluded from it. He faces the challenge of inspiring communities different from his own, communities whose aims and precepts differ divergently. He must function in a world that changes dramatically every year, with new technological innovations that transform lives and, in doing so, generate social changes of their own.

At such times it seems easy to shelter oneself in ancient commandments and to avoid the uncertainty of change. From America to Asia leaders hark back to a golden past and urge their constituents to emulate historical practices, while demonising new practices and those that practise them.

Yet the application of medieval precepts meant for a largely illiterate populace and contextualised in a pre-modern situation cannot offer a solution to the increasing changes in our lives. On the other hand, a complete embrace of the present without understanding its implications can equally lead to misery. This is a delicate balancing act that can strain even the wisest. There are hardly any precedents, and leaders must begin what seems an adventure in morality.

The Hindu worldview offers a unique perspective and guidance to leaders embarking on a journey of moral exploration. Hinduism is extremely different from the monotheistic religions since it does not have a unified scripture or prophets proclaiming the truth as exclusively revealed to them. It defines rightful conduct in an extremely complex manner, keeping in mind that there can be a multiplicity of situations and a diversity of lifestyles. It provides a framework for understanding one's moral context and enables a person to determine the likely course of action that may be pursued.

Helping to clarify this understanding are the two great Epics—the *Ramayana* and the *Mahabharata*. Ostensibly the two epics are heroic tales with the *Ramayana* concentrating on the exploits of Prince Rama while the *Mahabharata* is a composite book that is centred on the travails of the Pandava brothers who fight a great war against their cousins. While the battles fought by them may seem on the surface like other heroic narratives, it is the issues that they faced in their lives as well as the way they intervened in the lives of others that hold significance for those who hold the epics in reverence.

The epics serve to clarify the elusive nature of Dharma, or right conduct. Right conduct is very much an individual action based on exigencies of situation, the betterment of the community and appropriateness of context. It is intensely individual so that the Dharma of one person may be different from that of his neighbour. The stories described in the epics serve as vital instruments of reflection and inner guidance as the reader examines the conflicts and final decisions of the characters as portrayed. The *Ramayana* and the *Mahabharata* are to Indian civilisation and Hindu culture what the *Iliad* and *Odyssey* are for Western civilisation. The two epics have influenced life, politics, society and culture, not just in India but across south-east Asia where Indian culture spread in the historical past.

The roots of Dharma

Hinduism sets forth four goals of life known as Purusharthas, which are essential to attaining perfection. The four goals are: Dharma or an ethically sound life; Artha or material prosperity; Kama or aesthetically beautiful expression of desires and natural instincts; and Moksha or spiritually free life (Sharma, 1982). Dharma is concomitant with morality and right conduct; Artha with wealth and economic interests; Kama with desire and the satisfaction of sexual, emotional and artistic life; Moksha with salvation and the liberation of the spirit (Klostermaier, 1994). Artha and Kama are legitimate aims but are instrumental and not intrinsic ends, and hence are subordinate to Dharma. These should be acquired and enjoyed in such a way that one does not slide back in terms of spiritual evolution.

To show Dharma is to order one's thoughts, passions and affections in accordance with prescribed rules. In the concept of Dharma, there is no simple rule for distinguishing between right and wrong since much is left on the discrimination of the individual. Further, the content of Dharma changes according to time and region so that the law responds to the needs of the situation. Dharma as a code of conduct is eternal but its content depends on the conditions of society at the time.

The Raja-Dharma (or the Dharma of kings) enjoins the king to care for his subjects, to protect them, to collect taxes without harming them, to maintain high personal conduct, to engage in self-reflection and to solicit feedback. This essay focuses on Dharma with a special focus on Raja-Dharma. We shall understand its implications for leaders by analysing the actions of the principal actors of our two epics: Rama, the prince of Ayodhya in the *Ramayana*, who chose self-exile to fulfil his father's vow, and Yudhishthira, the King of Hastinapura in the *Mahabharata*, who gambled away his kingdom.

The *Ramayana*

The *Ramayana* is centred on the figure of Rama who is considered to be an Avatar or divine incarnation of Lord Vishnu, the deity worshipped by the Vaishnavas as supreme God. He is the eldest of the four sons (by three wives) of King Dasharatha. The king's wives are Kaushalya, Sumitra and Kaikeyi, and all three have born sons to the King. Kaushalya's son is called Rama. Sumitra has given birth to twin boys, Lakshmana and Shatrugna. Kaikeyi, the King's third wife, presents him with his fourth son, Bharata.

Rama, the first-born son, is thus the legal and presumptive heir, popular across the kingdom for his exemplary personal conduct; his father decides to crown Rama as king. It was often the practice of rulers in ancient India to crown one of their children as junior king and retire to the role of an advisor or to renounce the world in order to live as a hermit.

However, a spanner is thrown in the works by Kaikeyi, the King's third wife. She initially agrees to the coronation of Rama but changes her mind on the advice of her maid Manthara, who plays to her fears, suggesting that Rama would kill his brothers, and advises her to stop the coronation of Rama and to insist on the coronation of Bharata, her own son.

The king had once given her two boons after she had saved his life on a battlefield, and she decides to use them now to fulfil her ends. Accordingly she summons the king and reminds him of the promises. The king, full of joy in view of the coming coronation of Rama, repeats the promises and Kaikeyi drops the bombshell.

Kaikeyi's first wish is that Bharata should become king; the second is that Rama should go into forest-exile for 14 years. The king is aghast but nothing could change Kaikeyi's mind. Rama is summoned to the chamber where he sees his father in a pitiable condition. On enquiry, Kaikeyi states that King Dasharatha has given her a promise, which she does not dare to express due to fear of Rama. If he agrees to abide by the truth, irrespective of the content of his father's promise, she will relate it. Rama promises that he will abide by his father's wishes, whatever they may be. Thereupon, Kaikeyi informs him of the boons she has extracted from Dasharatha.

Rama is not perturbed, and states:

Mother! This is all right. I will do it. To fulfil the king's promise I will wear the garb of a hermit and leave for the forest . . . Yet I am unhappy that the king did not himself inform me of Bharata's coronation. Should you yourself order it I will surrender the kingdom and my entire property to Bharata. And if the king orders me to do so to fulfill your objectives I will do it gladly. You should inform him of my acceptance. Why is he weeping with his eyes turned towards the floor? Call for Bharata! I will go to the forest immediately.

Kaikeyi is overjoyed to see her objectives fulfilled. She is also interested in ensuring that Rama leave as soon as possible so as to ease the succession of her son Bharata. She tells Rama that he should leave immediately because until he leaves the king will not perform his ablutions. On hearing these words the king collapses. But Rama tells her that he is a follower of Dharma set by the sages and will abide by the promises made by his father.

Filial duty is the greatest Dharma. Nothing is greater than it. Even though he has not stated it to me I will go to the forest for 14 years.

Devi, you have complete control over me. If you had given me the same orders I would have followed them without hesitation. I will inform my wife Sita and my mother of these developments and leave for the forest.

Hinduism is clear about the obligations of children towards parents, and therefore so is Rama. In Indian philosophy parents are the direct and visible manifestation of the masculine and feminine aspects of divinity on earth. Later in the argument Rama repeats this aspect of the parent's status. Rama leaves for his mother's palace and immediately stops all royal observances due to him.

His brother, Lakshmana, disagrees with his decision to accept his father's ruling.

Older brother! You think that if you do not abide by paternal wishes, Dharma would be violated. Besides it would cause doubt in the minds of people about your ability to aid them follow Dharma as a ruler, if you did not obey your own father. You also think that if you do not accept his wishes then others will not do so which would lead to anarchy. To remove these doubts you wish to leave for exile immediately. This is unfair and illusory. You are giving undue importance to a thing like 'fate'. If someone as brave and capable as you ascribes events to fate that is the product of illusion. This is the view of ordinary persons who are incapable of changing their lives and hence take recourse to giving exaggerated importance to fate.

Lakshmana draws out the deeper reasons for Rama's decision, which Rama could hardly make explicit. In doing so he attempts to demolish the assumptions on which Rama bases his decision. Lakshmana further criticises both King Dasharatha and his third wife Kaikeyi.

Why do you not question the motivations of those two sinners? You are well aware that there are many hypocrites who maintain a posture of religiosity. Those two want to dismiss a principled person like you, in order to fulfill their own personal ends. If the fact about the boons was true, it would have been brought into operation before this coronation.... You must accept that this is a false tale that has been circulated to place obstructions in your coronation. Following a hypocritical dharma has been criticized by all. How can you think of fulfilling the desires of these sexually passionate sinners? Only those who are cowards and who do not have valour place their faith in fate. Those who are respected by the world do not revere fate. The person who can subdue fate does not sit in dejection over obstructions. Today the world will see whether fate is more powerful than a man's power. Those who have seen your downfall as the result of fate will see this fate destroyed by my efforts. Like the majestic elephant that does not care for the ropes that bind him I will drive away this fate by the force of my valour. The folk of the three worlds cannot stop me. Those who have supported your exile will themselves go into exile . . . .

Rama wipes off the tears from Lakshmana's face and will not be dissuaded. Kaushalya, his mother, protests that she will follow him to the forest. Rama says:

Mother! Kaikeyi has betrayed the king and I'm going to the forest. If you leave him now then he will surely die. You should be with my father as long as he is alive . . . The king is your and my master. As long as he is alive you should not feel orphaned. Bharata too is a good man and he will serve you. You should take care that he does not die due to the shock he has experienced . . . .

Rama's wife Sita proclaims her intention of accompanying her husband into exile. She will not be dissuaded and Rama has to give in. Meanwhile Lakshmana also expresses his desire to accompany them. In vain does Rama ask his brother to stay behind and look after their parents. The trio now move to Kaikeyi's palace, where the entire palace retinue have by now gathered to bid a final farewell to their father. On seeing them the father can no longer control himself.

Son! I'm bound by the boons given to Kaikeyi. Imprison me and become the king of Ayodhya.

Here the king offers an excuse to Rama to usurp the throne. Since his actions are bound he attempts to ask Rama to circumscribe his actions. And since it is well known that the will of the king is with Rama, the people and the court would honour and perhaps even welcome such a decision.

However Rama will not agree to such a course of action. He says that he will return after 14 years. Dasharatha now bursts into tears.

Son! Go in peace. May your road be without obstacles . . . You are the embodiment of Dharma and it is impossible to change your mind.

Just wait one more night so that I may see you one last time. Having experienced the luxuries one last time you may go in the morning. You are acting to please me, but this is not pleasing to me. I do not like that you have to go to the forest. This woman Kaikeyi is worse than the fire that lies hidden behind the ashes. She hid her cruel intention and prevented me from acting on my intention. She has committed a great betrayal. You want to free me from the humiliation that her actions have inflicted on me. You want to make your father a truthful person. This is not surprising since in age as well as qualities you are my eldest son.

Dasharatha makes one last attempt to dissuade Rama. The request to spend one more night is actually not so innocent. The luxuries that Rama had possibly never cared about since they were available freely to him on account of his status would assume deep significance on the realisation that they were available only for a single night. By the morning it would be a Herculean decision to wrench oneself from them. Rama would then be tempted to opt for rebellion in order to savour those luxuries.

Rama refuses to stay a single moment longer.

If I do not travel today I will lose the benefits which will not be available tomorrow. Instead of enjoying desires I prefer to leave now. You may give this entire land to Bharata. I have never desired to take the kingdom for my own happiness or for the happiness of my near and dear ones. I desired coronation only to obey your commands to this effect. Remove your misery and do not shed such tears. Just as the ocean who is the master of all streams does not get perturbed so should you not leave morality out of your misery. I want neither this kingdom, nor happiness, neither land nor luxuries, neither heaven nor even this life. My only desire is that you should be truthful and that your word is not seen to be a lie.

Rama realises the temptation before him and decides not to let it lure him. He tells the king to be truthful and adhere to the path of Dharma. He further reminds the king of his duty to comfort everyone instead of himself wallowing in emotion.

It is your duty to console all these people who are weeping here. Why are you overcome with emotion yourself? I have left this town, kingdom and entire land so that you can give it to Bharata .....

Dasharatha faints. Efforts are made to convince Kaikeyi but she refuses to change her mind. Dasharatha now orders that the army and royal treasury accompany Rama in his journey to the forest. Kaikeyi immediately protests since it would leave her son Bharata without the instruments of kingship. Dasharatha turns the tables on her by pointing out that when she asked for the boons she had not specified that Rama go alone without the army or the treasury. Kaikeyi's response is that Rama should leave immediately and that the gate of the kingdom should be closed behind him as their ancestor King Sagara had turned out his own son Asamanjas. At this point Rama interjects.

> O King! I have left behind all luxuries. Now I have to subsist on the produce of the forest. I have left all desires so I do not need the army either. I permit you to grant these to Bharata. The maids can give me the skins and rags that I need to wear as well as implements that will be useful in the forest.

Kaikeyi has discarded all sense of shame by now. She brings the garb of mendicants for the brothers as well as Sita. Wearing these, the trio leaves for the forest, accompanied by most of the citizenry of the kingdom. It is only later when everyone else is asleep that Rama slipps away to begin his life in exile with just his wife and brother.

The *Mahabharata*

A somewhat similar choice is recounted in the *Mahabharata*. The *Mahabharata* is the tale of a fight between two sets of cousins—the Pandavas, who are rightful heirs of the kingdom of Hastinapura, and their first cousins, the Kauravas, who have usurped their kingdom. The Pandava brothers, along with their mother, initially wander in exile to escape the intrigues of the Kauravas under the nominal control of King Dhritarashtra, their uncle. After several years of wandering they manage to grow powerful by winning the hand of Princess Draupadi in marriage. Forced by the fact that their cousins have powerful allies, the Kauravas partition the kingdom and give half to the Pandavas. The Pandavas, under the eldest brother Yudhishthira, make it into a flourishing kingdom and conduct several sacrifices. Their wealth dazzles their cousins, who become jealous of their prosperity. Since they cannot be defeated in battle, the Kaurava brothers invite the Pandavas to a game of dice in which Yudhishthira loses his kingdom and the brothers are forced to spend years in exile. At the end of their exile the Kauravas refuse to return their kingdom, resulting in a terrible war in which the Pandavas are finally victorious.

The passage quoted below recounts the decision of Yudhishthira to agree to the game of dice while knowing that there is a plan to oust him from his kingdom.

The scene begins with King Dhritarashtra asking his stepbrother Vidura, who is well respected by the Pandavas, to go to them and invite them for a game of dice. Vidura understands well the intrigues of the Kaurava court and protests against the motives of the king. Dhritarashtra, however, refuses to cede ground and orders him to go on the mission. Forced by Dhritarashtra, Vidura goes to the city of the Pandavas and meets Yudhishthira, who notices that the former is morose. He asks Vidura whether everything is normal in Hastinapura. Vidura responds thus:

> King Dhritarashtra along with his relatives is happy and contented. He has sent a message that he has built a hall similar to yours and has invited you and your brothers to see this hall. Here all relatives and friends can play the game of dice together. The Kauravas will be pleased to meet their relatives and celebrate by playing together.
>
> The king has built several places for gambling. You will see cunning and shrewd gamblers sitting in these places. I have come to invite you for gambling at this place.

Vidura reveals the intentions of the Kauravas plainly. Yudhishthira is perturbed by this invitation:

> O Vidura! Gambling leads to quarrels and fights. No wise person can prefer to gamble. What do you think? We will obey your directives.

Vidura responds:

> I am well aware that gambling is the root cause of misfortune. I have tried to stop this. However Dhritarashtra has forced me to visit you. You have heard me. Now you should do as you wish.

Yudhishthira responds:

> Which other gamblers will be present over there apart from the sons of Dhritarashtra? Please identify those gamblers with whom we may have to gamble over our wealth?

Vidura replies:

> Over there is Shakuni, the prince of Gandhara. He is skilled in throwing the dice according to his choice. He is also well versed in the art of gambling. He will be accompanied by other gamblers such as Kings Vivishanti, Citrasena, Satyavrata, Purumitra and Jai.

Yudhishthira is astounded.

> That means that the place is filled with extremely evil and wretched gamblers. This world created by God is under the control of fate. It is not independent. I'd like to abide by the wishes of King Dhritarashtra and visit him. The son always loves the father. Therefore I will abide by your directions. I do not want to gamble. If King Dhritarashtra had not invited me to gamble then I would have never played with Shakuni. However it is my rule that I will never refuse when invited.

Yudhishthira realises that an elaborate strategy has been hatched to deprive him of his kingdom. Yet he decides to agree to the game of dice on the grounds that he has been invited to the game by a father, Dhritarashtra. In his opinion it is his duty to abide by that decision. Interestingly, the narrator of the epic is appalled at this blind obedience and makes a telling comment.

> Just as bright light blinds the sight of a person so does fate remove his intelligence. Motivated by fate a person moves under the control of the creator as if bound by ropes.

The implication is clear. Having lost his sense of discrimination, Yudhishthira is now a pawn in the hands of circumstances.

Yudhishthira now makes plans to travel to Hastinapura. On the way he is met by Vidura who explains the entire strategy of the Kauravas and the actual aims behind the game of dice. Thus the full planning of the Kauravas is now revealed to Yudhishthira, yet he refuses to retrace his steps.

Accompanied by his brothers, Yudhishthira enters the gambling hall where he is invited by Shakuni to play a game of dice. Yudhishthira criticises the game.

> Gambling is a kind of cheating and a cause of sin. There is nowhere the chance to display the valour of a warrior nor does it have a policy.

> The only respect that gamblers have is for the propensity to cheat and lie. Wise persons do not praise such a 'respect'. You should not behave like a cruel person and try to win over us through the use of unfair means.

Yudhishthira makes it clear that he is aware of that the game is just a ploy to cheat the Pandavas out of their wealth and attempts to debate with Shakuni on the nuances of Dharma. Shakuni is far too cunning to be involved in a debate on philosophy and only defends the game itself.
Shakuni responds.

> The real player of dice is the person who can counter his opponent's cunning, enthusiastically participate in the throwing of dice, and has knowledge of all the facets of the game of dice. He can bear the machinations of his opponents. If the dice are unfavorable it can defeat one side. Victory and defeat are therefore under the control of fate. Fate is responsible for the fault of defeat. Even we can possibly be defeated yet we play. O king, you should not doubt and should not delay. Come and play.

Yudhishthira counters this argument:

> The sage Asit-Deval, who travels across the world has said that the person who plays with cunning in a game of dice commits a sin. The only way rightful victory is assured is through battle so Kshatriyas[1] should meet in battle not in a game of dice. Gentlemen do not raise their voices unjustly at another and do not behave with cunning. The mark of an upright person is fighting without deceit and cunning. Shakuni, you should not try to use the game of dice to deceitfully seize our wealth that we use to protect the Brahmins. I am not a person who wishes to gain wealth through deceitful behaviour. Wise men do not favour the work of a gambler.

Yudhishthira is saying that the Kauravas should meet them in war in the way of warriors if they desire their wealth instead of using a cowardly technique like the dice game.
Shakuni responds:

> When a wise scholar goes to debate with another scholar he uses cunning to defeat his opponent. The scholar defeats his adversary only through deceit but the community does not see it that way.

O King of Dharma, the person who is well versed in the game of dice easily wins over those who are neophytes in a similar manner. Even the skilled warrior who is well versed in archery uses cunning to defeat a weaker warrior. Yet it is not seen in that manner by the community.

So if you come here and fear the use of cunning then you should not play.

Yudhishthira is stung by the barb.

O king. I do not withdraw from an invitation. This is my definite rule. Fate is strong. I'm controlled by fate.

I'd like to know who I will be playing with among the people gathered here. Who will be my adversary in the game of dice? Decide this so that we may start.

Duryodhana is waiting for this response:

O King. I'll put the money and jewels at stake but my uncle Shakuni will play on my behalf.

Yudhishthira offers only a weak protest:

I do not think that it is right that one person should play on behalf of another person. This should be understood. However, we may begin the game.

This is the most important point of the game. Yudhishthira could still upset the plans of the Kauravas by rightfully protesting that substitution of players is in violation of the rules of the game. The Kaurava strategy would be smashed immediately. Yet Yudhishthira allows this contravention of norms to pass unnoticed. In doing so he seals his family's fate. In the ensuing game the cunning Shakuni strips him of his wealth and kingdom and sends him and his brothers into exile.

Understanding the issues of Dharma in the actions of Rama and Yudhishthira

Dharma in terms of personal conduct

The similarity between Rama and Yudhishthira lies in the intentions behind their actions. Both strive to obey the commands or bonds laid down by a parent. In Indian philosophy parents are the direct and most visible manifestation of the masculine and feminine aspects of divinity on earth. A popular tale about a contest between Ganesha and Karttikeya, the sons of Goddess Parvati and Lord Shiva, illustrates this belief. The sons, like all siblings, squabble constantly with each other. Finally they decide to hold a contest whereby the one who travels around the universe in the shortest time would be accepted as superior. Karttikeya, the commander of the Deva armies, immediately sets off on his peacock, confident of winning over the corpulent Ganesha, who has a mere rat as his vehicle. Ganesha, however, is up to the challenge. To the amazement of all, he circumambulates around his parents and proclaims that he has accomplished the task and has won. His contention is that parents are the symbol of the universe. Hence having moved around them he has already completed travelling around the universe. The thesis is universally accepted, as poor Karttikeya finds out at the end of his long journey. If parents are the symbols of divinity on earth then their wishes have deep significance for their children who have a duty to revere them.

Thus, Rama's father, King Dasharatha, has the power to demand that his son accept his wish to renounce the kingdom and move into exile. And it is clear from the very beginning that Rama is ready to fulfil this duty. The repeated and striking references to Dharma in his conversations with Lakshmana and Kaushalya are testimony to his commitment. Similarly, Yudhishthira is intent on obeying Dhritarashtra even though it may mean being betrayed in the end. Are both individuals doing the same thing? Is Dharma then merely a case of blindly obeying the wishes of a parent? If so then it is no different from rote obedience to commandments.

However, this is a superficial conclusion that comes from a cursory reading of the epic, and does not seem to have been seen as constituting Dharma by Rama. Dharma is not just a matter of fulfilling obligations to a father. It is true that there are repeated statements by Rama about the necessity of following the wishes of one's father, but these statements are later qualified. Dasharatha is projected as a just and fair ruler, as well as a loving father. Hence his wishes, in Rama's opinion, deserve to be accepted. As a corollary to this, one could say that if Dasharatha were not a fair ruler and treated his sons differently, then it would not be a duty to follow his wishes. Rama is giving Dasharatha the status of a Shishta (upright) and deeming his wishes worthy of obedience.

This is not the stand taken by Yudhishthira, who merely repeats the precept of filial obligation like a parrot. It is ironical since Dhritarashtra is neither a just ruler, nor his father. On no account could he be deemed a Shishta and therefore worthy of obedience. All that he deserves is a general respect given to those who are elder. The situation is further clarified in the *Ramayana* by Lakshmana's interjection. He protests against Rama's defence of Dasharatha and roundly curses both Dasharatha and Kaikeyi. It follows directly from Rama's observation about the character of Dasharatha, which Lakshmana seeks to demolish by reflecting over the events in Kaikeyi's palace. In fact Lakshmana uses the term 'Kamasakta' for the king, which means a person who is completely immersed in passion. Such persons are universally despised and recognised for their inability to make coherent judgement. Kama is an acceptable Purushartha along with Artha, but both Artha and Kama have to be subordinated to Dharma. A person who is unable to balance them is seen as a person who has fallen from Dharma. Consequently those under him have no obligations due to him. Following him is then an act of Adharma (Lack of Dharma) and the argument of pursuing filial obligations would have no merit.

In the *Mahabharata* it is well known that King Dhritarashtra is merely a puppet in the hands of his children. It is also well known that he does not have any love for the Pandavas, who are rival claimants for the throne. Since it is evident that he is an enemy, the deference accorded to him by Yudhishthira is by no means indicative of Dharma.

Leadership by tradition

From a contemporary perspective, the debate about respect to elders can also be seen as a parallel to the debate about the kind of sanctity that should be accorded to older traditions. The epics seem to forward the view that a leader should neither denounce old traditions nor embrace them completely. Leaders should see sets of traditions as a library containing descriptions of alternatives. They need to be applied properly and intelligently. Rama chooses the action of respecting his father's promise not only because his father commands it, but because his father is worthy of being obeyed. Yudhishthira is castigated because he does not judge whether Dhritarashtra is worthy of obedience and blindly applies the principle.

Dharma from the view of followers

The above discussion is about personal action. Leaders have an even greater responsibility because their personal actions have public consequences affecting entire organisations. In Rama's and Yudhishthira's cases the decisions affect entire kingdoms and multitudes of people.

This perspective receives prominence in the *Ramayana*. Lakshmana is well aware of the way in which Rama thinks, and makes an astute observation, which Rama cannot accept but does not deny. The real issue is that if Rama does not respect his father's wishes and rebels, he will fall in the eyes of his subjects who would have grave doubts about following a person who has disobeyed his own father. Even if he becomes king, he would be one by use of force not by law. Consequently there would be a diminution of respect. It is explicitly stated in the *Ramayana* that Rama is universally loved for his conduct; the way in which (almost?) the entire citizenry deserts the city to accompany him in his exile is testimony to the deep bonds he has established with the people.

But if he were to rebel there would always be a blemish on his character. He would be seen as an embodiment of Adharma by some, which in turn would have serious consequences for the prestige of the family to which he belongs. Rama is cognisant of these implications and does not deny them when they are expressed by Lakshmana. He cannot have expressed these sentiments openly but, as the rejection of Dasaratha's request to rebel would reveal, his decision is far more complex than a simple obedience of parental wishes.

If the action were simply one of obeying the wishes of their father, then Dasaratha has given Rama the freedom to rebel. He has explicitly asked Rama to imprison him and become king; but this is an immoral action. Dharma is not about blind obedience. The reason why rebellion is not a viable option is that in obeying the letter Rama would be violating the spirit.

The king is supposed to be a model of Dharma because only a just and moral king could ensure that his citizens live a moral and upright life. In practice, this was not always the case, and Ancient India is replete with instances of citizens overthrowing their kings or leaving the city. Rama's ancestor, King Sagara, had a cruel son named Asamanjas who took delight in tormenting young children. In the end, the citizenry told the king to choose between them and his son, forcing King Sagara to exile his son permanently. This incident seems to have been imprinted on the royal line, since the incident is brought up twice during the event under discussion—first by Kaikeyi, to defend her action, and then by the courtier Siddhartha, who clarified the reasons for the exile of Asamanjas. The lesson was imprinted on the dynasty of Raghu, and no king ever wanted a repetition of the situation. The lesson was not just to ensure that a prince like Asamanjas did not exploit the citizens, but to ensure that the royalty of Ayodhya won a place in the hearts of the people by practising the cornerstones of Dharma—truth, compassion, purity and charity. If Rama had chosen to rebel, he would violate the truth on which Dharma is based.

Rama's real reason for honouring the wishes of his father is the example that it presents to his subjects. Leadership is not a one-way process. Any actions by a leader are evaluated by both potential and actual followers. A leader is not just a human being but an image that crystallises the hopes of a people. Actions that confirm the respect of a people strengthen their support, thereby strengthening a leader's legitimacy. On the other hand, actions out of synchronicity with followers' expectations destroy the very foundations on which leadership is based. In the case of Rama there is an expectation that the prince would always take a principled stand. In the short run, subjects would support a potential rebellion by Rama due to their antipathy to the machinations of Kaikeyi but that action would also demolish the reverence that they had built for the young prince. Taking the shorter and easier way would demean not only Rama but the very institution of kingship itself since there could be little respect for an individual who twists ideals for his own purposes.

When Rama is steadfast in his resolve, the king tries another way to make his vow less effective. Seizing upon the exact letter of the boons, he points to Kaikeyi that he could send the royal army and treasury with Rama. The boons do not specify that Rama is to go alone, and he could be accompanied by the wealth and the force of the kingdom. Kaikeyi has not thought this out and she is momentarily disconcerted before Rama shoots down the suggestion, since such a step would violate the sanctity of the promise. It would cast a stain on the reputation on the royal line of Ayodhya who would henceforth invite the charge that they 'gave out with one hand and took it back with the other'. Rama is thinking not just about the present but the future. While everyone around him is wallowing in emotion and anger, he has the long-term interest of his family in mind. He would willingly be the sacrificial lamb so that the family's reputation remains intact.

In total contrast is the case of Yudhishthira, in the *Mahabharata* epic, who makes no attempt to understand the public consequences of action. He has several responsibilities. He has younger brothers and a wife who are dependent on him. More importantly he has the responsibility of looking after the people of his kingdom. At no point does Yudhishthira ever dwell on the effect of his actions on those for whom he is responsible. This is a case of double jeopardy.

It is important to note that leaders are not just figures of flesh and blood but exist as images in the minds of their followers. In his book *Clearings in the Forest* Nathan Harter (2006) reflects on the perspective of primal images given by the nineteenth-century philosopher Eric Voegelin. According to Harter, primal images are the images individuals use to see the world, and any society has several primal images that are shared by its members. He goes on to point out that the primal image is embodied in an historical person who exemplifies an attribute or way of living. In doing so the image exerts a disproportionate influence on the rest of humanity who are affected by it. Such persons have affected history as others have sought to emulate them over time, and historical changes have occurred when primal images of one era or place have lost importance to primal images of another.

From this context Rama's denial of the kingdom makes greater sense. Not only is he fulfilling the image of the virtuous prince, but by becoming the bearer of this primal image he is engaging in a proactive influence over the people of the kingdom who would be influenced towards a greater pursuit of virtue. By becoming a model of self-sacrifice, Rama is not just conforming to social ideals, but reaching outward to affect larger numbers of people with the ideal he embodies. Of course, given the continuing popularity of the *Ramayana* and the wide geography of its popularity he has been more successful than he could have anticipated.

We do not see this perspective in the case of Yudhishthira, whose aim is to conform to a precept, not exemplify an attribute. This subtle difference needs to be clarified. The reason Rama exemplifies an attribute is his vigorous espousal of it. Rama repeatedly rejects the kingdom as well as any wealth that could be gained and goes with pride and dignity into exile. His exit impresses the entire assembly and influences them so much that they are ready to leave the city and spend their lives in exile with him. Yudhishthira, on the other hand, makes repeated references to fate and his own powerlessness in its face. There is no pride or dignity, but only defeatism and shame. Not surprisingly then that even to this day the most charitable attitude towards him is one of pity, while in the popular imagination he stands scorned.

Dharma in terms of moral adventure

The *Ramayana* offers guidance about moral action in the face of stark choices. Most situations, however, are ambiguous and it is not possible for grand and eloquent stands. What then is the path of the leader? In this respect the *Mahabharata* is more instructive by describing the mistaken actions of Yudhishthira.

When Yudhishthira meets Shakuni, Yudhishthira offers a seemingly sound and reasoned critique of the evils of gambling. Yudhishthira also shows awareness of the fact that the dice game is merely a ploy to rob him and his brothers of their wealth. But he offers a half-hearted response that Shakuni should not try to rob them of their wealth in such an illegitimate fashion. Shakuni and Yudhishthira then engage in a debate on the legitimacy of the game of dice. Shakuni makes the claim that there is nothing immoral about the dice game since the way in which the dice fall is controlled by fate. It is just a game of chance. Yudhishthira points out that the duty of a warrior is to use the strength of his arms in order to achieve a win over his opponent. This is in conformity with the Varna Dharma of a Kshatriya, or warrior. Kshatriyas are supposed to test their strength in the battlefield, and the victor claims the riches of the vanquished. Yudhishthira has performed the Rajasuya sacrifice only recently, in which his brothers had defeated kings across India and had brought honorary tribute, which augmented their wealth.

Until now Yudhishthira has had the upper hand. He is asking Shakuni to engage in a fair contest based on the strength of arms and skill in weapons, which was moral by the Varna Dharma. Given the fact that the Pandavas are militarily superior, Shakuni and the Kauravas would surely be defeated. This, however, is just what the Kauravas want to avoid. At this point Yudhishthira could have taken the high moral ground and refused to play the game. This opportunity is allowed to pass, and the conversation with Shakuni continues. Shakuni rejects the arguments offered by Yudhishthira. He goes on to make the claim that a cunning strategy lies at the root of every victory. This is plausible since any victor has to devise a strategy to defeat his opponents. What is incredible is the claim that it justifies the use of any tactic without moral restraints. Yudhishthira should have been quick to point out that the basic fault in Shakuni's reasoning is that there is no restraint inherent in the argument. The philosophy of dharma is essentially based on the principle of restraint. Dharma allows enjoyment of wealth (Artha) and pleasure (Kama) but enjoins the individual to do so with restraint. This is the second opportunity lost, whereby Yudhishthira could have brought the debate to a conclusive end. Yudhishthira makes an even greater mistake by allowing himself to be affected by the challenge issued by Shakuni that he is a coward. Yudhishthira prides himself on his knowledge of Dharma and should know that the barb thrown by Shakuni is meant to incite him towards hasty action. Despite being aware of the intentions of the Kaurava court, he allows himself to be swayed by the challenge when he could have counter-challenged Shakuni by calling into question his intentions since he had refused to enter into a reasoned debate.

Yudhishthira makes two interesting statements. Firstly, he says that it is his definite rule that he would not withdraw from invitations. Here he makes no arguments on the morality of such a rule that he has unilaterally fashioned for himself. As observed earlier, Yudhishthira has no understanding or sensitivity towards the public consequences of his actions. Secondly, he says that he is controlled by fate. Essentially, he abandons his hopes of finding a face-saving way out, and throws his hat in the ring. In the *Ramayana* epic, Rama initially says that his change in fortune is due to fate, but that sentiment is later abandoned.

Yet there is a final strategy that could still turn the tables on the Kauravas and defeat the plans of Dhritarashtra while conforming to the dictates of Dharma, as believed by Yudhishthira. It is a measure of the despondency and fatalism of Yudhishthira that he fails to correct the severe violation of rules by which the game of dice was played, in which Shakuni illegally substitutes himself for the unskilled game-player Duryodhana. By accepting this illegal violation Yudhishthira seals his fate.

Dharma, as espoused by the narrator of the *Mahabharata*, is not just passive acceptance of virtues and practices but encompasses both strategy and courage. The overriding duty of Yudhishthira is to look towards the needs of those who are dependent on him. In doing so it is necessary that he seek a way to defeat his enemies by concentrating on their weaknesses, and be full of courage and initiative instead of taking the role of the prisoner awaiting his fate.

The debate between Shakuni and Yudhishthira makes evident his lack of preparation. Despite being aware of the Kaurava strategy, Yudhishthira has prepared an extremely weak defence leaving the matter in the hands of fate. The arguments against Shakuni lack depth, and Yudhishthira is capable of far more eloquence and sophistication. Possibly Yudhishthira's will has been sapped by the implications of obedience so that even the barest of defences seems to be a defiance of this precept.

It is also necessary to point out that, unlike Rama, who debates the issue with Lakshmana, Yudhishthira does not discuss the issue with his wife and brothers who are co-rulers of the kingdom and whose advice would have surely benefited him greatly. Yudhishthira makes Dharma a private enterprise instead of a communal one, forgetting that Dharma is practised not in isolation but in the midst of society. Dependent only on himself, it is not surprising that he falls into despondency when he should have taken the initiative. Fortified with the support of his brothers and with clarity about the nature of Dharma, he would have been able to pick out the chinks in the armour of the Kauravas and defeat them in their own game.

Conclusion

The epics see the relationship between the leader and his Dharma as a constantly evolving one. The leader is not a passive follower of an 'ancien regime': he collaborates with tradition to evolve the right conduct for himself. The epics see tradition as providing a set of worthy alternatives that, however, need to be evaluated and qualified, and applied with care. Personal duty must be balanced by public responsibilities and the leader must strive to see the effects of his actions on others. Dharma does not involve giving ground to those who would violate its spirit, and requires adherents to strategise effectively to counter such attempts. Above all, the practice of Dharma is neither literal nor passive, but an exploratory adventure involving courage and determination to make a new future.

Note

1. Warriors, the second caste in the Hindu caste system, following the Brahmins.

References

Biardeau, Madeline. (1989) *Hinduism: The Anthropology of a Civilization*, Translated from French by Richard Nice, Delhi: Oxford University Press.

Chennakesavan, Saraswati. (1978). *A Critical Study of Hinduism*, Delhi: Asia Publishing House.

Harter, Nathan. (2006) *Clearing in the Forest*, West Lafayette: Purdue University Press.

Klostermaier, Klaus K. (1994). *A Survey of Hinduism*, Albany, NY: State University of New York Press.

Mahadevan, T.M.P. (1971). *Outlines of Hinduism*, Bombay; Chetna Ltd.

Sharma, Arvind. (1982). *The Purusarthas: A Study in Hindu Axiology*, South Asia Series, Occasional Paper No. 32, Asian Studies Center, Michigan State University, East Lansing, Michigan.

Weis, René, ed. (1998). *Henry IV, Part 2, The Oxford World's Classics*, New York, NY: Oxford University Press.

Wilson, Troy (1970). *The Hindu Quest for the Perfection of Man*, Athens, OH: Ohio University Press.

13
The Leader as Poet: Tennyson, Whitman and Dickinson

Barbara Mossberg

A New Heroics for an Age of Change: Alfred, Lord Tennyson, Walt Whitman and Emily Dickinson

> Like dark matter in the universe, chaos comprises a great deal of the reality of the leader's world. An intrinsic element of human experience, chaos is depicted by canonical writers of the nineteenth century in a vision that is integral to leadership studies.

'The world is too much with us', sighed William Wordsworth in 1802. Yet if he would flee the world's realities, fellow poets in the literary pantheon of the nineteenth century did not. In form and theme, Alfred, Lord Tennyson (1809–92), Walt Whitman (1819–92) and Emily Dickinson (1830–86) are worldly. At first glance, the iconic Lord, Bard of the barbaric *yawp*, and fluttery Myth of Amherst have little in common, much less relevance to leadership studies. While Tennyson was an official poet laureate, and descended from a king, Whitman was a self-appointed (and self-promoting) people's poet, and Dickinson, although a congressman's daughter, described herself as 'nobody'. Tennyson wrote commissioned pieces for royalty. Whitman charged himself to write for the masses to promote democracy. Dickinson was a private poet in self-exile, unable to participate in or contribute to the public sphere. Tennyson was famous, Whitman was a literary outsider who self-published and felt largely ignored during his life, and Dickinson was unpublished in her lifetime. Tennyson flowed in blank verse, Whitman flooded a re-engineered epic bursting poetic bounds, and Dickinson clenched and fisted quatrains. For all their differences, these poets engage the world Wordsworth characterises as 'too much'. Taken together, their writing sheds light on an aspect of the human experience so pervasive that it comprises the 'dark matter' of leadership studies: chaos.

The reality of chaos dominates orderly structures of art and leadership. Turbulence, tumult, unmanageable forces and fragmentation: this is how people so often suffer the modern world. There seems increasingly less coherence, connection, community, stability and predictability. Chaos is what the leader must engage, and chaos theory illuminates what is visible from the leader's perch—or trench: a system in motion, or set of dynamical systems. These systems are 'whole' but characterised by change and complexity. Diverse sets of interest and points of view—which are interdependent—compete, collide, conflict, contradict, overlap and shift. This wild system behaviour (or misbehaviour) that can be confusing, demoralising, lacking in meaning, unpredictable and unintelligible is the leader's world. Fraught and frightful, this is also the world that poets do not turn from but boldly front. The chaotic nature of the world is expressed in chaotic ways. Indeed, readers confront daring perturbations of traditional poetics. Poems in irregular forms embody contradiction and turmoil. Even Tennyson gives voice to chaos. At the heart of the self-styled, free-styled disorderly aesthetics of Tennyson's iambics, Whitman's sprawling epic and Dickinson's dense lyric compressions is an understanding intrinsic to leadership of the chaotic inner and outer experience of humanity in a dynamical world.

The student of leadership—and of literature—can very well ask: How can weepy Laureate Tennyson be an authority on leadership and chaos in his cobblestone London–Freshwater–Cambridge Apostle digs; or Whitman, the flamboyant lover–journalist nursing Civil War soldiers; or least of them all, Dickinson, retreating to her upstairs room as a Yankee princess gone to seed? Yet in their own ways the chaotic world was very much with them. They each were intimately involved in the day's politics and imaginatively engaged with its leaders' greatest issues. They wrote about current and historical leadership, royal, democratic, elected, appointed and self-appointed. The headlines of the fractured and turbulent civic world pulsed in their themes of war and peace, their expression of civil crisis and their depiction of human development. Through the lens of their own personal experience with chaos, they shape the political, social, psychological and spiritual confusion of their day into a heroic consciousness that incorporates chaos into a creative worldview.

What canonical, iconic—even celebrity—nineteenth-century authors show is a poetics that is explicitly irregular, disruptive and unruly. As different in style as are Whitman, Dickinson and Tennyson, each departs from structured models and forms readers expect. Their poetry is dynamical. It destabilises and reforms traditional modes to capture individual and civic life as one ceaseless ebb and flow of break down and build-up, growth and death, violence and peace. It takes up themes and reiterates them in variations with a constantly revised text.

There are many manifestations of chaos in literature, including 'fractals', structural repetitive fractures of text, narrative disruptions and interruptions, syntactical tumult and fusion, and contradictory arguments within the whole. We will track one aspect of chaos in the poetry of Whitman, Dickinson and Tennyson—who themselves are representative models of creativity relevant to leadership studies: turbulence, and its social and psychological manifestation, strife. Turbulence is seen in imagery, theme and form in all three poets. Turbulence is re-created in art that reflects the wars, perturbations and storms in the world and the inner world, in the polis and the mind that leaders, and leadership studies, will recognise as the dark matter of creativity.

Walt Whitman

Brain of the New World—W.W.

Whitman is the poet perhaps most identified with a concern with leadership of a dynamic society; he writes of and to democratic leadership, using his 'authority' as a poet to declaim on what is needed for the nation. He explicitly embraces chaos as a principle of the poet's creativity in harmony with nature's laws:

> (Thou canst not with thy dumbness me deceive,
> I know before the fitting man all Nature yields,
> Though answering not in words, the skies, trees, hear his voice—
> And thou O sun,
> As for thy throes, thy perturbations, sudden breaks and shafts
> Of flame gigantic,
> I understand them, I know those flames, those perturbations well.)
> ('Thou Orb Aloft Full-Dazzling', from *Noon to Starry Night*)

In fact, Whitman criticises leadership that does not encompass a comprehensive view of the dynamic nature of the world:

> To A President
> All you are doing and saying is to America dangled mirages,
> You have not learn'd of Nature—of the politics of Nature you
> Have not learn'd the great amplitude, rectitude, impartiality,
> You have not seen that only such as they are for these States,

And that what is less than they must sooner or later lift off from
These States.

(From 'By the Roadside', *Leaves of Grass*)

In this vision of reality, Whitman deliberately sets out to make his
poems in form and content contain the whole USA. His epic poem,
'Song of Myself, by Walt Whitman, American', within the larger *Leaves
of Grass*, develops his own leadership as a poet providing us an inclusive
story in which we can each see ourselves. He is poet Walt Whitman, the
individual man, and the voice of the diverse emergent country itself.

> . . . of these one and all I weave the song of myself.
> I am of old and young, of the foolish as much as the wise,
> . . . Maternal and well as paternal, a child as well as a man,
> Stuff'd with the stuff that is coarse and stuff'd with the stuff that is
> fine,
> One of the Nation of many nations, the smallest the same and the
> largest the same,
> A Southerner soon as a Northerner, a planter nonchalant and . . .
> A Yankee . . .
> Of every hue and caste am I, of every rank and religion,
> . . . I am the poet of the woman the same as the man,
> . . . Walt Whitman, a kosmos, of Manhattan the son,
> Turbulent, fleshy, sensual, eating, drinking and breeding . . .
> Through me the afflatus surging and surging, through me the current
> and index.

He aspires to make his language flow the way consciousness experiences complexity, in 'perturbations'. The true nature of the world does
not exclude anything: the inclusiveness appears chaotic but everything
belongs. Whitman is aware his inclusive list of all the components that
make up a cosmic self or nation is chaotic:

> Do I contradict myself?
> Very well then I contradict myself,
> (I am large, I contain multitudes.)

And in this, he defines himself as the natural world, simultaneously
coexisting realities. Although he is a multitude of diverse elements,
like any dynamical system, men and women, eastern and western,

urban and rural, free and slave, young and old, he sees this as ultimate harmony:

> Do you see O my brothers and sisters?
> It is not chaos or death—it is form, union, plan—it is eternal life—it is Happiness.

Many features of Whitman's poetry, considered innovative in form, so fresh as to be slightly disreputable (he himself said his legacy was not as great 'literature') illustrate the theory that explains chaos as behaviour of the natural world, and a greater, if messy and irregular, form of order. His lines are not neatly hemmed nor are they bordered with rhyme; they are not contained in metrical order. He writes a 'free verse' deliberately constructed to be free of order, to be perturbations, authentic, rustic and grounded in a democratic context. For Whitman, a self-described turbulent spirit, his poetic form is not intimidated, nor does it bow to authorities of traditional bounded poetics. His lines and poems repeat and sprawl, jagged as a storm-pressed coastline; they flow like a river, sometimes smoothly, sometimes turbulently; they belch and have gas, and possess dignified oratory and calm reflection in a tragic mode:

> You oceans that have been calm within me! How I feel you,
> fathomless, stirring, preparing unprecedented waves and storms.

The 'dark matter' of a world he celebrates for its boisterous freedoms as an emergent democracy he also finds tragic; his poems are about mourning the losses in a war he sees first-hand as a nurse to the soldiers. He begins his book opus, *Leaves of Grass,* mindful of a muse, 'Terrible in beauty, age, and power,' asking him, 'Know'st thou not there is but one theme for ever-enduring bards?/And that is the theme of War'; but Whitman answers that although he also does 'sing war', it is 'a longer and greater /one than any,/ . . . the field the world,/For life and death, for the Body and for the eternal Soul'. War is a 'seething principle! . . . with all its angry and vehement play of causes,/(With vast results to come for thrice a thousand years,) . . . my book and the war are one'. Whitman's vision integrates a darker understanding of human nature and society along with a buoyant sense of hope.

Whitman specifically addresses chaos in context of a larger order that contains psychological, spiritual, political and social forms of dissolution and integrity. He sees himself as 'Me Imperturbe', a play on 'imperturbable',

standing at ease in Nature,
Master of all or mistress of all, aplomb in the midst of irrational
things,
Imbued as they, passive, receptive, silent as they,
Finding my occupation, poverty, notoriety, foibles, crimes, less
important than I thought...
Me wherever my life is lived, O to be self-balanced for contingencies,
To confront night, storms, hunger, ridicule, accidents, rebuffs, as the
trees and animals do.

In 'Savantism', he sees 'each result and glory retracing itself and
nestling close,...every-day life, speech, utensils, politics, persons,
estates;/Thither we also, I with my leaves and songs, trustful, admi-
rant....' and in his 'leaves of grass', his poems, 'I hear America singing.'
Much of this voice is dark matter, but it is all 'consciousness, these forms,
the power of motion', and thereby, in Whitman's view of chaos, he is
singing in 'ecstatic songs' 'what has come to the surface after so many
throes and convulsions'.

Emily Dickinson

> *I once perceived that chaos reined.*

As a natural and essential feature of the human landscape, turbulence
is present even in a sheltered spare upstairs bedroom of a woman who
never left home. Whereas Walt Whitman was a New York City boy, who
lived in Washington, DC, much of his life in the corridors of leadership
and on-going national dramas, Dickinson lived in a white frame house
on Main Street, in bucolic Amherst, Massachusetts, and with almost no
exceptions never entered the fray of public life. In spite of her famous
poem, 'Wild Nights', she is not what is normally thought of as a 'wild
woman'. But the mind expressing and portrayed in Emily Dickinson's
poetry is wild. Just as Walt Whitman wrote of himself in contradictory
ways as a complex organic system, 'I am large, I contain multitudes',
Emily Dickinson describes herself in an existentialist paradox: 'I'm
Nobody! Who are You?/Are You—Nobody—Too?' In fact, her poems
describe the chaos within consciousness as the self fragments in strife
that parallels the Civil War and a nation's crisis of a ruptured national
identity: 'Me from Myself—to banish—/Had I Art-.../And since We're
mutual Monarch—/How this be/Except by Abdication—/Me—of Me?'
The integrity of the self at war is dismantled—by definition—when
incompatible realities overlay each other in psychic chaos.

Like Whitman's plural and pluralistic identity of fragments of diverse regional and cultural peoples, she conceives herself as a turbulent nation; specifically, her polis is a repudiation of a country that denies her rights to contribute leadership. She is wry and rueful when she relates that her role in society is to be daughter of a candidate for state or national leadership when '... I know all about Daniel Webster, and the Tariff, and the Law?' 'I don't like this country at all, and I shan't stay here any longer. My country is Truth.' Loyal to the 'native land' of the mind, she lives as an ex-patriate poet: 'I have no life but this, to live it here'—that is, on the page. In this country, she has a voice; her identity is her creative self. When she describes her brain torn, she speaks from a leader's vantage, a 'head of state' which confronts tumult; in Lincoln's assassination, the loss of the nation's 'head' creates political chaos. Dickinson describes her own mind at war with itself. In 'One need not be a chamber to be haunted', there is an explicit division between the (female) mind and the (male) body 'who borrows a revolver' to fend off gothic terrors. Her psyche is in strife. In 'The first day's night had come', she describes what is probably a mortal wound, at least to one's sanity. She has initially survived an attack, and instructs her 'soul to sing'. Her soul is too damaged, and the poet sets about to try to put the pieces together again for a coherent voice. The poem ends, however, from a time long since past, and yet the 'brain keeps giggling—still'. She wonders if this is 'madness'.

But it is as much in style that Dickinson expresses turbulence of consciousness as a creative principle. Her poetry appears in startled bursts, dashed and breathless, with meteoric insights, while the grammar intensifies the release of suppressed energy, fusing parts of speech. Words almost rhyme in quatrains; metre is established only to break it up in irregular gusts or trailing sighs.

> On a columnar Self
> How ample to rely
> In Tumult—or Extremity—
> How good the Certainty
> That Lever cannot pry—
> And Wedge cannot divide
> Conviction—That Granitic Base—
> Though None be on our Side—
> Suffice Us—for a Crowd—
> Ourself—and Rectitude—
> And that Assembly—not far off
> From furthest Spirit—God

Although embattled, she is heroic in defying the forces that would 'bind' and 'imprison' her soul and voice. Her verses were so 'irregular' in rhyme, metre and form that early editors did not conceive them as poetry. She was advised not to publish by editors she consulted. She admitted in a letter that when she tries to organise herself, she explodes her force. She cannot be contained.

Alfred, Lord Tennyson

Chaos: only leaders need apply

Tennyson's poetry engages with a chaotic vision of turbulence that is essential to a heroic self. His poetry is broadly concerned with leadership as a theme. One of Tennyson's most famous poems is 'Ulysses', an imagined monologue in the voice of the protagonist of Homer's *Odyssey*. Recounted in Shakespeare's iambic pentameter, the poem is a 'natural' form and does not rhyme. It proceeds in fitful starts and sighs, interrupting itself, bringing in new themes, changing the tone, and making the mind at work complex and rife with turbulence. An aged king is speaking about his retirement as a leader. After the war, after the long monster-studded voyage home, no turbulence is in sight:

> It little profits that an idle king,
> By this still hearth, among these barren crags,
> Match'd with an aged wife, I mete and dole
> Unequal laws unto a savage race,
> That hoard, and sleep, and feed, and know not me.

It is a quiet, still world. But within this framework is a swelling resistance and spirit of longing which erupts into an impatience with a stable status quo, finally crashing with vehemence in the final urgent message: let's go! Let's get out of here!

> I cannot rest from travel: I will drink
> Life to the lees: all times I have enjoyed
> Greatly, have suffered greatly, both with those
> That loved me, and alone; on shore, and when
> Through scudding drifts the rainy Hyades
> Vexed the dim sea: I am become a name;
> For always roaming with a hungry heart
> Much have I seen and known; cities of men

> And manners, climates, councils, governments,
> Myself not least, but honoured of them all;
> And drunk delight of battle with my peers;
> Far on the ringing plains of windy Troy.
> I am a part of all that I have met;
> Yet all experience is an arch wherethrough
> Gleams that untravelled world, whose margin fades
> For ever and for ever when I move.
> How dull it is to pause, to make an end,
> To rust unburnished, not to shine in use!
> As though to breathe were life. Life piled on life
> Were all too little, and of one to me
> Little remains: but every hour is saved
> From that eternal silence, something more,
> A bringer of new things; and vile it were
> For some three suns to store and hoard myself,
> And this grey spirit yearning in desire
> To follow knowledge like a sinking star,
> Beyond the utmost bound of human thought.

Halfway through the reflection the speaker interrupts himself to introduce his son who will inherit his civic leadership duties 'to make mild/A rugged people':

> This is my son, mine own Telemachus,
> To whom I leave the sceptre and the isle

The way he describes this work in terms of 'labour', 'slow prudence', 'soft degrees', 'subdue', suggests what it is about it that makes Ulysses reject this managerial role for his own. While he holds his son 'blameless', the staidness of respecting 'common duties', what is 'decent', 'useful and the good', is not for him: 'He works his work, I mine.' What is inferred is his own perception about the difference between himself and his son as leaders:

> —
> Well-loved of me, discerning to fulfill
> This labour, by slow prudence to make mild
> A rugged people, and through soft degrees
> Subdue them to the useful and the good.
> Most blameless is he, centred in the sphere
> Of common duties, decent not to fail

> In offices of tenderness, and pay
> Meet adoration to my household gods,
> When I am gone. He works his work, I mine.

Ulysses then breaks off his comments in what now gradually appears to be a highly rhetorical rousing speech to recruit a team for his next adventure. When Ulysses refers to 'my mariners', we could imagine the community of spirits he is thinking about; but suddenly, the flow of thoughts is interrupted with a direct statement revealing his real audience: 'you', his mates. We as readers move from people with whom he is sharing his reflections as he rocks on his metaphoric porch, to cronies he might yet induce to join him in what will certainly be a last hurrah adventure ending in death.

> There lies the port; the vessel puffs her sail:
> There gloom the dark broad seas. My mariners,
> Souls that have toil'd, and wrought, and thought with me—
> That ever with a frolic welcome took
> The thunder and the sunshine, and opposed
> Free hearts, free foreheads—you and I are old;
> Old age hath yet his honour and his toil;
> Death closes all: but something ere the end,
> Some work of noble note, may yet be done,
> Not unbecoming men that strove with Gods.
> The lights begin to twinkle from the rocks:
> The long day wanes: the slow moon climbs: the deep
> Moans round with many voices. Come, my friends,
> 'Tis not too late to seek a newer world.
> Push off, and sitting well in order smite
> The sounding furrows; for my purpose holds
> To sail beyond the sunset, and the baths
> Of all the western stars, until I die.
> It may be that the gulfs will wash us down:
> It may be we shall touch the Happy Isles,
> And see the great Achilles, whom we knew
> Tho' much is taken, much abides; and though
> We are not now that strength which in old days
> Moved earth and heaven; that which we are, we are;
> One equal temper of heroic hearts,
> Made weak by time and fate, but strong in will
> To strive, to seek, to find, and not to yield.

Leaders can find in 'Ulysses' multiple ideas about leadership at war within the poem: a civil war of internal conflict. At first, it seems as if the speaker's life is exhausted. As a retired king, he is through. But when he considers his son Telemachus, he offers another view of leadership which he rejects. Ulysses's leadership world is chaotic, and he thrives on it: it is 'noble'. It requires great energy: pushing off, smiting, seeking relentlessly unto death. Both thunder and sunshine are embraced joyously. Telemachus's kind of leadership is rejected because it lacks the vitality of chaos, the dynamical, risky turbulence and the defiant and heroic spirit which is required to engage such a world. For Tennyson's Ulysses, Telemachus ensures the social order. For the land-lubbers, he is a do-gooder, and Ulysses's contempt for the low stakes of his son's work is barely disguised. The insertion about Telemachus seems superfluous and gratuitously, even aggressively, dismissive. In fact, the speaker hardly even bothers to acknowledge his wife, who neither merits being named—her thanks after all those years of fending off suitors—nor graced with any word except 'aged'. Thus we are not altogether shocked when Ulysses goes out of his way to condescend to the nature of his son's duties. What we see is that the rejection of the domestic life is a rejection of the kind of order that stifles the spirits.

Ulysses is addicted to strife: he wants the tumult, the turmoil, the roil of turbulence, because this is where life is. Ulysses knows how to live: life is in the spray, the splash. It would seem that two models of leadership are presented here, but Tennyson's interpretation of Ulysses rejecting the happy ending that 'Ithaca' represents suggests that Telemachus's leadership, while 'useful' to civic society, does not promote heroic outcomes of a people. In Homer's version, Ulysses spends 20 years trying to get home; Ithaca is a destination goal. A goal which is always there, but never achieved? I don't know what Ithaca meant to Ulysses, and perhaps this phrase could be clearer. But Tennyson in the nineteenth century cannot imagine an island retirement as a happy ending. Leadership must be heroic, risky, self-sacrificing.

Readers of world literature have seen the dynamics of leadership described in this way. For today's readers, in fact, Tennyson's Ulysses seems a twentieth-century hero, updated from Shakespeare's 'once more, good friends, into the fray', tragic leaders who willingly front the tumult. He (Tennyson) chooses the unpredictable universe Ulysses has had to encounter on his journey home—storms, monstrous forces, stalls and delays, which defined the world of Homer's Ulysses. In contrast, Ithaca is characterised as a dull place. The second word in the poem is 'little', and the language is belittling, confined: an *idle* king, *still* crags, *barren, aged*: nothing is happening there; it's all decline. It's *pause, rust,* dis-use, breathing, not life. Even his invocation to his mates argues against the decline of ageing when things are slow: 'come, my friends', he says, finally breaking out of his exposition, making his case with this flip-chart Power Point: 'It little profits ...' This is a management seminar to the board in terms of cost–benefit analysis. But he brings his board on board; when Ulysses engages his group, he speaks to them with affection, claiming them as 'my friends'. A newer world is not dull: it is the way the poet physicist E E Cummings describes the 'great happening illimitably earth'. Now Ulysses makes the leader's case statement, beginning with the mission: 'for my purpose holds ...' He does a risk assessment: 'It may be that the gulfs will wash us down.' They might go to hell—and he wants to follow knowledge beyond known boundaries: he proposes to take his community to the edge of consciousness where life—if also death—is happening. Tennyson's version of Ulysses opens our insight into leadership itself as a dynamical, turbulent enterprise requiring a heroic sensibility embracing chaos for the larger life.

Conclusion

In the English-speaking world, both nineteenth-century Great Britain and America experienced increasing social and civic instability and fragmentation on the heels of progressive rights movements upheaving the political world in the eighteenth century. Issues of race, class and gender were now exploding beyond national borders. Leaders faced turbulence not only of war and peace but in changing laws and values on human and civil rights. They entered the fray, and in the process perturbed the political systems through their governance, whether elected or royal. Their role was to help society through chaos. In this way, the challenge of the leader is the same as the poet's: fearlessly to grasp complexity and change and incorporate chaotic realities into a form of unity of theory and practice that governance and poetry represent. In the examples of the age's iconic poets, we see minds at work not resisting the world as 'too much', but making order of chaos in a way that respects its formative role in human consciousness and behaviour. Contradiction and tension are expressed in terms of civil war of the psyche, whether a nation or self, imagined leader or 'nobody'. In these poets, chaos is a creative principle. Seemingly so different in temperament, culture, experience and literary style, the century's great iconic poets engage with worldly chaos in a way that expresses creative solutions to age-old human challenges leaders have always had to face. Therefore, understanding how they engage with chaos illuminates a creative aspect of the leader's world and work.

The way that poets conceive and express chaos is useful for leaders in recognising and illuminating a common, yet fearsome, feature of their daily work and world. For all that these writers express and even model chaos in their poetry, they also show how imaginatively they have creative control of it. Chaos becomes a conscious and conspicuous part of their force and power as artists. Similarly, understanding how chaos energises and organises a writer's mind illuminates the mandates and opportunities for the essentially creative work of the leader.

Impassioned by their own intent to speak authentically for and to their fellow citizens about life and death matters, Tennyson, Whitman and Dickinson express a heroic energy. Their poetry reflects the turbulence, strife and tumult of their world, whether they describe inner and personal struggle, current political affairs of war and peace, or historical events. Yet it orders this perception and experience of chaos into art. The poets show an approach to life's dilemmas in the content and form of their writing that is inextricable from the way leadership strives to organise civic chaos and complacence into effective governance. The leader's vision is a 'story' that expresses individual and community values and needs. In the process, the leader contributes to an ethos of common understanding of purpose and meaning upon which civic society is based. For societies undergoing rapid transitions and flux, leaders can find insights into the challenges and possibilities of their work in poetry organising the human spirit in heroic stance and stanza.

Bibliography

Dickinson, E. (1960). *The Complete Poems of Emily Dickinson.* Edited by Thomas H Johnson. Little, Brown: New York.

Lord Tennyson, Alfred (1891). *Works.* Two volumes. Macmillan: London.

Whitman, W. (1981). *Leaves of Grass: The First (1855) Edition.* Penguin Classics: London.

14
Leadership and Tradition: Rabindranath Tagore

Satish Kumar

Early life

Rabindranath Tagore was born into a wealthy and cultured Hindu family in Calcutta in 1861, the youngest of many children. He was educated mainly at home, and during his youth travelled widely with his father. In 1878, the year in which his first poems were published in India, he went to study in England with the intention of becoming a barrister, but returned home without a degree in 1880. For the next decade, he immersed himself in his poetry and other writings. He married in 1893. In 1890, at his father's choice, he began managing the family's vast estates in East Bengal (now Bangladesh). At the same time, he continued to write and to edit an influential magazine; and he founded a school in 1901 where he could put his ideas on education into practice. Through publishing his poems and other writings, Tagore was becoming a well-known writer in his native land. For the rest of his life, he was to expand his interests and apply his ideals, and he was always to keep his connection with the land and with farming.

The Nobel Prize

Rabindranath Tagore went on to achieve great worldly success. He visited England again in 1912, this time as an established poet, and to great effect; such was the impact of his poetry that he was awarded the Nobel Prize in Literature in 1913. In 1915, he was knighted: a distinction that he was to repudiate in 1919, after the British massacre in Amritsar, when over 400 Indian protestors were shot down by Brigadier-General Dyer. Tagore was *au fait* with political developments, but unlike his friend and admirer, Mohandas Gandhi, he did not lead a political movement or play an active day-to-day role in national politics. Rather than playing the role of leader himself, Tagore was the person to whom the leaders went for ideas, inspiration and evaluation; and Gandhi, whom Tagore recognised as the Mahatma or Great Soul, was to acknowledge his contribution to the foundation of a new India, not only free of British rule but finding its own way forward to an unbiased future.

Rural reform: Santiniketan

Tagore founded the Institute for Rural Reconstruction at Santiniketan in 1921, in association with the English agronomist and social reformer Leonard Elmhirst (1893–1974). The Institute remained an important part of Tagore's life and evolved into a university which remains active today. Elmhirst and his wife, the American heiress Dorothy Whitney Straight (1887–1968), went on to purchase Dartington Hall in Devon in 1925. With Tagore's involvement, the Elmhirsts made Dartington into the centre for progressive education and rural reconstruction that remains active today. Tagore continued to write, travel, reform and publish for the remainder of his long and highly productive life, during which he never ceased from exploring new activities and interests; so that when already in his seventies, for example, he became a painter.

Rabindranath Tagore was awarded a doctorate of letters at Oxford University in 1940, and died at his home in Calcutta at the age of 80 in 1941. His wife had died many years before, and they left several children.

His achievements and reputation

Mahatma Gandhi called Tagore 'Gurudev' (the divine teacher) and Western writers and scientists such as W B Yeats, Bernard Shaw and Albert Einstein called him 'the greatest son of India'. In his native place he was known as 'the voice of Bengal'. He inspired millions in India as well as abroad through his novels, short stories, plays and paintings and more especially through his songs and poetry. He wrote more than a thousand poems and over two thousand songs, and they are popularly recited and sung in every corner of Bengal as well as wherever there are Bengalis, and have been translated into all major languages of the world including English, French, Spanish, German, Russian, Chinese and Japanese.

Tagore started to paint only when he was in his seventies, and in the last ten years of his life he produced three thousand paintings. In 1913 he was awarded the Nobel Prize in Literature for his collection of poems,

Gitanjali, an offering of sacred songs; at this stage his international reputation was probably at its highest point.

The unity of life

For Tagore writing, painting and singing were vehicles to communicate the profound unity of life, the sacred, mystical and divine quality of the natural world and to inspire his readers to connect with the universality of the human spirit. He never subscribed to the idea of 'art for art's sake' or even to art and poetry as a means of self-expression. For Tagore poetry and art were to serve the human spirit and to affirm the unity of life and to protect the integrity of the sacred earth.

Recommending Tagore for the Nobel Prize, the Swedish poet Verner von Heidenstam wrote, 'The loving and intense religious sense that permeates all his thoughts and feelings, the purity of heart and the noble and unaffected elevation of the style—all amount to a total impression of deep and rare spiritual beauty.'

Tagore on leadership

A friend of Rabindranath Tagore, Ananda Coomaraswamy, once said, 'An artist is not a special kind of person but every person is a special kind of artist' (Coomaraswamy, 1934). Tagore would echo that in terms of leadership. Everyone is potentially a leader but often the quality of leadership is suppressed through social, religious and cultural conditioning. This is why Tagore established a school for children so that children are able to grow in self-confidence, free from fear and cultural conditioning.

To be a true leader one has to lead one's own life fearlessly in the direction of one's own idealism and courage of convictions. One cannot lead others unless one is able to lead oneself. As Tagore's friend, Mahatma Gandhi, said, 'Be the change you want to see in the world.' One cannot bring about change by preaching or expecting others to change unless one has put oneself on the line. Setting an example speaks louder than a million words. Tagore was able to influence others because he led his own life with great discipline, with tenacity and with courage, irrespective of opposition and criticism from others.

'Even if no one listens to you or follows you, walk alone, walk alone, walk alone. Even if the night is dark and the path goes through dense forest walk alone, walk alone,' he wrote in one of his songs. This song became a favourite of Mahatma Gandhi and a popular chant of the Independence of India Movement. Paradoxically, when one is prepared to go it alone others usually want to come along; but in the heart of the true leader there is no expectation that this will happen. This rare 'spiritual beauty' is as evident in Tagore's poetry as it is in his plays and novels.

The Post Office

My favourite play by Tagore is *The Post Office*, which attracted worldwide attention. It was performed in Dublin, London, Berlin and Warsaw and was broadcast on French radio in Andre Guide's translation. The young hero, Amal, is very ill; almost on his deathbed; and he is confined to his room by his anxious father. From his window, Amal connects with the outside world and talks to passers-by. One of them is a lovely girl collecting flowers, which creates a deep longing for love in the heart of Amal. He also talks to a wandering sadhu, a milkman, a guard and other village people, who include boys, somewhat younger than he, who borrow the toys he can no longer use. Amal is envious of their freedom, and yet seems to have reached some sort of acceptance of his status in seclusion; this is conveyed in the poetry of the language in which this play is offered, as much as by the dialogue itself.

In the distance, Amal sees a building with a flag flying on it, which is the Post Office. Amal dreams of getting a letter from the king, and he becomes excited and thrilled at the idea. He is looking out of the window morning after morning waiting for the postman to bring him the letter from the king. Amal is talking to everyone about his longing for this letter.

The village head is deeply touched and moved by this innocent fantasy of Amal, and so he informs the king about Amal's obsession to receive a letter from him. Impressed by Amal's childlike desire, the king not only sends a get-well message but also a healer to treat the dying young man. Amal, however, does not want healing; he wants liberation. The letter is enough. It is the note of freedom. He is emancipated. Filled with love the flower girl comes to offer flowers to Amal; but he has gone to sleep forever. In Tagore's own words 'death to the world of hoarded wealth and certified creeds brings him awakenings in the world of spiritual freedom'.

Gora

In the equally well-known novel *Gora*, Tagore elaborates the transcendental quality of the human spirit. The hero of the story is a fair-colour, orphaned, Irish child who is brought up by an Indian family in a Hindu tradition. As the boy grows up he rejects the Hindu orthodoxy, but falls in love with a beautiful Hindu girl.

When the young hero realises that he is not a Hindu but an Irishman whose father died in the mutiny of 1857, he struggles through an identity crisis as well as the crisis of love. Eventually love triumphs and the two souls are united. They transcend racial, cultural and geographical limitations and embody the universal human spirit. Again and again, whether it is a story, or a play or a poem, Tagore never fails to convey the essential longing for liberation and spiritual freedom.

To appreciate Tagore's passion one needs to go no further than to read his poem in *Gitanjali*, the Nobel Prize-winning book.

> Where the mind is without fear and the head is held high,
> Where knowledge is free;
> Where the world has not been broken up into fragments by narrow
> domestic walls;
> Where words come out from the depth of truth;
> Where tireless striving stretches its arms towards perfection;
> Where the clear stream of reason has not lost its way into the
> dreary desert sand of dead habit;
> Where the mind is led forward by thee into ever-widening thought
> and action—
> into that heaven of freedom,
> my Father,
> Let my country awake.

Education

In addition to his passion for writing, singing and painting, Tagore was a social activist, a cultural reformer and a radical educationalist. Although he himself never attended a school proper or a university he encountered many young people who had been victims of the disciplinarian, materialist and utilitarian system of education imposed by British rulers. In exasperation and in protest against 'job-seeking education' he started a school with five children, which grew and grew, and became India's greatest experiment in holistic learning.

Tagore's love of nature came over clearly and explicitly in the way his school operated. Classes took place under the trees. 'You have two Teachers', Tagore would say to his pupils. 'The human teachers are of course your teachers but, equally important, if not more so, are the trees. They are your true teachers. Learn from the book of nature as much as you learn from the books of humans because the book of nature is even older and is also more authentic.'

Knowledge from experience

For Tagore, knowledge by itself is not enough; it must be complemented by experience. When knowledge and experience come together, wisdom is born. Theory is of no use without practice, and therefore children must learn to use their hands and nourish their hearts as much as they educate their heads. Gardening, cooking and arts and crafts were an essential part of the school from the very start. Feeding the intellect is only half the story, for Tagore believed that the real purpose of education is to nourish the human imagination. That is why he called his school 'a poet's school'. At the same time he believed that 'education should never be disassociated from life'.

Agriculture

Within walking distance of the school Tagore started a centre for rural reconstruction. He encouraged his own son to be educated in the art and science of agriculture. He persuaded Leonard Elmhirst, an agronomist from the United Kingdom, to work at this new centre in order to put new energy and respect into the working of the land. For Tagore, agriculture was the soul of the Indian economy. All other economic activities were for him like icing on the cake because agriculture was not merely a source of livelihood, it was the poetry of life itself; he believed that industrial development at the expense of agriculture would bring tears and tragedy.

Tagore's heart was in the land because he had experienced the rural life of India at close quarters. His father, who owned an agricultural estate in East Bengal, now Bangladesh, chose his poet son to manage it, and through the experience of working closely with farmers Tagore understood the deep-rooted culture of people living on the land. Therefore, Tagore's vision of India was of a country where agriculture was respected and loved. Agriculture was a simple and natural way of being close to nature, and being close to nature was being close to God.

Nationalism

Tagore was a great friend of Gandhi and was the first to call him 'Mahatma', yet he did not wholeheartedly agree with Gandhi's view of nationalism. Tagore was as much for the independence of India as Gandhi, and had rejected the knighthood offered to him by the British government; but he was also enthralled by the idea of synthesising and integrating the world views of East and West. Tagore would distance himself from xenophobic nationalists who would throw away the baby with the bath water. Tagore wanted to retain the good aspects of British culture, like science and technology. For Tagore, science and spirituality were complementary. Naturally, Tagore joined Mahatma Gandhi and other leaders of the independence movement to free India from British colonial rule, although sometimes he considered their political outlook too narrow; for he was never a simple-minded nationalist.

Divinity

Tagore's poetry and politics, as well as his views on education and agriculture, were firmly founded in a religious and spiritual worldview. Tagore's father was a great Sanskrit scholar of the Upanishads and a Sufi mystic. Being brought up in such an environment and being inspired by Baul musicians who sang devotional songs in fairs, fields and bazaars, Tagore absorbed their ancient spiritual tradition and grew up as a poet of the soul. The divinity present in people, nature and the land became his muse and the guiding principle of his life. Beauty in nature, and harmony between nature and humans, was his religion. He urged Hindus, Muslims, Christians, Buddhists, Jains and Sikhs to transcend their sectarian differences and seek truth, beauty and goodness through harmony and interdependence.

Conclusion

Tagore led his life with commitment to his place, to his people, to the planet and to the universe. His love for the particular as much as for the universal came over through his songs so vividly and strongly that when India achieved independence, the country adopted his song 'The Fate of the Universe Is the Fate of India' as its national anthem. Another of his songs expressing his love for the land of Bengal became the national anthem of Bangladesh. It is a rare honour that a country with a Hindu majority, India, and a country with a Muslim majority, Bangladesh, should both adopt his songs as their national anthems. Such songs transcend national and religious limitations and boundaries.

Tagore was a leading figure in promoting new approaches to life in general, as well as a spiritual leader. He explored new territories in the spheres of poetry, fiction and the arts. He also travelled in new directions to discover sustainable, spiritual, imaginative and resilient ways to build strong communities. He introduced holistic vision into the fields of education, agriculture and religion. That vision of integrity, spirituality and simplicity is even more relevant today. The challenges facing humanity in the twenty-first century are monumental. The greatest of them is the disconnection and breakdown of the human–nature relationship and the urgent need to find ways of reconnecting human activities with the natural world so that people and planet are in harmony with each other. The life, thoughts and poetry of Tagore can act as a beacon of inspiration to guide us in the right direction.

Rabindranath Tagore's example is as inspiring today as it was one hundred years ago.

References

It is difficult to reference Tagore's works and quotations, since some of the information needed is not readily available. Here are some representative references.

www.nobelprize.org:

Chakravarty, A (1961) A Tagore Reader. Beacon Press, Uckfield, East Sussex. (Now owned by The Pureprint Group, Uckfield, East Sussex.)
Coomaraswamy, A K C (1934) The Transformation of Nature in Art. (This appears to have been privately published.)
Tagore, R (1913) Gitanjali (A Collection of Poems). Macmillan, London.
Tagore, R (1977) Collected Plays and Poems of Rabindranath Tagore. Macmillan, London.

15
Leadership and Acceptability: Plato and the Odium of Truth

Nathan Harter

Probably the most authentic presentation of the philosophical beliefs and ideas of Socrates is Plato's *Apology*, a recreation of his legal defence against charges of impiety and corrupting the young. There, Socrates explained his life's purpose and method for improving Athens by serving as a gadfly to rouse the people to think critically about what they are doing and choose those ends that conduce to well-being. Socrates claimed to confer a benefit on his community as he confronted leaders and prospective leaders to give account of their knowledge. As a result of these dialogues, Socrates exposed their ignorance and thereby undermined their authority with the people, while at the same time inspiring generations of citizens to undertake critical thinking for themselves.

Plato's *Apology*

About six years after Socrates was executed, his most gifted admirer wrote an account of his legal defence, a forensic *tour de force* that lost the case and won lasting admiration. Although not a dialogue in the manner popularly associated with Plato's Socrates, *The Apology* has been considered by scholars such as Eduard Zeller to be the most authentic representation of the beliefs and ideas of that singular character who is widely regarded as the founder of critical thinking (for example, Zeller, 1955, Page 116). In these passages, the accused philosopher laid before the people of Athens his mission, method and justification for conducting a series of dialogues with leaders and prospective leaders—dialogues that resulted in demonstrating their ignorance and in provoking his listeners to reflect on their own lack of knowledge about the most important questions.

As Plato's subsequent dialogues make plain, he was profoundly distressed at the fate of his beloved elder and furious with the people of Athens for tolerating such an unjust verdict. That bitterness motivated him to demonstrate how wrong they had been to order the execution. However, the trial of Socrates was more than a miscarriage of justice: it was also symbolic of the tensions inherent in civic life.

Three citizens of Athens brought the following charges against an elderly Socrates: impiety and corrupting the young. The charge of impiety included two parts: a failure to recognise the official gods as well as the introduction of 'strange daimonic doings' (Reeve, 1989, Page 76). These are separate and distinct charges. Corrupting the young follows from impiety, since the accused allegedly tended to foster impiety in them (26b). So, in effect, the charge of impiety underlay the charge of corrupting the young. According to Gregory Vlastos, the bare charge of impiety was not actionable unless Socrates were trying to proselytise someone (1991, Page 295), so alleging the corruption of the young does add a necessary component to the indictment. Confusing matters, however, one of the accusers under direct examination during the trial admitted that the indictment was really meant to charge Socrates with atheism—this despite the claim that he had introduced new divinities, a contradiction Socrates was quick to exploit (26c–27e). 'How does an atheist introduce new divinities?' he asked. Nevertheless, Socrates stood trial for impiety and corrupting the young.

The Apology is comprised of three parts in accordance with Athenian trial procedure. In a case of this sort, 501 jurors sat in judgement. The prosecution would be conducted by the accusers and not by an elected official. We have no record of the actual prosecution in this case. At the conclusion of the prosecution, the defendant would be given an opportunity to reply. It is this portion of the trial that opens *The Apology*. Once the jury had rendered a verdict of guilt with a count of 280 votes for conviction, the trial entered into a new phase. In this second phase, the accusers proposed a penalty and the defendant made a counter-proposal; then the jury simply picked between the two proposals. By inference, we know that the accusers sought the death penalty in this case, yet this second portion of *The Apology* includes only Socrates's counter-proposal. Finally, after the decision had been handed down and he was officially condemned to death, Socrates delivered an impromptu speech that was not part of the formal procedure and yet appears at the conclusion of *The Apology*.

We can refer to these three sections as the Defence Phase, the Counter-Penalty Phase and his Extra-Legal Remarks.

The Defence Phase itself can be broken into four sub-parts. Socrates opens by disclaiming expertise at forensic speech and pledging simply to speak the truth. Next, he protests that he stands accused by two different indictments. There is the formal charge brought by the accusers, to which he would turn his attention shortly, but Socrates had been criticised and ridiculed for decades in the court of public opinion. The judgement of the jurors might be clouded by their prejudice, which is why Socrates deals with his general reputation first, before responding to the official indictment. The Defence Phase concludes with a peroration, when Socrates begs leave to depart from customary practice and refrain from emotional pleas and other histrionics.

The Counter-Penalty Phase that follows the vote can be broken into two sub-parts. Socrates tells the jury what he thinks he honestly deserves before making the official counter-proposal of paying a fine. The Extra-Legal Remarks at the end can also be broken into two sub-parts, in which he addresses those jurors who voted to acquit separately from addressing those jurors who voted to condemn.

The structure of Plato's *Apology* therefore looks like this.

1. Defence Phase (17a–35d)

   a. opening;
   b. countering public opinion;
   c. countering the official indictment;
   d. peroration.

2. Counter-Penalty Phase (35e–38b)

   a. what I deserve;
   b. what I propose.

3. Extra-Legal Remarks (38b–42a)

   a. to those who voted for condemnation;
   b. to those who voted against condemnation.

It is probably useful to mention that, in contrast to some interpreters of *The Apology* who find Socrates engaged in all sorts of misdirection such as irony, issuing playful jests and boasts, and actually choosing tactics designed to *lose* the trial so he could be put to death, here we treat his remarks as straightforward and sincere (Brickhouse and Smith, 1983, Page 41; Reeve, 1989, Page xiii). This is not to say that Socrates failed to see the irony in these proceedings, but we will proceed as though he meant what he said when he began his defence by telling the jury he would speak only the truth (17b).

The mission of Socrates

At the heart of his defence against the central charges of impiety, Socrates demonstrates his piety by disclosing his service to the divine, as expressed both by the Oracle of Delphi and by a personal *daimonion* or angel that advises him in daily affairs.[1] He even says, 'I have been ordered to practice [philosophy] by the gods, as I affirm, from divinations, and from dreams, and in every way that any divine allotment ever ordered a human being to practice anything at all' (33c; contra Reeve, 1989, Page 66). This piety inspired a devotion to the community, which consisted of improving the moral character of the people of Athens. It was divine will that they learn to govern themselves without dependence on sophists and demagogues, whose knowledge of the good proved to be inadequate and therefore destructive. In order for Socrates to accomplish this divine mission, however, it became necessary for him to confront people with the extent of their ignorance and confusion. In other words, he argues that in contradiction to the charges of impiety he was being brought before a court of law precisely because he had been doing the bidding of the gods.

Socrates denies that he could have been impious once he undertook the mission given to him by the god Apollo, for it was towards the fulfilment of the god's purpose that he had spent his life questioning others about their beliefs. Plato has subsequently given us numerous examples of this behaviour in the so-called dialogues, where Socrates engaged a range of people to talk about beauty, truth, justice and love. At first, Socrates says that he did so in order to help interpret the prophecy from the Oracle at Delphi 30 years earlier, which stated that no one was wiser than Socrates. He had found this utterance puzzling, inasmuch as he thought of himself as ignorant. Nevertheless, as he probed further, the ignorance of others became evident, beginning with the political leaders of Athens (20c–22a). Thus, Socrates concluded that the only reason he might be wiser lay in the fact that at least he *knew* he was ignorant; everyone else seemed not to be so aware of their own ignorance.

Thereafter, Socrates continued his inquiries with anyone he could find, in hopes that by exposing them to their own ignorance, they would see to the care of their own souls and seek wisdom. During these dialogues, he was also questioning himself. As C D C Reeve put it, he set out 'to purge himself and others...of the hubris that they possessed expert knowledge of virtue...' (1989, Page 45). In this way, Socrates revealed that the people of Athens were, according to the Czech philosopher Jan Patočka, an 'errant people, blindly wandering' (2002, Page 84). How exactly did Socrates do this?

The method of Socrates

Socrates engaged fellow citizens in conversation about the meaning and purpose of their lives, frequently beginning by asking the interlocutor to define a key term—a term that person would presumably understand because of his public office or a term that he had used as the basis for some particular course of action. By a series of questions that gradually led the interlocutor to come up against some internal contradiction, Socrates avoided preaching to his neighbours about right and wrong and instead invited them to practise the art of critical thinking for themselves. He led them to uncover (and resolve) their own contradictions. Even when his fellow citizens aborted the dialogue in frustration and anger, as was often the case, youthful listeners would have witnessed an example of the Socratic method.

Socrates avoided lecturing others. This one-directional method of persuasion—typical of Sophists and their students—at its best failed to do more than impress an opinion onto the minds of the listeners like a stamping. Even if it were the correct opinion, listeners would not know it to be true if they had not arrived at the conclusion for themselves. So Socrates used questions to probe an interlocutor's understanding, drawing him along until he stumbled into a contradiction. Reeve has explained this process as 'an argument directed against one of the person's sincere ethical beliefs, the premises of which are drawn from other propositions to which his commitment is greater' (1989, Page 48). Later, Aristotle was to label this type of argument *peirastic*, meaning that Socrates refutes the other person by using his own beliefs (Vlastos, 1991, Page 94). The goal was to spur the other person to go back and think more critically about what he believed and why, so he could eventually give a rational account. Socrates assumed that people wanted to know the truth. It was his objective to help them recognise when they did not know the truth. Sometimes, it is true he could be harsh during these interrogations, but with cooperative companions he joined them in a more collaborative spirit (Reeve, 1989, Page 47).

In response to the charge that Socrates was playing purely a 'destructive' role, casting doubt without helping the interlocutor to find the truth, Laszlo Versényi has argued that readers of the Platonic dialogues would not be able to see his positive influence in the text because it would have taken place after the dialogue ended and the interlocutor, stung by the awareness of his ignorance, struggled to overcome that ignorance. In other words, it happened out of sight because it happened later and it happened in the privacy of the interlocutor's soul (1963, Page 119). In that sense, therefore, Socrates *could* claim to the jurors that he did not directly teach anyone: if anyone learned anything, it was because they did it themselves (1963, Page 121).

The philosopher Karl Jaspers was to characterise what was happening in the following manner: 'At first those who converse with [Socrates] simply seem to become more ignorant, but only because they are freed from pseudo-knowledge' (1957/1962, Page 18). This 'disencumbering' of the mind was a 'necessary step' towards greater humility and therefore the concomitant possibility of virtue (Burnyeat, 1992, Page 58, citing Plato's *Ion*, *Hippias Minor*, *Euthyphro*, *Laches*, *Charmides*, *Lysis*, *Protagoras*, and *Meno*).

What Socrates found objectionable was reproachable ignorance—the very sort of ignorance displayed by the political leaders who sought to squelch evidence of their ignorance rather than undertake an examination of their own thoughts and beliefs. Socrates was amenable to correction. Not everyone was.

Since nobody came forward to testify against him as having corrupted them, why did anyone have reason to make the allegation? Socrates apparently felt that he had to answer that question. Why indeed would these charges even arise in the first place? Socrates understood that his method incurred hatred from many who in fact did not learn, but rather resented being exposed publicly as ignorant (21b–23b). In other words, he was not harming those who might have learned something from him. Rather, he was injuring the pride and reputation of those who *refused* to learn anything from their encounters. Many of these ingrates were leaders or aspiring leaders in a democracy who had a particular stake in their reputations. It is also evident that many of the young who had witnessed these various exchanges probably adopted Socratic methods and made themselves odious by challenging those who exercised authority in their own lives, for which Socrates was being blamed (23c–23e). That is, Socrates had set an example that influenced young men to question the status quo.

The disturbing effect of Socratic method

It would be rare for anyone to enjoy being exposed by Socratic questioning, especially for leaders and prospective leaders in a regime where leadership was ostensibly dependent on public approval. The Socratic method tended to undermine a leader's authority by revealing his ignorance about the very things he would have been expected to understand. Socrates compounded the insult, however, by inspiring his youthful followers to adopt similar methods of critique. Thomas West acknowledges that Socrates represented 'a challenge to the most authoritative opinions [and] an attack on...paternal and political authority' (1984, Page 18).

The disturbing effects were personal and not just political. Socrates held forth a standard of rigorous thinking about life's worth, such that anyone present would have occasion to stop and reflect anew. In other words, Socratic questioning induced doubt, and doubt is an experience that motivates a person to alleviate that doubt. Like a gadfly, therefore, Socrates stung the conscience of the people to acknowledge their ignorance and work their way towards moral character (30d–31a). For this, he brought odium upon himself.

Compounding this disturbing effect, Socrates here stood before the jury and pronounced that because his was a divine mission, he would persist in his philosophical practice even if they were inclined to let him go, for he was doing this for their own good (29d–30b). He was a gift of the gods to the people of Athens. Not surprisingly, many jurors took offence at such grandiose claims (for example, 20e). Undeterred by their grumbling, however, Socrates would later open the Counter-Penalty Phase of the trial by asserting that what he deserved was to be fed at public expense in the hall of champions and benefactors (36b–36e). Rather than incur hatred, he should have been celebrated.

Nevertheless, he did incur hatred. At line 37d, as Socrates submits his counter-penalty, he observes that his habits of conversation have apparently been regarded by the jurors as 'grave and hateful' (to quote from the West & West translation) or 'too irksome and disagreeable' (to quote from the Fowler translation) or 'grievous and odious' (to quote from the Jowett translation). Interestingly, the first of the two terms in Greek suggests being heavy to the point of becoming burdensome and wearying and just too much to bear (Liddell and Scott, 1940), whereas the second term suggests evoking a hatred based on envy or jealous passions (Liddell and Scott, 1940), a self-tormenting poison that spurned lovers, for example, or what critics might feel towards those who have become successful (Atsma, 2000–08). Socrates indicates that the interlocutors and jurors have become unable to tolerate him, that is, that the problem lay in their reception of his life's divine work and not in anything he has ever actually said or done.

Critical thinking in a democratic regime

A regime ostensibly dependent on public approval will reflect the character of its people. Socrates took the position that its leaders had an obligation not only to *reflect* their character but also to *improve* it. This requires empowering citizens to use their minds and engage one another in conversation about ultimate questions, even to the extent of challenging the regime itself. The fact that not only leaders but everyone tends to resist being challenged in this way presents those who would defend democracy with a predicament. Such a regime will resist precisely what it needs.

Socrates had previously served the city in several capacities, most notably as an exemplary soldier, yet he refrained from putting himself forward to lead the regime politically. If he presumed to want the best for Athens, then why had he never entered politics? Wouldn't that be the most obvious way to lead his fellow citizens towards virtue? In response to this obvious question, Socrates points out to the jury that he had been involved in politics twice—once during an oligarchy and once during a democracy—and in each instance he found that his devotion to truth and justice put him in defiance of the regime (32a–33c). If he had persisted in that career, no doubt he would have invited immediate wrath, for politics did not seem hospitable to men of virtue (31e–32a; 32e). This is an assertion that would have angered partisans of democracy and most especially their leaders who, by negative inference, must not be men of virtue.

Socrates did add, by the way, that his personal *daimonion* had warned him against such a career, so he felt his non-participation in politics had divine endorsement (31c–31d). Instead, Socrates was political in other ways, going so far as to claim elsewhere that he was the only person to understand politics (*Gorgias* 521d6–8). It was his purpose therefore to identify and cultivate prospective leaders by his dialectical methods, so that, ironically, the young, whom the prosecutors suspected were being corrupted, were in fact being *improved* for public service (Reeve, 1989, Page 159; see note 61). Towards this end, Socrates set 'himself up as the exemplar of civic excellence' (West, 1984, Page 21). He was doing what any worthy citizen in a democracy should be doing.

These claims about preparing the next generation of leaders would have struck his accusers as particularly risible, inasmuch as Socrates was known to have influenced more than one young man who had subsequently troubled the regime with their tyrannical and impious ways (33a). Among those who had once followed Socrates were Critias,

Charmides and Alcibiades, and although by law Socrates could not be held responsible formally for their scandalous behaviour, people remembered and deplored what they had done (West, 1984, Page 85, n. 60). In their minds, Socrates must have had a hand in their corruption.

Socrates did not regard his method exclusively as a means to an end, such as inculcating successful leadership in the young; critical thinking is also the most worthy activity in and of itself. One does not engage in these dialogues just for the sake of becoming a leader. *One becomes a leader in order to enable people to engage in activities such as these dialogues.* That is a very different thing. Socrates discloses that he expects to continue his inquiries after death, where there would be no ulterior motive (41b–c). We might put this into perspective by saying that authority for leadership rests on its ability to improve the virtue of its people, so they can worship the gods best by tending the soul in conversation with each other about the loftiest themes. *Democracy exists for the sake of dialogue, more so than that dialogue exists for the sake of democracy.*

For Socrates, then, critical thinking is both the end of political life as well as a necessary means. Critical thinking helps leaders in a democratic regime to avoid reproachable ignorance—or, to be more precise, it helps to prevent hubris, even if it never completely removes a leader's ignorance. Critical thinking also helps the citizenry choose leaders wisely, so they can detect hubris in prospective leaders by means of inquiry. For leaders to suppress critics by using the powers of office is therefore an ignoble approach to leadership (39d). Critical thinking also helps citizens to govern themselves, thereby reducing their dependence on leaders in the first place. They learn to govern themselves by avoiding what Thomas West referred to as 'civic dogmatism' (1984, Page 16). Finally, critical thinking will have become the objective of leadership, as ordinary people come to participate in communal deliberations about the most worthy topics and are not distracted by deprivation, civic turmoil, or other ills the leaders will have been chosen to remedy. Another way of saying this is that leaders are responsible for preserving the *agon* or public space within which a free people assemble and improve themselves.

The example of Socrates

What Socrates said is probably less important than his example—the example of his life in dialogue, to be sure, but perhaps more importantly his death as a martyr on behalf of critical thinking, when he exhibited a peculiar patriotism to Athens and a piety unto death. It is his life's example that we must ultimately consider.

Socrates explains his motives to the jury, though he doubts they would understand (38a). He had chosen to subordinate all other goods or values to the cause of virtue (Vlastos, 1991, Pages 233–5). His conscience was clear. Happiness appears to consist in fulfilling the purpose of the gods, wherever that service leads. In his particular case, it led to a verdict of guilt and drinking the hemlock.

A twentieth-century protégé of Socrates was the Czech philosopher Jan Patočka. Like Socrates, he had lived on the margin of politics during unsettling times. Finally, he undertook to influence others by means of teaching philosophy, despite being prohibited by the prevailing Marxist-Leninist regime. Upon becoming a spokesman for the Charter 77 movement as a 70-year-old man, Patočka was picked up by interrogators and died in their custody. During his career, it turns out he had plainly harkened back to the example of Socrates. In mid-life, for example, he had written about the supreme freedom that comes with defying an unjust regime. Such a man has fulfilled himself, he wrote. The highest sacrifice, as seen from an external viewpoint, might be the logical next step for someone dedicated to the truth (2007, Pages 94, 96).

Acknowledgement

For reading this manuscript with insight and grace, the author owes a debt to Tiberius Popa, PhD, of the College of Liberal Arts and Sciences at Butler University.

Note

1. Gregory Vlastos argues that the *daimonion* was not so much a being as a sign or emanation from a divine source (1991, Pages 280–7). It is for similar reasons that Reeve refers to 'strange daimonic doings' (1989, Page 76).

References

Atsma, A. J. (2000–08) *The Theoi Project: Greek Mythology*. Date accessed: 26 August 2009 at http://www.theoi.com/.
Brickhouse, T. and Smith, N. (1983) 'Irony, arrogance, and sincerity in Plato's *Apology*', in Kelly, E. (ed.). *New Essays on Socrates*, pp. 29–46, University Press of America, New York.
Burnyeat, M. (1992) 'Socratic midwifery, Platonic inspiration', in Benson, H. (ed.). *Essays on the Philosophy of Socrates*, ch. 4, Oxford University Press, New York.
Gilbert, D. (2006) *Stumbling on Happiness*, Alfred A. Knopf, New York.

Jaspers, K. (1957/1962) *The Great Philosophers: The Foundations*, pp. 15–31, H. Arendt (ed.); R. Manheim (trans.), Harcourt, Brace & World, Inc., New York.

Liddell, H. G. and Scott, R. (1940) *A Greek-English Lexicon*, revised and augmented throughout by Sir H. S. Jones, with the assistance of R. McKenzie, Clarendon Press, Oxford. *Perseus Digital Library Project*, G. R. Crane (ed.) (2009) Tufts University. Date accessed: 26 August 2009 at http://www.perseus.tufts.edu.

Patočka, J. (2007) 'Ideology and Life in the Idea' (E. Manton, trans.), *Studia Phænomenologica*, 7: 89–96 (Original work published 1946).

Patočka, J. (2002) *Plato and Europe* (P. Lom, tr.) [Cultural Memory in the Present]. Stanford University Press, Stanford.

Plato. (1960) *Gorgias* (W. Hamilton, trans.), Penguin Books, New York.

Plato. (1984) 'Apology of Socrates', in Plato & Aristophanes (eds). *Four Texts on Socrates: Plato's 'Euthyphro', 'Apology', and 'Crito' and Aristophanes' 'Clouds'*, pp. 63–97 (T. West and G. West, trans.), Cornell University Press, Ithaca, NY.

Reeve, C. D. C. (1989) *Socrates in the 'Apology': An Essay on Plato's 'Apology of Socrates'*, Hackett, Indianapolis, IN.

Reeve, C. D. C. (2002) *The Trials of Socrates: Six Classic Texts*, Hackett, Indianapolis, IN.

Versényi, L. (1963) *Socratic Humanism* (L. Conversi, trans.), Yale University Press, New Haven, CT.

Vlastos, G. (1991) *Socrates: Ironist and Moral Philosopher*, Cornell University Press, Ithaca, NY.

West, T. (1984) 'Introduction', in Plato & Aristophanes (eds). *Four Texts on Socrates: Plato's 'Euthyphro', 'Apology', and 'Crito' and Aristophanes' 'Clouds'*, pp. 9–37 (T. West and G. West, trans.), Cornell University Press, Ithaca, NY.

Zeller, E. (1955) *Outlines of the History of Greek Philosophy* (13th edn.) (L. R. Palmer, trans.), A Meridian Book, New York.

16
Ten Great Works for Leadership Development

Robert Adlam

This chapter was born out of two striking experiences. Both concerned failure. The first followed upon Nietzsche's (2002) correct observation that there is something undeniably visceral about the use of evocative language. Language can 'move' us. It can quicken the heart and set off the dreams that make life worth the struggle. Reading the funeral oration given by Pericles of Athens, or hearing Paul Schofield's Thomas More in *A Man for All Seasons* is riveting, heart stopping, inspiring. I wanted the most senior management course at the institution in which I was working to include some practice in the art of oratory on its timetable. I thought that part of the leader's repertoire must include the ability to mobilise and focus, through the magic of language, the positive energies and warm feelings of subordinates. My proposal, however, was immediately dismissed. Why? Well, it was because the future leaders would 'refuse to do it'. It was then that I realised that the programme of senior management development was not about leadership at all; along with being an induction into the Establishment, its main concern was to produce a kind of system-functionary.[1] The world had gone 'systemic'.

The second failure has been documented in some of my earlier work (Adlam, 1999, 2000): it concerned my inability to secure the serious study of ethics—both professional and applied—on the leadership development curriculum. Ratings culture held sway in the institution. 'Ethics', though, is hard work, unsettling and confronting; it is not the kind of subject that has immediate appeal. It does not lend itself to the popular 'feel-good' sentiment. However, even if the methods I chose, or the educational designs I produced, or the 'personality' I had, were not good enough to please the course members, following O'Neil (2002) and Richards (1993), I am convinced that public service managers and leaders must be people we can trust. We need to be assured of their professionalism as well as their commitment to work for morally desirable ends through morally acceptable means. We need to know that they are there 'for us'. We need to know that they measure up to the rights, privileges and status that they enjoy. Professional ethics *should* be a theme for study on public service programmes; however, it must not be reduced to facile moralising or simply involve making earnest resolutions 'to do better'. Kleinig (1990), Kleinig and Leland Smith (1997) and Richards (1993) have already identified the moral terrain that should be traversed.

Since these (and other) failures, I have developed an approach to leadership that attempts, through the use of literary works, to establish the groundwork or principles upon which leadership practice might be based. I have chosen ten books that I think are sufficient to get things going. Ideally, one or two lectures would accompany the reading material. Here, I want to pick out the key issues for leaders—for those people who make a claim to lead—that are surfaced in each of the ten texts.

I start with Plato's *Republic*. Although regularly identified as one of the great works of world literature, I have been surprised to discover that it is rarely read in its entirety. It constitutes a reasonably coherent outline of Plato's model of the ideal state and reflects his deeper philosophical beliefs.

Plato, the *Republic* and the Philosopher-ruler

Turmoil and political problems in the city-state of Athens gave Plato reason to lose faith in politics: he concluded that a society watched over and guided by philosopher-kings would be preferable even to democracy. Although initially concerned with defining the nature of justice, Plato, through Socrates, challenges the reader with a question that is rarely asked outside the disciplines of politics and sociology: What are the underlying principles of any society? Socrates immediately focuses his analysis by examining how a community comes into existence. First, he identifies the principle of mutual need: society originates because the individual is not self-sufficient. Individual persons have many needs that cannot be met alone. Mutuality and interdependence lie at the very core of society. Second, Socrates identifies the principle of different aptitudes: 'No two of us are born exactly alike. We have different aptitudes which fit us for different jobs.' He goes on to say that it is best for all if each of us concentrates on developing his or her particular aptitude.

It is possible to link this principle with the contemporary emphasis on specialisation—or even 'diversity'.

It is worth dwelling, for a moment, upon these very basic ideas. The first principle counters an ideology of the individual. In essence, it reminds us that we are 'in this together' and that we cannot do very much on our own. It emphasises sociality—and reminds us about the fundamental character of public service, that is, an organisational framework designed to help meet needs that cannot always be met by individuals alone. It even links to the idea that there is no such thing as an individual but individuals-in-relationship. The second principle underpins the idea of respect. It counters arrogance. Different individuals, in virtue of their specialisations, maintain and advance society. Persons are valued because of their powers and abilities. They all have the potential to contribute to the common good. They all have the opportunity to enjoy the fruits of the common good.

In practical terms, the principles that Socrates finds are, *prima facie*, worthy of very serious consideration in the practice of leadership and, particularly, public sector leadership. They help to ground the public service in its proper context, that is, the wider idea of society, and begin to provide two of the foundational ideas or cornerstones of the public sector leadership role. In short, they say: 'We are about the greater good.'

Socrates moves on to give an account as to how societies develop. He describes the emerging classes and argues that justice and harmony will only prevail if everyone 'minds their own business' and adheres to the primary virtue commensurate with their societal function. He then argues, in Part 7 Book 5 that: 'there will be no end to the troubles of states ... of humanity itself, till philosophers become kings of the world, or till those we now call kings and rulers really and truly become philosophers'. In effect, he declares that society will only work well if it is governed by philosopher-rulers. Socrates then identifies the nature of the philosopher—the person who is best fitted to rule. He believes that the philosophic character comes naturally to some people and he thinks that this character is identifiable from an early age. At the heart of the philosophic character lies a passion for knowledge. Plato's philosophy underlines that this is not superficial knowledge; it is something far deeper and, to a modern consciousness, is more akin to discovering the laws that underlie nature, etc. Socrates, in Part 7, Book 6, is then asked by Adeimantus to explain why the philosophic character will be equipped with exemplary qualities and dispositions.[2] He does this using both deductive arguments and empirical observations. First, he asks his interlocutor to imagine what *has* to be associated with a passion for knowledge—the sort of knowledge that yields insight and wisdom. The answer is truthfulness; the philosopher will never willingly tolerate an untruth. Again, truthfulness means much more than simply telling the truth: it is to go beyond the surface and conventional views on reality; it rejects the world of appearances.

Truth, on the Socratic account, is a pre-condition for wisdom. Socrates then asks what would be the result if one were to aim for the whole truth from the earliest years of life. His answer is significant because he begins to portray a person who will be immune from distractions and venality. He finds that if the current of a person's desires flows towards knowledge then his pleasures will be entirely in things of the mind. Physical pleasures will pass him by. The mind of the philosopher will be set on higher things and, if he is the genuine article, he will not be diverted from his search for knowledge by material goods or money. The philosophic character will also be free from meanness and pettiness; these are incompatible with the search for the highest truth. Socrates also finds that the true philosopher will not be afraid of death. By implication, mean and cowardly natures will be disqualified from dealings with philosophy. Socrates declares that the philosophic character, in virtue of his or her nature, is neither mean, nor cowardly, nor irascible, nor unjust. At this point, Plato, again through the voice of Socrates, restates the fact that these attitudes and dispositions cluster together in a person's nature and that this nature is identifiable from an early age. The potential philosopher-ruler will, from a young age, be 'just and civilised' not 'un-co-operative and barbarous'. To this analysis and description Socrates thinks that a philosophic nature will learn easily, will remember what he or she has learned, and will have grace and a sense of proportion. At the end of this account Socrates remarks to Adeimantus:

'Do you agree, then, that we have now been through a list of characteristics, which all go together, and which the mind must have if it is to grasp reality fully and completely?'

'Yes, it must certainly have them all,' replies Adeimantes.

Socrates continues:

Can you, then, possibly find fault with an occupation for the proper pursuit of which a man must combine in his nature good memory, readiness to learn, breadth of vision and versatility of mind, and be a friend of truth, justice, courage and discipline?[3]

Adeimantus duly agrees and Socrates concludes his remarks with:

> Grant, then, education and maturity to round them off, and aren't they the only people to whom you would entrust your state?

The account of the philosophic character is important, not because of the listing of character traits but because the whole tone of the discussion constitutes a rejection of the liabilities and limitations to which humans are susceptible: it is a design to combat the corruption wrought by power. There is no place in Plato's scheme for 'driven' personalities, no place for personal ambition, no place for self-indulgence. As a text it begins the process of helping a leader to make sure his claim to lead is based on defensible and commendable foundations.

While Plato's prose is often poetic and always evocative it is still philosophical writing. It has, as Murdoch (1978) puts it, a kind of crystalline quality. A more straightforwardly literary idiom marks Plutarch's *Lives*. How strange to think that some of the great moments in the iconic imagery of leadership are based on the writings of a priest at the Temple of Apollo in Delphi.

Plutarch's *Lives*: The construction of heroic leadership

Written in about 100 AD, Plutarch's *Lives* contain, *inter alia*, vivid accounts of the lives of 'noble' Greeks and Romans. Duff (1999) in the first recent monograph on Plutarch for 25 years finds that the *Lives* are written to what he calls a 'moralising programme'. They do not attempt to provide full biographies but instead contain ethical discussion through the telling of life stories. The moralising programme is not, however, 'resolved'; it aims at what Goldhill (2000) regards as a 'more open-ended and exploratory didacticism'. Plutarch's agenda is, to a greater or lesser extent, educational. Duff pinpoints the device of synkrisis as central to his method: synkrisis is the formal pairing of two lives (for example, Antony and Demetrius or Brutus and Dion) along with the subsequent act of comparing and contrasting the paired lives. Duff insists that a life is not meant to be read independently of its comparator. Goldhill (2000) asserts that 'this reading of the *Lives* as an integral process of contrast and comparison feeds directly back into the moralising agenda' and he continues: 'It is by exploring such narratives that your own life finds both its paradigms and evaluations.'

Overall, the *Lives* can scarcely be read without the feeling of being in the company of something extraordinary and exceptional. The personalities, network of relationships, the shifts in location, the sheer number of military campaigns, the intensity and extremes of feeling, the violence, the political intrigues and the susceptibility of history to 'personality' all swirl together in spectacular and dramatic fashion. Superimposed on this are the vivid references to the way the Fates—the portents, auguries and prodigies—exert their influence on the psychology of the central characters and (perhaps) foretell the outcome of events.

Plutarch also provides some highly sophisticated narrative in which alternative perceptions of reality are debated.[4] Added to this he abstracts a form of practical wisdom drawn from the individuals about whom he writes. For example, of Caesar he remarks: 'There is no beginning so mean, which continual application will not make considerable and . . . will make it at last irresistible.' We are given effectively a lesson in the value of perseverance and an intimation of the triumph of the will.

The heady, larger-than-life character of the *Lives* is also strangely familiar. The form and content of the narrative seems reprised by Tolstoy or Dickens. Pushed in a mytho-fantastic direction they might have been written by Tolkien. Pushed into the discipline of anthropology they exemplify the great storytelling traditions that lie at the heart of most cultures. More simply, the *Lives* impress as terrific tales; their more recent counterparts are the great Hollywood epics. Plutarch profiles truly spectacular and remarkable characters; he delineates the forms of life that define the mood and conduct of leadership. He pictures and establishes the dominant narrative characterising alpha males (Braden, 2004); it may be that he is the originator of our underlying assumptions and even our hopes for the ideal leader. He also identifies the importance of rhetoric and oratory in the careers of his heroes; and, he hints at the significance of 'spin'—the ability to 'colour' events to suit one's purpose.

While Plutarch's intention, as Duff (1999) points out, was to provide role-models, the more significant aspect of his *Lives* lies in the way they were used by Shakespeare and in the subsequent impact of Shakespearean drama on the Western consciousness.

Scholars agree that Plutarch's *Lives* is the major classical literary source informing Shakespeare's 'Roman' plays. Goldhill (2000), for example, notes that the *Lives* were once 'the staple read' for Shakespeare and other major literary figures such as Chesterfield and Macaulay. Greenblatt (2004) tells us that one of Shakespeare's 'favourite' books was Sir Thomas North's translation of the *Lives*. He goes on to say that Plutarch was a 'principal source' for *Julius Caesar*, *Timon of Athens*, *Coriolanus* and, most of all, *Anthony and Cleopatra*. The *Lives* also provided for Shakespeare a template for heroic and inspirational leadership in plays such as *Henry V*.

Shakespeare had 'throughout his entire career' (Greenblatt, 2004, Page 46) been fascinated by the charismatic power of royalty including the excitement such charismatic figures 'awakened in crowds'. By the time he wrote *Julius Caesar*

> ... had come to understand the dark sides of this power ... he had taken in the pride, cruelty, and ambition that it aroused, the dangerous plots that it bred.
>
> (Greenblatt, 2004, Page 46)

Shakespeare saw in Plutarch's life of Anthony the chance to explore the power and magic of commanding eloquence. But, for Shakespeare, Plutarch's *Lives* also underlined a view he had already begun to include in some of his earlier plays. Thus, Shakespeare saw that vaunting ambition led to chaos and an ungovernable, murderous factionalism. And this is exactly what is expressed in the play *Julius Caesar*. However, despite the fact that leadership development programmes include moments of the kind of inspirational leadership shown by Henry V or by Mark Anthony, the *Lives* of Plutarch are themselves imaginative and poetic constructions: they are themselves partly fanciful: for example, the life of Anthony—'a very beautiful youth'—is linked directly to the mythicised super-human Hercules. Of Anthony's appearance Plutarch writes: 'He had ... a very good and noble appearance; his beard was well-grown, his forehead large and his nose aquiline, giving him altogether a bold masculine look that reminded people of the faces of Hercules in paintings and sculptures.' Plutarch underlines this association by saying: 'it was moreover an ancient tradition that the Anthonys were descended from Hercules'. The comparison between Anthony and Hercules was even manifested in his 'fashion of dress' and image management: 'Whenever he had to appear before large numbers of people he wore his tunic girt about the hips' and he carried a broad sword. Plutarch gives us the picture of a man fashioned on the iconography of antiquity. This image is sustained throughout most of the history of Anthony. Not only is he shown to be capable of extraordinary endurance and stunning feats of leadership, he even justifies his fathering of Cleopatra's children as a replication of Hercules's strategy for 'seeding' greatness and unity.

But while Plutarch is not afraid to discuss Anthony's weaknesses, such as his liberality and debauchery, the Anthony in Shakespeare is a transformational character: and this image was subsequently made famous in Joseph Mankevicz's 1953 film *Julius Caesar* through Brando's performance. In fact, Brando's performance was so powerful that it subverted the intentions of the director and producer.[5]

Plutarch's *Lives* stand in a complex yet profound relationship to conceptions of leadership. On the one hand, they seem to model one ideal of leadership and they have provided the loam from which great drama has sprung. In turn this great drama has created an image as to 'how it's done'. On the other hand, the *Lives* themselves are informed by older mythic narratives—in virtue of which they are unrealistic, implausible and impossible. In this respect they raise some cautionary tales for leaders: do not live a fantasy; choose your words with care; never underestimate the arational.

The third work of literature establishes a different and more reflective mood; it is the great Russian novel *Anna Karenina* that was originally published in serial form between 1873 and 1877.

Uncovering the male psyche

Anna Karenina is a great work of fiction. It gives us a portrait of Russia at the onset of modernity. Deeply realistic, at times the text seems to rise out of the ground itself; there are moments when we feel the chill at sunrise, feel the dew on our boots, hear the lark sing or watch the bright moon fade into the light blue sky. But that is almost incidental: wherever the prose may go, it is the relationships that grip us and make for such compelling reading.

Anna Karenina, the woman, is striking in her beauty, striking in her virtue. She glitters and sparkles—a red ruby scattered over black velvet. I love her passion, her courage, her hypnotic presence. I want her to find enduring happiness; I want her to live happily ever after. But, as Tolstoy gives us his tragic Anna, I realise that this is a novel about the psychology of men.

Some years ago a quietly desperate woman wrote to the *Times Literary Supplement* asking the readership to recommend a work of literature to 'educate' her 'yuppie daughter'. It was a great question. The readers duly sent in their selections and, finally, a list was published: at the top was Jane Austen's *Pride and Prejudice*. If that woman had asked for a work that might educate the world about men I would choose *Anna Karenina*. Why? Well, Anna's husband, Karenin, a person we are supposed to revile, is a profoundly damaged man. Emotionally wrecked, he allows Tolstoy to raise the awful prospect that men who seek power are wounded, pathological people. Count Vronsky, Anna's lover, although brilliant, urbane and sophisticated, is driven by ambition: he never finds the resources to help Anna through her crises. Stepan, brother of Anna, remains a hopeless sensualist, a chummy but useless *bon viveur*. Even Konstanin Levin, who trudges manfully through the dramas, is riven by the narrowness of common sense and gauche naïveté. And so it goes on. These sketches of individual character merge into the idea of a single, more generalised, psyche: Tolstoy is uncovering what it is to be a man: he shows us that the best we can ever hope to get is nowhere near perfection.

Small but true psychological touches are scattered throughout the novel: for example, as Christian (1969) notes, when Levin and Oblonsky dine together, for all their bonhomie 'each was thinking only of his own affairs and was not concerned with the other' and, later on, 'Levin both liked and did not like the peasant, just as he liked and did not like men in general' (Part 3, Chapter One).

Tolstoy's psychological portraits stimulate a dual process of development. On the one hand, he establishes an objective register. We can look at each of his finely nuanced characters and understand their nature, their fragility, their dispositions and ways of coping. We can even go beyond this and make connections with the depth psychologies—such as the analytic psychology of C G Jung. In relation to Jung's psychological types, Stepan is a sensing-feeling type while Vronsky is an intuitive thinker. We can go beyond depth psychology, enter the realm of humanistic psychology and explore the fine detail of emotional literacy. On the other hand, Tolstoy's writing enables the reader to embark on a more personal and subjective inquiry. It might even culminate in the kind of insight displayed by Primo Levi: he indicated that he knew himself sufficiently well to predict exactly how he would react in the company of an oppressor—a former concentration camp official. Tolstoy invites us to compare ourselves with the particular characters and encourages us to ask or confront the question 'what is it that a life is aiming towards?'

Anna Karenina also resists passing judgement on the different characters; it suggests that society is the villain of the piece. As Christian (1969) writes:

> It is possible to sense in the novel a rooted dissatisfaction with society in the widest sense of the word, an aversion to materialism and a groping towards spiritual values.

> (Christian, 1969, Page 175)

The novel encourages its reader to begin the long process of exploring how a society makes its people and to critique its structures and conventions. In conclusion, it is difficult not to agree with Christian's summary that:

> In *Anna Karenina*, Tolstoy demonstrates his immense range of knowledge of human nature, his breadth of sympathy and an anger tempered by charity. His extraordinary powers of observation, his vivid and detailed depiction of contemporary life…allied to a seriousness of purpose and a deep concern with the fundamental issues of life in society make his novel one of the truly great works of European literature.
>
> (Christian, 1969, Page 211)

We need to read *Anna Karenina* because it is one of those novels that, on completion—as we read the final paragraphs and close the cover—we know that we have been in the presence of a masterpiece and that we are more fully human as a result.

A case study in leadership

Hermann Hesse's philosophical novel, *The Glass Bead Game* charts the career of Joseph Knecht who rises to hold the highest office in the state of Castalia. Published in 1943, Hesse's beautifully written work analyses the complex tension between the individual and society. His genius lies in his ability to disinter and criticise some of the most basic assumptions lying at the heart of contemporary Western culture; he prompts an exhilarating re-evaluation of the way we live now. How does he achieve this?

First, he attacks the ideal of individualism: reprising Socratic ethics, he reminds us that we should commend the person who suppresses or obliterates individuality in favour of service to the wider social order. Next, in place of the 'gigantic consumption of empty whimsies' he proposes an 'heroic counter-movement' that prizes self-discipline and the cultivation of the human intellect. Finally, he questions the idea that our lives should ultimately be concerned with the pursuit of happiness. In a riveting piece of post-Aristotelian scholarship he proposes that 'serenity' is the better goal; it is not a reclusive serenity: rather, it is one entailing authentic and committed action in the world. Hesse can be read as saying that the stress on image and 'the look', the extraordinary 'genitalisation' of our culture—as well as the caricatures and distortions presented through the media—are disastrous for humanity. He is not, though, a naïve idealist. He thinks that however we try to solve the problems of living, a 'degenerate morbid form' lies latent in our best designs and social arrangements. That is his warning.

Right now, across the Western world, there is, in the main, a curious lack of inspiring political leadership: we are chained, it seems, to an economic treadmill of increased production and consumption. But, Hesse's *Glass Bead Game* shows us that we already have everything we need. It is an optimistic account: he demonstrates that a better future lies close at hand 'in the cool blithe light' of the world's forenoon.

Hesse's account can also be read as a case study in the life trajectory of a leader. It is an object lesson in the discipline of taking up public office. Here, three features of this trajectory will be picked out. The first is the importance of debate. Joseph Knecht is strengthened, tempered and extended through debate, especially with his friend and adversary Designori. Designori is a man of the world—the so-called 'real world'—in which 'there were loving mothers and children, hungry people... newspapers and election campaigns...' Designori, in his criticism of Knecht's more sheltered and assured world, obliges Knecht to acknowledge that this real world not only existed but that:

> The great majority of human beings on the globe lived a life different from that of Castalia, simpler, more primitive, more disorderly, less sheltered. And this primitive world was innate in every man; everyone felt something of it in his own heart, had some curiosity about it, some nostalgia for it, some sympathy with it.
>
> (Hesse, 1970, Page 95)

From this perception, Knecht is able to make the following resolution: 'The true task was to face it, to keep a place for it in one's own heart, but still not to relapse into it.'

Second, Knecht learns of the importance of history and, within history, the establishment of congregations and orders. Father Jacobus 'perhaps the most eminent historian of the Benedictine order' declares that:

> For me... the most attractive and amazing aspects of history, and the most deserving of study, are not individuals and not coups, triumphs or downfalls; rather I love and am insatiably curious about such phenomena as our congregation. For it is one of those long-lived organizations whose purpose is to gather, educate and shape

men's minds and souls, to make a nobility of them...a nobility as capable of serving as of ruling.

(Hesse, 1970, Page 159)

Hesse challenges the tendency in histories to focus on exceptional individuals. Instead it is communities of shared values that merit study and understanding.

Third, Hesse provides an extraordinary study of duty—of the subordination of preferences, inclinations and desires to the requirements of role. Joseph Knecht becomes 'enveloped and isolated by the gravity and austerity of his office as if by a shining glaze that had been poured over him' until it had hardened. Knecht discovers that his sheer devotion to his organisation saw him 'so thoroughly converted into an instrument that such personal matters as friendship vanished into the impossible'. As Knecht achieves the highest rank he finds his strength 'almost devoured'. Although Knecht recovers and impresses the Order with his exemplariness, he never stops learning, observing and acknowledging the intimations from himself. He knows that his Order is too isolated, too immune to the world surrounding it, and that something of himself remains unfulfilled. He resolves to leave the Order and Castalia to engage more fully with life-in-the-world. As Hesse puts it:

He...had reached the point at which great men must leave the path of tradition and obedient subordination and, trusting to supreme, indefinable powers, strike out on new trackless courses where experience is no guide.

(Hesse, 1970, Page 278)

Part of the problem in the practice of public service sector leadership is that it mirrors Castalia. It enjoys a certain immunity from the real and the harsh. And part of it can be read as an elaborate game with its own exclusionary discourses. Hesse's novel, as it profiles the life of Joseph Knecht in the state of Castalia—along with his ultimate rejection of its artificiality and alienation—is a superb manifesto for a type of principled and insightful leadership.

The concepts we live by

Written in 1920, Zamyatin's *We* was authored at a time when there was abundant evidence of progress through science. *We* is a breath-taking novel. One of the most overlooked masterpieces of twentieth-century writing, it is an intellectual and literary jewel: every page sparkles with vivid description, challenging theory and brilliant insight.

Zamyatin uses the diary entries of 'D-503', a design engineer and mathematician, to tell us about life, work, love and resistance in the totalitarian 'One State'. 'Tables of Hourly Commandments' regulate almost every aspect of social behaviour; conformity to the system is assured through automated processes of socialisation as well as the ominous Bureau of Guardians; plasma screens work as the eyes and ears of the State; the roseate glow of sex unfolds during the two 'Personal Hours'. It is the apotheosis of the disciplinary society.

Initially, D-503 reveals extreme rationality in his consciousness. He apprehends the world through the crystalline clarity of mathematics and the concepts of natural and physical science. He has no real quarrel with the One State: after all, 'freedom has been replaced by happiness'! But then he meets the enchantress E-330. Through her, he discovers the magic of anthropology, the transformative power of sexual love and the existence of an alternative society living on the margins of the 'One State'.

D-503 finds himself like 'a crystal, dissolving into E'—becoming 'smaller and smaller yet un-encompassable'. Bit by bit, his mode of apprehending the world is shot to shreds. The story, though, ends in tragedy. The revolution, for which the gorgeous E-330 has been fighting, begins to stutter. She is captured and tortured in the 'Gas Bell Jar': Later, with other revolutionaries, she is taken away for liquidation. D-503 is broken and rendered back into the society of the One State.

We, a precursor to Orwell's *Nineteen Eighty-Four*, remains an empyrean achievement; the quality of perception and the expression of artistic sensibility is unrivalled. It is the finest post-utopian novel I have ever read. It is particularly important because it represents a way of looking at the world through the prism of concepts. It illustrates the second half of Kant's remark 'Sensations without concepts are empty. Concepts without content are meaningless' (1999). In this case the conceptual framework is that of science and mathematics: Zamyatin's D-504 cannot 'see' the world except in rational-scientific terms. By drawing his central character in this way, Zamyatin invites the reader to ask: What are the major concepts that are *now* used to view reality? The question can be extended and we can ask: What is the dominant sensibility of our times?

There are two strong candidates concerning the structuring of modern consciousness. The first derives from Heidegger's (1953) insights. In the 1950s and 1960s Heidegger began to see the increasing dominance of modern technology with the result that a 'measuring, reckoning, calculating logic is applied to everything'. Collins (1999) summarises this aspect of Heidegger's thought as follows:

> Human activity is to be governed by efficiency—maximum output for minimum input. Nature is to be commanded and manipulated. Technological thought sets no limits to itself. It is infinitely expandable and erodes other modes of thought.
>
> (Collins, 1999, Page 160)

Heidegger, according to Collins, saw 'an unrestrained, complete technicizing of the world and of humans' where:

> Even human discourse will be consigned to electronic thinking and calculating machines, circulating information as an end in itself.
>
> (Collins, 1999, Page 160)

Heidegger found that the metaphor most appropriate for describing our times lay in mining. Everything is 'stock' to be 'set upon'; everything is apprehended in terms of its 'potential' to yield value for its possessor.

An aspect of the Heideggerian insight is recognised by Foucault (1981) in his exploration of the disciplinary society. Everything (and everyone) is to be made docile, manageable, normalised. Order, control, routine and predictability are prized; deviance is recast as exotica or spectacle. 'Is it surprising' asks Foucault, 'that our hospitals resemble prisons which resemble schools etc.?' (Page 228).

The idea of the 'spectacle' links to the second mode of modern consciousness. This mode is the result of a technological achievement that is still under-theorised: it concerns the ubiquity of screen culture and the implications of the Internet. How is the modern mind 'cast' as a consequence of the sheer presence of the screen? What are the consequences of not being able to govern except through the management of the media? What happens when reality becomes a pale grey version of the media constructed hyperreality? What happens when information and knowledge are so distributed, so available, that depth and the slow process of crafting are rendered obsolete?

Plainly something rather strange has occurred in modern society— something that *We* foreshadows. It is the evolution of pervasive regulation. This is a major theme in Orwell's *Nineteen Eighty-Four*.

A reflection on the human condition

Nineteen Eighty-Four has a legitimate claim to be *the* novel of the twentieth century. It is simultaneously an essay about the nature of political power, a reflection on the human condition and an invitation to critique the society that surrounds us. We are also given a lesson in the use of language and its relationship both to thought and reality.

Something unnervingly hard—the iron-fist of state politics—is written into the text itself: one false move and you're done for. Set in London and the State of Oceania, *Nineteen Eighty-Four* finds Winston Smith, a minor party official working in the Ministry of Truth, engaged in the falsification of history. He cannot resist thinking for himself and begins to record his 'heretical' thoughts in a diary. In a grimly totalitarian, bureaucratic and cynical world, he encounters the spirited and sensual Julia: a love affair unfolds in which both find a form of liberation. However, the 'Thought Police' have them in their sights: they are caught, interrogated and tortured until they betray one other. Through the manipulation of fear they are neutralised and rendered back into society. It is a riveting but dreadful tale. *Nineteen Eighty-Four* has been seen as an update on the human condition (Pimlott, 1989) who adds: 'What matters most is that it reminds us of so many things we usually avoid'—such as the ease with which pure irrational hate can be elicited. More simply it has a terrible message: 'everything that exists— even the spirit of man itself—can be destroyed by totalitarianism' (Boit, 1958).

Since its publication in 1949, British society has steadily tracked its way along a number of the paths identified in the novel. We have seen the rise of surveillance, the emergence of managerialism and the wall-to-wall hyperreality of the telescreen; image is all; surface has triumphed over depth. We even have a culture that is now being told that globalisation is the reason for everything! But other developments have taken place that qualify these trends, namely, commitments to human rights and the rise of multiculturalism. Thankfully, the world is not entirely Orwellian.

Significantly, *Nineteen Eighty-Four* has come to enter the British psyche: we are deeply suspicious of the way language is used and have grown accustomed to being deceived by 'spin'. We have little trust in official pronouncements or government claims, and we remain sceptical about authority. We also cherish a certain freedom of thought and expression. All this is due, in no small way, to Orwell's tremendous achievement. However, it is worth considering the implications of

Orwell's insights concerning the tendency by the powerful to 'colour events' to suit their purposes.

Warnock (1995) has addressed the consequences of the fact that the UK is suffused by a 'culture of spin' (truth-shaving, manipulation, evasion, etc.).[6] Warnock finds that a correlate of spin culture is a decline in trust along with the spread of cynicism—both of which have negative consequences for social cohesion. Her main thesis is that, although we are a better-educated nation than we used to be, we are becoming a nation of cynics, that is, incredulous of human goodness. People, as a matter of fact, do know more and, because there is such a lot of information available, they come to 'hanker after the truth'. However, as Warnock puts it:

> People...would like what they are told to be true; and when it turns out not to be, when what they are promised is not delivered then naturally they turn cynical. They become extravagantly cautious. They cannot accept anything they are told whatever the evidence, and they refuse to believe that there exists anyone among their rulers, advisers or teachers who is prepared disinterestedly to seek out and present the truth. Whatever anyone says the presumption is that he says it only in order to gain something to his own advantage.
>
> (Warnock, 1995, Page 104)

This raises a key requirement: people must be taught to distinguish what can from what cannot be believed. They need a critical attitude with which they will distinguish between rhetoric, advertisement and propaganda. Propaganda is the real enemy: 'The commonest form of propaganda is selective truth telling which avoids actual lying but only lets the good news be known' (Page 105). Warnock thinks that 'we all begin to believe that propaganda is everywhere; that all official statements are propaganda'.

What, then, is to be done? The answer Warnock proposes is a policy of openness or, to use the more modern idiom, transparency. But there are problems: it is not always possible to be completely open and there is an ignorant and scandal-seeking press to deal with. There is also a tendency to adopt the principle 'honesty is the best policy'—which means 'making sure one is not caught lying'. So, for Warnock, more than honesty is needed: candour is the paramount requirement.

> Candour goes beyond honesty. It is an absence of reserve that carries openness and genuineness on its face. It is a readiness to tell the

truth without bias, to speak disinterestedly, to admit, if necessary, that things have gone wrong, that one's opponents may have points in their favour.

(Warnock, 1995, Page 113)

In making this assertion Warnock thinks that she is advocating a 'great initiative':

What is needed is a new way of disseminating the truth so it can be believed. Professional people as well as politicians should learn a new style of presentation that commands belief. But this style must not be mere rhetoric.

Echoing Orwell's essay on *Politics and the English Language* she urges politicians and journalists not to be advertisers or propagandists. Her hope remains that a good system of education allied to a new ethos of candour and truth will produce critics rather than cynics. Orwell saw that there was 'a connexion between the decay of language and the stifling of freedom, that the immediate enemies of truthfulness are the Press Lords, the film magnates and the bureaucrats' (Boit, 1958). It seems that we are obliged to work very hard to discern truth and find it just as hard to speak the truth.

Playing with the unconscious: *Titus Groan* by Mervyn Peake

Titus Groan is a unique literary achievement: like all great works of art it has its source not in history nor in politics but in magic. This is a long-haul book: set in the extraordinary world of Gormenghast, a dreamy, fantastic tale slowly unfolds. Yet somehow it is all very familiar, very English: everything creaks and groans and crumbles. The sere laws and arcane rituals, the dripping landscapes and leaden skies, the weird characters, the social divisions, the hope and resignation, intrigues and loyalties—all are emblems of a nation and a culture.

Here's the story. Little Titus—a boy with violet eyes—is born the 77th Earl of Groan. The society around him is static, becalmed, fetishised, frozen. However, just as the future seems secure, Steerpike, a truly remarkable literary creation, at once heroic, ambitious, psychopathic and truly evil, makes his appearance. A dark agent of change, he gradually engineers the destruction of the hierarchy at Gormenghast.

By the time this brilliant work ends, four of the major characters are dead or missing, the sacred library at Gormenghast has burned to the ground, and Titus is still only two years old. Steerpike has achieved the impossible: he has insinuated his way into the ageing corridors of power and is poised to challenge the future authority of Titus himself. His fate and that of Titus await us in the sequel, *Gormenghast*.

The work is so beautifully crafted in such gorgeous prose that it's difficult to imagine how better the English language can be used. In this sublime piece of fiction, Mervyn Peake takes us to the very edge of the possible: if the mind is always dreaming then *Titus Groan* is dark nectar for dreams richer still.

The novel is an antidote to the intellectual, ethical and spiritual aspects of leadership that have been surfaced in the preceding works. In fact, it is hardly about leadership at all; its strength and power lies in its capacity to attune the reader to the mysterious and the fantastic. Murdoch (1978) in her discussion on 'philosophy and literature' states that 'art is close dangerous play with unconscious forces' and that 'we enjoy art because it disturbs us in deep, often incomprehensible ways'.

Titus Groan leads the reader to the edge of the close dangerous play with unconscious forces. For example, Steerpike, despite his psychopathy, is strangely appealing. Flay, the faithful servant, simultaneously attracts and repulses us. The rituals, though detached from their original meaning, still serve to reassure us with their continuity and serve as a kind of scaffolding that preserves the basic structure of society. *Titus Groan* has been the object of brilliant literary criticism: Gardiner-Scott (1989) has explored how Peake assimilated his own experiences into his writing while Mills, in her search to 'find a way to understand this amazing, daunting, mystifying' (Page 2) and 'unforgettable author' takes a complex psychoanalytic perceptive and explores 'stuckness' in the writing of Peake as a whole. Mills's analysis is always wonderfully suggestive: like Hesse, she attends to the problem of authenticity that befalls a ruler; she finds that the Earl Sepulchrave is really 'the first servant' of Gormenghast and that 'each of the rituals that he performs is . . . a flawlessly dutiful image of [himself] that is held up every morning for him to identify with, an unauthentic self' (Page 99).

Overall, on a less technical level, Gormenghast castle can serve as a metaphor for the whole personality: its characters reflect the divergent energies that reverberate within ourselves. Engaging with *Titus Groan* helps raise the question: How far can a leader both constrain and enable irrationality and work outside the limits of reason?

Reason and science: the engineering of good citizens

One by David Karp is a heart-stopping novel. It examines the extremes to which a society might go in order to secure control of both thought and behaviour. It can seem like reading one's way through a slow-motion nightmare. There is a moment in the drama, so shocking, so terribly sad, that it is almost impossible to continue reading.

The story unfolds in the Benevolent State—a state that has succeeded in taming its citizens; they stay indoors living out lives of anodyne banality. But the State is proud of itself: all the indices of social 'well-being' are positive; it has even dispensed with the concept of punishment: heretics are either re-educated or eliminated. Against this backdrop an extraordinary encounter unfolds: Professor Burden, who genuinely believes that he is a good citizen, finds himself brought into the Department of Internal Examination for questioning. Little by little, his examiners find him guilty of the worst kind of heresy: Burden prizes both his personal identity and his independence of thought. The chief interrogator, Lark, sets out, remorselessly, to rid Burden of his 'illness'. Using every terrible means at his disposal he gradually re-engineers Burden's mind. Finally, Lark takes the most drastic step of all: he obliterates all traces of Burden's identity. A new person, Mr Hughes, is constructed and released back into the world of work, the world of social relationships.

But, will this extreme experiment work? Or, is there lodged within most of us, an inviolable sense of autonomous selfhood? To Lark's dismay, it turns out that his creation, the good Mr Hughes, still has the capacity to make up his own mind. This time, then, there is no alternative: Mr Hughes is cordially invited to the Department—for execution.

David Karp's *One* is nothing short of brilliant: the dialogues are riveting, the issues are profound and his capacity to evoke the bleak amorality of bureaucracy is unsurpassed. This is a novel that shows us why it is worth striving for a safe, just and tolerant society.

It is also a novel that reveals the extraordinary dangers consequent upon simplistic analyses of history and society. As the incarcerated Professor Burden contemplates his predicament he finds himself making explicit the immediate 'history' preceding the Benevolent State:

> He knew about the psychotic tensions of the twentieth-century world, the terrors, the brutalities, the incredible bestiality recorded in

the history books. It had been a sick, tortured, frenetic world . . . It had to be made over in a new image. The benevolent state was the new way.

(Karp, 1953, Pages 110–11)

To this false view of history is added an inadequate diagnosis:

The mercantile philosophy, the concept of their cultural progenitors, had failed; the myth of self-gratification had failed; the great religions had failed; terror had failed; war had failed; technology had failed. Character was the only thing left. (Page 112)

As a result, a conceptually flawed solution is proposed based on the idea that 'character' could be treated independently of the social and technological processes in which people participate. 'Character' was to be engineered through reason and science: the Benevolent State was devoted to 'the deliberate, systematic, tortuous method of breeding human of character, believing in one another and in their systems of government' (Page 114).

Karp's portrayal of the simplistic nature of Professor Burden's rationale for the Benevolent State is unsettling because it echoes a tendency in contemporary leadership and management discourse that reduces complexity and trades in slogans.[7] It also points to a wider problem concerned with testing the quality of factual information and exploring the meaning of the concepts that find themselves deployed. In essence, Karp's text stimulates the process of asking serious questions about the realities of current society and the diagnostic accounts that are given concerning its nature and its future. He also provides a story that intersects with Foucault's (1981) analysis of the science of discipline and the techniques by which people are normalised and made into model citizens.

The black flower of civilisation: *Waiting for the Barbarians* by J M Coetzee

Some philosophers think that the best modern philosophy is being done by writers such as J M Coetzee. *Waiting for the Barbarians* shows why: the text reads like a brilliant extended lecture on the nature of human limitations; it grapples with 'the black flower of civilisation'. It is a short novel about pain, suffering, politics and truth.

It's a 'no-hiding place' novel: Coetzee tells of an ageing magistrate, quietly filling his role in a remote frontier settlement; he embodies the benign lie an empire tells itself when times are easy. Then, he is shocked by the cruelties of the security police who are sent to quell insurrection on the borders of the empire. He tries to act, to do the right thing and, after a devastating set of realisations, sets out on a mission to return a tortured girl to her nomadic people—the enemy, the 'barbarians'.

On his return he is imprisoned for 'treasonable consorting'; he is a threat to the state. Then, he is gradually so degraded, so brutally abused that he screams and howls—because there is nothing else that he can do.

Twice, in the course of the narrative, an awful feeling of horror mixed with fear reached into and around my heart. I get that feeling when I have terrible nightmares. This feeling—this chill—stayed with me for a surprisingly long time. Part of me thinks that we should not stray too far from this, from the emotional grain of the novel. But Coetzee also embeds in his text a philosophical exploration of 'No-saying' and its consequences as well as a critique of the way civilisations exclude or deny other ways of being. On top of this, he succeeds in telling us a story about what happens as men grow older, about their search for intimacy and meaning and, finally, about how to die. Written in a seemingly spare and economical style *Waiting for the Barbarians* is an extraordinarily evocative piece of writing.

The magistrate, from whose vantage point the story is told, is reduced, through humiliation and torment, to a subhuman level. And, as he later reflects, he learns one of the great lessons of the twentieth century:

> When (the torturers) first brought me back here ... I wondered how much pain a plump comfortable old man would be able to endure in the name of his eccentric notions of how the Empire should conduct itself. But my torturers were not interested in degrees of pain. They were interested only in demonstrating to me what it meant to live in a body, as a body, a body which can entertain notions of justice only as long as it is whole and well, which very soon forgets them when its head is gripped and a pipe is pushed down its gullet and pints of salt water are poured into it .... They came to my cell to show me the meaning of humanity, and in the space of an hour they showed me a great deal.
>
> (Coetzee, 2000, Page 126)

An anonymous commentator noted that 'hardly a moment of the story doesn't read like a what-to-expect-next playbook from the American Empire of the early Twenty-First Century'; he continues: 'Hardly a moment doesn't call upon the subjects of Empire to see more clearly the folly of their "civilised" society and its fears.' His remarks should not be limited to the 'American Empire'.

Salvaging civilisation

Let's cut to the chase: Cormac McCarthy's *The Road* is a remarkable and brilliant achievement. This work is chosen as the last text for a course devoted to the education of leaders.

Set amidst the ash-laden wreckage of a burnt-out America, McCarthy explores a primal psychology of the human male. Edging, bit-by-bit, along the road, a father and his son struggle to stay alive in a post-cataclysmic world stripped of its resources. Staying close to the grain of human experience, McCarthy moves us through the data of their senses, tracks along their memories, dwells in their dreams and unearths the big enduring truths that make life worth living and death worth welcoming.

His prose is deceptively simple: alongside seemingly spare description he details the inventive genius of our cultural heritage. Echoing Bronowski's (1973) celebration of human artefacts in the *Ascent of Man*, McCarthy confronts us with the things it has become simply too easy to overlook: canned food, the cleat on a boat, a ratchet, tools and toolboxes, oil in plastic bottles, fashioning a bullet, telegraph wires, a spatula, a cistern. This may be the most powerful and damning message in the book: how is it that surrounded by a wealth of technological and social achievements we have produced bored people, casual people, ungrateful people, helpless people?

In the short clipped dialogues between father and son, moments of terrible profundity emerge. As they cope with the dramatic episodes on the road, a philosophy for life begins to emerge. Together, father and son 'keep the fire alive'; together they try to remain 'good guys'. And, the good guys keep hoping and keep going on. That's what they do.

McCarthy's writing carries with it a sense of urgency: everything really could come to a halt—and we might have to start the process of building a society from the very beginning. If it is the case that we are creatures of enduring limitations then our civilised and genteel moral codes may not command sufficient authority and the power of the word may give way to the power of the fist, the boot and the iron bar.

Conclusion

In her discussion on philosophy and literature, Murdoch examines several fundamental features of literature as art. Her discussion illustrates why, in general, leaders would benefit from engaging with good art, with good works of literature.[8] She points out that 'literary modes are very natural to us, very close to ordinary life and to the way we live as reflective beings' (Murdoch, 1978). She then observes that:

> When we return home and 'tell our day' we are artfully shaping material into story form. So, in a way as word-users we all exist in a literary atmosphere, we live and breathe literature, we are all literary artists, we are constantly employing language to make interesting forms out of experience which perhaps originally seemed dull or incoherent.
>
> (Murdoch, 1978, Page 232)

This is the most basic argument as to why leaders should engage with good literature: the 'literary atmosphere' might counter any tendencies to dullness. Murdoch goes on to explore the nature of literature and finds that, like philosophy, it is a truth-seeking and truth-revealing activity: 'Think how much thought, how much truth a Shakespeare play contains, or a great novel' (Murdoch, 1978, Page 236).

Here is a more significant argument: literature is about the world and can 'stir us to the effort of the true vision'. Murdoch is convinced that most of the time we fail to see the big wide real world at all because we are blinded by our own psychology, but that great art liberates us and helps us to take pleasure in what is not ourselves.

Each of the ten texts identified in this chapter does not converge on a single truth but excites a more general search for the kinds of truth relevant to the expressions of leadership.

Notes

1. I have become used to seeing these system-functionaries on news bulletins and those media occasions where the senior managers of 'service delivery' talk to us in that curiously alienated language of jargon-laden narratives.
2. Later in the discussion, Socrates describes why the philosophic character can easily be corrupted as a result of living in the confines of popular and conventional culture.
3. These latter virtues are the very ones that will best support the stability and effectiveness of Plato's ideal society.
4. Plutarch's life of Brutus, for example, includes a passage in which Stoicism is contrasted with Epicureanism.
5. For a riveting analysis of Mankievicz's *Julius Caesar* see, Wyke (2004).
6. Spin culture overlaps with a culture of 'faking it', manifested in, for example, the 'sham' curriculum vitae, the practice of 'winging it', falsifying expense claims, exposés of improper practices of, for example, plumbers, security firms,

etc. Even in the field of documentary film-making or reality TV it turns out that scenarios are pre-scripted.

7. Training packages in the field of leadership and management are replete with simplistic models and catchy slogans that have instant appeal.

8. Murdoch acknowledges that most art is bad art, that is, it expresses false values and is sentimental, pretentious and fanciful.

References

Adlam, R. (1999) We need a night shift: notes on the failure of an educational design for police leaders and managers. *Educational Action Research* Vol 7, No. 1, pp. 34–51.

Adlam, R. (2000) *Culture change: an attempt to teach ethics to police leaders and managers within a traditional institution and changing social milieu*, Unpublished Ph.D. thesis, Department of Educational Studies, University of Surrey, Guildford Surrey.

Boit, G. (1958) Introductory essay, in Boit, G. (ed.) *George Orwell: selected writings*. London: Heinemann Educational Books Limited.

Braden, G. (2004) Plutarch, Shakespeare and the alpha males, in Martindale, C. and Taylor, B. (eds) *Shakespeare and the classics*. Cambridge: Cambridge University Press.

Bronowski, J. (1973) *The ascent of man*. London: BBC publications.

Christian, R.F. (1969) *Tolstoy: a critical introduction*. Cambridge: Cambridge University Press.

Collins, J. (1999) *Introducing Heidegger*. Cambridge Icon Books.

Coetzee, J.M. (2000) *Waiting for the barbarians*. London: Vintage.

Duff, T. (1999) *Plutarch's Lives: exploring virtue and vice*. Oxford: Oxford University Press.

Foucault, M. (1981) *Discipline and punish*. Harmondsworth Middlesex: Penguin Books.

Gardiner-Scott, T. (1989) *Mervyn Peake: The evolution of a dark romantic* (American University Studies Series IV, English Language and Literature). New York: Peter Lang Inc.

Goldhill, S. (2000) Review of Tim Duff's 'Plutarch's Lives: exploring virtue and vice' Cambridge: *Bryn Mawr Classical Review* 10.08.2000 pp. 444.

Greenblatt, S. (2004) *Will in the world: how Shakespeare became Shakespeare*. New York: W.W. Norton and Company Inc.

Heidegger, M. (1953) The question concerning technology, in Krell, D.F. (ed.) *Martin Heidegger: Basic Writings*. London: Routledge.

Hesse, H. (1970) *The Glass Bead Game*. London: Jonathan Cape.

Kant, I. (1999) *Critique of Pure Reason*. London: Cambridge University Press.

Karp, D. (1953) *One*. London: Victor Gollanz Ltd.

Kleinig, J. (1990) Teaching and learning police ethics: competing and complementary approaches. *Journal of Criminal Justice* Vol 18, pp. 1–18.

Kleinig, J. and Leland Smith, M. (1997) (eds) *Teaching criminal justice ethics: strategic issues*. Cincinnati, OH: Anderson Publishing Company.

McCarthy, C. (2006) *The Road*. New York: Alfred Knopf.

Mills, A. (2005) *Stuckness in the fiction of Mervyn Peake*. New York: Rodopi.

Murdoch, I. (1978) Philosophy and literature, in Magee, B. (ed.) *Men of ideas—dialogues with fifteen leading philosophers*. Oxford: Oxford University Press.

Nietzsche, F. (2002) Beyond good and evil, in Horstmann, R.-P. and Norman, J. (eds) *Cambridge Texts in the history of philosophy*. Cambrige: Cambridge University Press.

O'Neil, O. (2002) *A question of trust*. Cambridge: Cambridge University Press.

Orwell, G. (1989) *Nineteen eighty-four*. Harmondsworth, Middlesex: Penguin Books.

Peake, M. (1968) *Titus Groan*. Harmondsworth, Middlesex: Penguin Books.

Pimlott, B. (1989) Introduction to nineteen eighty four, in Orwell, G. (ed.) *Nineteen eighty four*. Harmondsworth, Middlesex: Penguin Books.

Plato (1955) *The Republic*. Harmondsworth, Middlesex: Penguin books.

Plutarch (1992) Plutarch, in Clough, A.H. (ed.) *Lives of noble Romans and Grecians*. New York: Random House Inc.

Richards, N. (1993) *A plea for applied ethics*, in Thomas, R. (ed.) *Government ethics*, Volume 1. Cambridge: Centre for Business and public sector ethics.

Tolstoy, L. (1960) *Anna Karenin*. London: William Heinemann Ltd.

Warnock, M. (1995) *The uses of philosophy*. Oxford: Blackwell.

Wyke, M. (2004) Film style and fascism: Julius Caesar. *Film Studies*. Summer, No. 4, pp. 58–74.

Zamyatin, Y. (1972) *We*. Harmondsworth, Middlesex: Penguin Books.

Index

Printed and bound in the United States of America